Conservation of Human Resources

COLUMBIA UNIVERSITY, Eli Ginzberg, Director

LABOR MARKETS: SEGMENTS AND SHELTERS
  Marcia Freedman, with Gretchen Maclachlan

SUBURBANIZATION AND THE CITY
  Thomas M. Stanback, Jr., and Richard Knight

BRIDGES TO WORK
  International Comparisons of Transition Services
  Beatrice G. Reubens

Suburbanization and the City

Suburbanization and the City /

by THOMAS M. STANBACK, Jr.
and RICHARD V. KNIGHT ;
Foreword by Eli Ginzberg ,

LAND MARK STUDIES
ALLANHELD, OSMUN & CO. PUBLISHERS
UNIVERSE BOOKS

ALLANHELD, OSMUN & CO. PUBLISHERS, INC.
19 Brunswick Road, Montclair, N.J. 07042

Published in the United States of America in 1976
by Allanheld, Osmun & Co. and by Universe Books
381 Park Avenue South, New York, N.Y. 10016
Distribution: Universe Books

Second Printing 1979

LIBRARY OF CONGRESS CATALOGING IN PUBLICATION DATA

Stanback, Thomas M.
  Suburbanization and the city.

  (Conservation of Human Resources series;)
  (Land mark studies; 2)
  Bibliography: p.
  Includes index.
  1. Urban economics. 2. Suburbs. 3. Labor supply.
I. Knight, Richard V., joint author.
II. Title.
III. Series.
HT321.S73   330.9'173'2   76–472
ISBN 0-87663-800-0

The material in this publication was prepared under contracts numbers
21-36-73-51 and 21-36-75-20 from the Employment and Training Administration, U.S. Department of Labor, under the authority of Title
III, Part B of the Comprehensive Employment and Training Act of
1973. Researchers undertaking such projects under government spon-
sorship are encouraged to express freely their professional judgment.
Therefore, points of view and opinions stated in this document do not
necessarily represent the official position or policy of the Department
of Labor.
  Reproduction by the U.S. Government in whole or in part is permitted for any purpose.

Printed in the United States of America

Contents

Tables

Appendix Tables

Foreword

We are often aware, generally, of rapid social change, but we lack deeper understanding of the underlying developments. This gap reflects in the first instance the inevitable lag in data collection. In the United States we remain dependent to an extraordinary degree on the decennial census, which means that the data become available, on the average, three years after the decade has ended. The second principal cause for inadequate understanding is the domination of contemporary thinking by concepts and ideas developed in an earlier generation—a danger which John Maynard Keynes warned us about in the concluding paragraphs of his famous *General Theory*.

The simple facts of life that bound the social scientist who addresses contemporary problems help to set the stage for understanding the task that Professors Stanback and Knight set themselves in the present inquiry into the processes of suburbanization and metropolitan development and the freshness and significance of their findings and recommendations. It would be an exaggeration to say that theirs is the first study in depth about the processes of suburban expansion, but it is well within bounds to say that the present study is the first that focuses specifically on the role of manpower resources in the process. Moreover, it is distinctive in still another regard since it is informed by developments not in a single suburban community, but by systematic exploitation of the available data in ten of the nation's largest suburban rings. It thereby avoids the danger of generalizing on the basis of the idiosyncratic experience of a New York, Cleveland, or Houston.

The Conservation of Human Resources Project, Columbia University, under whose auspices the current investigation was designed and carried out, entered the field of urbanology approximately a decade ago when it recognized that there were severe limits to understanding the problems of manpower solely from the vantage of macro analysis.

At that point, the Conservation staff recognized that a deeper under-standing of how people acquire skills, jobs, and income had to be carried out within a spatial analysis, the limits being set by the distances that people are able to travel from their homes to work and back again.

It may be helpful to the reader if the more important of the metropoli-tan studies carried out by the Conservation staff, to which the present authors have been major contributors, are noted.

Ginzberg, Eli, and the Conservation of Human Resources Staff. *Urban Health Services: The Case of New York.* New York: Columbia Univer-sity Press, 1971.

Ginzberg, Eli, and the Conservation of Human Resources Staff. *New York Is Very Much Alive: A Manpower View.* New York: McGraw-Hill Inc., 1973.

Ginzberg, Eli (editor). *The Future of the Metropolis: People, Jobs, and In-come.* Salt Lake City: Olympus Publishing Co., 1975.

Knight, Richard. *Employment Expansion and Metropolitan Trade.* New York: Praeger Publishers, Inc., 1973.

Stanback, Thomas, Jr., and Richard Knight. *The Metropolitan Economy: The Process of Employment Expansion.* New York: Columbia University Press, 1970.

Yavitz, Boris, and Thomas Stanback, Jr. *Electronic Data Processing in New York City: Lessons for Metropolitan Economics.* New York: Columbia University Press, 1970 .

While many investigators have noted the serious consequences to the future economic well-being of the core city resulting from the outflow of a high proportion of the settled population to the suburbs and the loss of many jobs that preceded, accompanied, or followed upon this pop-ulation shift, particularly in manufacturing, headquarters activities, and residentiary services, relatively little attention has been directed to the longer-run implications of this demographic shift. What of the future? Will the suburban rings with their enlarged populations and increasingly diversified job structures keep growing, pulling still more people and jobs out of the central business district until the inner city becomes a burnt-out core?

The Stanback-Knight study started with a focus on the suburban labor market in an effort to assess the potentiality of future suburban growth. But it is critical to the understanding of the present work that the authors shifted focus early in their investigation because of their new perception that the suburb could not be studied as an independent economic entity sufficient unto itself and master of its own future. Nor, for that matter, can the future of the core city be assessed except in relation to its outer ring from which it draws many members of its work force and for whose population it provides many specialized services. Hence the authors' framework includes the dynamic relations between suburbanization and the city from a manpower vantage.

The authors have made it easy for the reader to extract the most important findings and implications from their detailed analysis of the people-jobs-and-income relations between the central city and the suburb. A close reading of the summaries in each analytical chapter will enable the reader to learn easily and quickly what the authors were able to distill from their detailed empirical analysis. Accordingly, this Foreword will single out for comment a few of the larger policy issues that can now be more sharply delineated because of the Stanback-Knight materials and analyses, issues that must be dealt with by every community that is concerned about its survival and growth.

Perhaps the most important policy-loaded finding in the entire study is the dependence of the suburb on the city. The authors' estimate that, on an average, 67 percent of the income of suburbanites is generated, directly and indirectly, by earnings in the city. In short, the suburbs today—and most probably tomorrow—are not close to the point of economic self-sufficiency. They are unable to generate the income required to sustain the standard of living of their populations. The relatively high standard of living that most suburbanites enjoy reflects the large numbers who are able to earn high incomes in the core city. This is further enhanced by the fact that the suburbs need not raise as many tax dollars per capita as does the city because the suburbs have succeeded, at least up to the present, in restricting the number of low-income people from taking up residence in their midst. A related benefit from the greater economic homogeneity of the suburban population is that the public dollars that are raised redound to the benefit overwhelmingly of the middle class that makes heavy use of the schools, the recreational facilities, and special services, in sharp contrast to the central city's urban middle class that is forced to seek such services in the private market.

The present situation is inherently unstable. The city cannot continue to cover the costs of caring for the large numbers of dependent people—a burden which the suburb fails to share at the same time that the well-being of the suburb depends on its residents holding down relatively high-paying positions in the city. The inequality in the distribution of social burdens between suburb and city, reinforced by tax burdens, has weakened the city to a point where its future economic viability is in question: a matter of the utmost concern to suburbanites whose future depends on the city.

Or does it? Can the suburbs go it alone, if not now, some years hence? Stanback and Knight offer some interesting and important insights into this critical question. They find, for instance, that despite their rapid growth, the suburbs have not encountered any serious constraint on their expansion from the side of labor supply. Whatever additional workers have been required have been forthcoming—first from among the married women and young men resident in the suburbs; next from city families relocating there in response to job opportunities; third from people moving in, or commuting daily, from exurbia; and finally from those who continue to live in the city but who commute daily to work in the suburbs. They conclude that manpower stringency will not limit the growth of suburban development.

But that is only a partial answer. The authors note that a major source of economic development for the suburbs these last several decades has been the growth of manufacturing and warehousing in the less crowded areas where modern plants can be erected at much lower costs—plants with easy access to the critically important interstate highway systems. But the authors are not sure that the future of manufacturing will continue to lie with the suburbs now that land is more costly, labor costs are relatively high, and taxes are continuing to go up steeply. Many manufacturing units are being relocated in rural settings which have a clear advantage on all these grounds: the cost of land, labor, and taxes. Jobs requiring a highly skilled work force or producing for regional markets are less likely to decline.

If the manufacturing base of the suburban economy weakens, what will replace it? The authors recognize that the growth in population has been the spur to the growth of residentiary services, particularly retailing. And more recently, more sophisticated services are expanding in the suburbs—hospitals, junior colleges, theaters, museums, and still others. But the authors question whether the critical business services— banking, insurance, law, architecture, consulting—which, through their dependence on each other provide so much of the dynamics of growth for our largest metropolitan areas, are likely to be relocated in suburban rings. Some firms have moved out and others will unquestionably do so, but the authors read their figures to suggest that the city is likely to retain for a considerable period its clear-cut advantage as the base of advanced business services.

If they are right in these forecasts that manufacturing is no longer likely to find the suburb as attractive as in the past, and that the suburb will prove a weak competitor when it comes to attracting the advanced business services from the core city—and if these forecasts hold up—it is difficult to see the future spring for rapid suburban development.

These questions are reinforced when one considers several additional trends—the slowed growth of population and rising costs of new styles of living. Each of the foregoing suggests a potential decline in the attractiveness of the suburb. It is difficult except for the poor and the rich to bring up a family of three or four youngsters in the city. The rapid growth of the suburb in the early post-World War II years was a direct outcome of the larger American family in which three, four, and even five children became typical. But unless the demographic trends undergo a totally unexpected change, families of one and two children are more likely to become the norm. And such families have less need for the space and the housing that were the principal allures of the suburbs.

The costs of automotive transportation are most certainly going to increase, probably quite rapidly, and it will prove increasingly restrictive for many families to maintain two or three cars as has been the recent trend in many upper-income suburban areas.

Closely linked to the foregoing is the question of the work attachment of the female population. The recent trends point to the desire on the part of more and more women, even in the childbearing years twenty to thirty-four, to remain attached to the labor force, or to withdraw from work for only a few years to minimize adverse effects on their career development. The more women become career oriented, the greater the attractions of a smaller family, and the greater the pull of residence in the city. For it is the city that offers a career woman wider choices.

The authors call attention to still another likely constraint on the rapid growth of suburban communities. The leadership in well-established suburban communities has come to recognize that their communities have little to gain, and possibly much to lose, from further growth. Their new interest is to preserve the quality of the environment. They are opposed to real estate and other interest groups that see their future linked to rapid economic expansion. And so more and more suburban communities are moving towards a no- or slow-growth policy.

The serious questions that have been raised about the future development of the suburbs should be read neither as a pessimistic forecast of their potentials, nor as a guarantee of the city's future; but rather as a challenge to both suburb and city to take stock, to recognize their interdependence, and to plan jointly for their future well-being. The absence of regional planning in the quarter century just behind us is no basis for projecting that major metropolitan areas have much to gain from another quarter century of unplanned development.

The situation as of 1975 comes to this: the people in the suburbs need access to the good jobs in the cities from which they draw a large part of their income. The cities cannot look to themselves to provide the number and range of talented managerial and professional personnel they require. They must attract a high proportion of these able people from those who make their homes in the suburbs. Suburb and city, each requires the other for continued stability and growth. The high-income populations now resident in the suburbs will not return to the city to live, at least not in the near term, among other reasons because there is inadequate housing for their needs. On the other hand, it is highly unlikely that the city will be able to disperse its large numbers of poor and dependent into its outer ring—if for no other reason than that the suburbs will not accept them and many of the poor would not relocate even if they could.

In the face of these facts—and it is hard to see how they will change, especially in the near term—city and suburb face the urgent necessity of cooperatively working toward joint solutions. The beginnings of such an alliance can be seen on the horizon: the new alignments that often find city and suburb in the same political camp in state politics; the assumption by the federal and state governments of some of the more costly services formerly provided by the city—particularly in welfare, health, education, transportation, environmental protection, and still other areas; the proliferation of authorities or commissions participated in by suburban and urban communities to plan and operate essential services for a large metropolitan area. But these are only a beginning and, more often than not, city and suburb continue to see each other as opponents, not collaborators. But if the moral of the Stanback-Knight thesis is not to be ignored, there is no future, surely no attractive future, for the suburb or the city to go it alone. They must cooperate. Among the openings that exist for constructive collaboration are the following:

The suburbs must recognize their stake in the future viability of the city and must cooperate at both the federal and state levels to lessen the burdens of the city. It is in their own self-interest to see that the city remains economically viable.

The city must look to itself to build on its strengths and to lower and remove the barriers to its continual economic development. As the authors suggest, there is need for the city to understand the specialized advantages which it possesses and to build on them. At a minimum, it must make strenuous efforts to increase the skills and competences of its new in-migrants, for a city without a strong diversified labor force is doomed. It will have to spend considerable revenue on supporting people until they are able to support themselves. Equally important, a city must be constantly alert as to the alternative use of its valuable space. If it puts too much into housing, the opportunities for productive employment may not be available, without which people cannot cover their rents. And if too much space is converted to productive purposes, the costs of attracting an adequate labor force from outlying areas may prove excessively difficult.

Thirdly, those who are concerned about the further well-being of the entire metropolitan area must remain alert to the importance of protecting the city's amenities, both for the sake of those who are urban residents, as well as for those who commute daily or visit occasionally. The quality of the central city with its dynamic economic institutions, its cultural amenities, its wide range of recreational attractions must be protected and enhanced if the metropolitan area is to flourish. If the central city becomes unattractive, unsafe, unclean, then not only it, but the suburbs on its outskirts, have a bleak future. That is the lesson that Stanback and Knight have to teach us.

Eli Ginzberg

Suburbanization and the City

Introduction

The postwar years have been marked by growth in population and employment which has centered on the suburbs. From 1950 to 1974, population in the United States increased by 56.6 million, of which 39.5 million (70 percent) was accounted for by growth in suburban rings (areas lying within metropolitan areas but outside of central cities), 7.9 million (14 percent) by central cities, and 9.2 million (16 percent) by rural areas. Moreover, although the most recent years of this period (1970-1974) have been marked by certain new trends—a number of central cities have declined in population and many nonmetropolitan areas have accelerated their growth—suburban areas have continued to grow.

These shifts in population and economic activity have brought with them a variety of problems—economic, sociological, and political. This study is concerned principally with the economic. What has occurred is essentially a reorganization of the metropolitan economy and, with it, a restructuring of metropolitan labor markets—of both labor demand and labor supply. Accordingly, we must examine what has taken place both in terms of the industry structure of cities and suburbs and in terms of the kinds of jobs people hold and the kinds of people who hold these jobs.

Moreover, the history of the postwar years has been one of changing transportation modes—the rise of automotive and air transport and the decline of railways—and of changing institutional structures. These have impacted metropolitan economies and must also be taken into account.

3

OBJECTIVES OF THE STUDY

The study has four principal objectives. The first is to determine whether the restructuring of industries and occupations varies among metropolitan areas and between cities and their suburbs. For example, are employment changes in a manufacturing metropolis such as Cleveland different from those of a service metropolis such as Atlanta? Do central cities and suburbs differ significantly in their industry and occupational employment mix, and in patterns of employment growth and decline? This requires the formulation of an analytical framework which permits us to treat economic development in different types of metropolitan economies and within cities and suburbs of such economies.

The second objective is to examine suburban growth and adaptation processes, including new institutional developments, and to consider the labor market flows and linkages between cities and suburbs. The expansion of metropolitan economies has loosened up the urban form in the sense that there are now longer average journeys to work. Disproportionate growth of higher-level occupations and greatly improved road systems have extended the boundaries of labor markets for higher income workers, enabling a wide range of choice among work places and residences. To what extent do professional, managerial and clerical personnel commute from distant suburbs to central business districts? Do higher-level wage and salary workers in suburban manufacturing plants commute from the central city and other suburbs? What effect do long commutes have on local labor markets? How are city and suburban economies linked, not only in terms of commuters pursuing work, but also in terms of where household purchases, services, and cultural and recreational facilities are located, where jobs are created, where employers look for their labor force, and where the tax base to support local services is developing? How have new and evolving institutional arrangements played a part in the adaptation process? How does the sex-age-race composition of the work force differ between cities and suburbs and to what extent do the differences reflect industrial mix and other factors?

The third objective is to evaluate the impact of loosely structured (i.e., geographically dispersed) metropolitan labor markets on different segments of the population. Who participates in which metropolitan and sub-metropolitan labor markets? Where are the good jobs found, and do they draw on city or suburban labor markets? How is economic opportunity created, or filtered down to those at the bottom of the opportunity ladder? How has suburbanization changed the traditional process of work establishment for the young and for the disadvantaged, both new migrants and older residents of the metropolis? To what extent has economic opportunity for low-wage workers shifted to the suburbs? Is the suburbanization process creating additional economic problems for the poor, particularly those remaining in the inner city?

The fourth objective is to achieve increased understanding of suburbanization and other employment expansion processes so that public programs and policies may be formulated in a more appropriate fashion. Particularly significant are signs of constraints on suburbanization and emerging problems, as well as new opportunities for suburban development. How may urban form affect development? At some point will the suburbanization processes be reversed, central cities revitalized, commuting distances reduced, and communities become more integrated and heterogeneous? To answer these questions, demographic forces underlying suburbanization and the probable impacts of emerging trends are reviewed, and the rising costs of energy and infrastructure considered.

THE METROPOLITAN AREAS STUDIED

Clearly, there is no way by which a sample of as few as ten can be made completely representative of the 259 metropolitan areas of the United States, or even of the largest fifty, for variations occur in many dimensions, including age and region. Nevertheless, the SMSA's selected comprise as representative a sample of large SMSA's as it was feasible to investigate, given the objectives of detailed data analysis which were held to be of critical importance to the usefulness of the study.[1] What stands out in the chapters which follow is that, in spite of differences in terms of a number of variables, there are solid generalizations which can be made regarding the nature of suburban development and its impact upon metropolitan labor markets.

The ten metropolitan areas (SMSA's) studied represent seven of the eight regions of the continental United States (the Far West is not represented). Although they vary considerably in size (from New York with a population of 11,580,000 to Atlanta with a population of 1,390,000), all rank within the top thirty-two metropolitan areas of the country. Six SMSA's (Atlanta, Boston, Denver, Houston, New Orleans, and New York) are classified on the basis of 1960 industrial composition as nodal places (i.e., service centers), two (Cleveland and St. Louis) as manufacturing centers, and one (Philadelphia) as "mixed with nodal characteristics."[2]

The data in Table A highlight certain key characteristics of cities and suburbs. The first is the wide disparity in population and employment densities among cities and between cities and suburbs. Population densities range from 26,345 per square mile in New York City to 2,841 in Houston. Even where suburban employment densities in suburbs

Table A. Selected Information Relating to Ten Metropolitan Areas Studied, 1970

Place and Region	Type of Place (1960)	Area	Population (000's)	Employment^a (000's)	Land Area (sq. miles)	Population per sq. mile	Employment per sq. mile	Average Distance to Central City (miles)[b]	Commuters to city[c] %
Atlanta	Nodal	SMSA	1,390	520.6	1,727.0	805.0	301.4		
Southeast		City	497	286.9	131.5	3,783.0	2,181.7	13.0	55.2
		Suburb	893	233.7	1,595.5	559.6	146.5		
Baltimore	Mixed[d]	SMSA	2,072	721.0	2,259.0	917.0	319.2		
Mideast		City	906	365.8	78.3	11,568.0	4,671.8	14.7	38.2
		Suburb	1,166	355.2	2,180.7	534.6	162.9		
Boston	Nodal	SMSA	2,755	978.5	987.0	2,791.0	991.4		
New England		City	641	372.2	46.0	13,936.0	8,091.3	15.0	56.7
		Suburb	2,114	606.3	941.0	2,246.2	644.3		
Cleveland	Manufacturing	SMSA	2,064	719.3	1,519.0	1,359.0	473.5		
Great Lakes		City	751	389.7	75.9	9,893.0	5,134.4	10.7	54.7
		Suburb	1,313	329.6	1,443.1	910.2	228.4		
Denver	Nodal	SMSA	1,230	454.2	3,660.0	336.0	124.1		
Rocky Mountains		City	515	272.7	95.2	5,406.0	2,864.5	25.2	41.6
		Suburb	715	181.5	3,564.8	200.6	50.9		

Houston	Nodal	SMSA	1,986	708.9	6,286.0	316.0	112.8	16.3
		City	1,233	533.0	433.9	2,841.0	1,228.4	24.0
Southwest		Suburb	753	175.9	5,852.1	128.8	30.1	
New Orleans	Nodal	SMSA	1,046	319.6	1975.0	530.0	161.8	23.2
		City	593	216.7	197.1	3,011.0	1,099.4	30.3
Southeast		Suburb	453	102.9	1,777.9	255.0	57.9	
New York	Nodal	SMSA	11,580	3,859.9	2,137.0	5,419.0	1,806.2	29.6
		City	7,895	2,877.8	299.7	26,345.0	9,602.3	18.6
Mideast		Suburb	3,685	982.1	1,837.3	2,005.6	534.5	
Philadelphia	Mixed[d]	SMSA	4,821	1,586.0	3,553.0	1,357.0	446.4	21.0
		City	1,950	769.2	128.5	15,175.0	5986.0	29.0
Mideast		Suburb	2,871	816.8	3,424.5	838.5	238.5	
St. Louis	Manufacturing	SMSA	2,364	803.6	4,118.0	574.0	195.1	15.2
		City	622	338.7	61.2	10,167.0	5,534.3	54.7
Plains		Suburb	1,742	464.9	4,056.8	429.3	114.6	

[a] At place of work.
[b] Calculated by weighting the distance from the center of each county in the SMSA to the central city by the total incommuters to the city from that county and averaging.
[c] As percentage of city employment at place of work. Employees from outside SMSA included in this calculation.
[d] Mixed with nodal characteristics.

Source: *Census of Population, 1970. Statistical Abstract of the U.S. 1971.* T.M. Stanback, Jr. and R.K. Knight, *The Metropolitan Economy.*

7

are relatively high (New York and Philadelphia), city employment densities are greater by factors of eighteen or more, and where suburban densities are low (Denver and Cleveland), they are in excess of forty. The second is that distance from suburb to city varies considerably from metropolis to metropolis, ranging from 13 to 30 miles. The third is perhaps the most interesting: that the role played by commuters from the suburbs and areas outside the metropolitan area in the city's labor market is of major importance. These commuters account for shares of total jobs in central cities by amounts ranging from 57 percent (Boston) to 19 percent (New York). The significance of these commuter flows will be examined in detail in subsequent chapters.

THE PLAN OF STUDY

Eight chapters follow. The next chapter, *The Nature of Metropolitan Development*, provides a conceptual frame describing the ways in which development may take place through growth, upgrading, and import substitution. Chapter 2, *Transportation, Institutions, and Other Factors Influencing Suburbanization*, discusses changes in the transportation system and selected institutional aspects of suburbanization. Chapter 3, *Industrial Characteristics*, investigates the changing industrial composition, as well as certain qualitative aspects, of cities and suburbs. Chapter 4, *Occupational Characteristics and Commuter Flows*, examines occupational composition of employment and the size of commuter flows and assesses the importance of commuter earnings in the suburbs. Chapter 5, *Labor-Market Characteristics*, examines suburban and city labor markets through analyzing participation and unemployment rates, detailed composition of the work force and commuter flows in terms of age, sex, race, and employment stability. Chapter 6, *Labor-Market Flows*, analyzes flows into suburban and city work forces (e.g., new entrants, in-migrants, out-migrants).

Chapter 7, *The Unskilled Worker in Cities and Suburbs*. examines the problem of the city and suburban unskilled workers as they seek employment in suburban labor markets. Finally, in Chapter 8, *Metropolis at the Crossroads*, we consider the possibility of revitalizing the city and examine the implications of the analysis for public policy.

REFERENCES

1. See Appendix A for a more detailed discussion of the SMSA's selected.

2. Thomas M. Stanback, Jr. and Richard V. Knight, *The Metropolitan Economy* (New York, N.Y.: Columbia University Press, 1970).

[1

The Nature of Metropolitan Development

The central business district (CBD), the rest of the central city, and the suburbs are interdependent and together comprise the metropolitan economy. This metropolitan economy is, in turn, part of a larger system of regional, national, and international economies, engaging in trade with its hinterland, with other metropolitan economies, and with the rest of the world. Its development hinges on its ability to adapt to external changes, while responding to the diverse needs of its own constituency.

At the same time, the metropolitan region must be regarded as an economy with an evolving differentiation between city and suburbs, each of which exhibits specialization in terms of work and residential functions. The more developed the metropolis, the greater the variety of functions and the more advanced the differentiation process (functionally and spatially) between these sub-economies is likely to be.

In the first section of this chapter, the metropolitan region is examined principally as a spatially undifferentiated economy. Attention focuses on growth and change in two broad sectors, the export sector and the local sector, and on the strategic importance of each.

The second and third sections examine patterns of spatial organization of various types of activities and move toward an analysis of city and suburbs within the metropolitan economy, observing the specialization of each in terms of export and local activities. This approach, which is followed throughout the remainder of the book, throws light on sources of growth in the suburbs arising out of development in its export and local sectors, on the difficult transition which many cities are undergoing as the industrial composition of their export bases changes,

9

and on the nature and extent of the interdependence which exists between suburb and city.

A fourth section examines the significance of the analysis for the formulation of developmental policies.

METROPOLITAN DEVELOPMENTAL PROCESSES[1]

EXPORT AND LOCAL SECTORS WITHIN THE METROPOLITAN ECONOMY

Activities which comprise the export sector involve the production (directly or indirectly) of goods and services for markets outside the given economy, or for nonresidents. Activities which comprise the local sector involve the production of goods and services for local residents (e.g., bakeries, schools, hospitals, retailing, police). The distinction between these two sectors of the metropolitan economy allows for examination of two sets of urban-growth processes. One set involves metropolitan relationships with the larger environment (the exchange of goods, services, ideas, people, and resources with the rest of the world)—the addressing of extra-metropolitan needs. The other set concerns how income originating from exports is spent to purchase goods and services produced locally, and how this local sector may expand through import substitution.

NEED TO DISTINGUISH BETWEEN QUALITATIVE AND QUANTITATIVE CHANGES

A distinction within the export and local sectors between growth processes that represent qualitative changes and those that represent quantitative changes is critical in the analysis of metropolitan growth and in the formulation of metropolitan development policies. Qualitative changes involve increased value added per worker; quantitative changes involve simply increases in employment. With the maturing of the metropolitan economy and the slowing of its growth rate, qualitative changes become more important than quantitative changes. Growth of leading sectors is offset by declines in lagging sectors, so neither the extent, nor the nature, of the transition and upgrading is revealed through examination of quantitative changes.

Each type of growth process implies a different type of metropolitan development. The quantity dimension concerns magnitude of net increments in population and employment, capital and labor. The quality dimension concerns processes of upgrading economic opportunity and business-social-cultural infrastructure. If, for example, a metropolis is expanding output without upgrading *(industry expansion)*, a filling-in of its less-developed areas is likely. Such development may be characterized as "more of the same," as metropolitan space becomes more completely utilized. If, on the other hand, quality is improving, and incomes of certain groups are rising, then we would expect new forms of growth, restructuring, and integration.

Quality improvements take place primarily in the central business district. They are accompanied by a shift of residents and residentiary functions to new suburban areas and by obsolescence of older areas in the inner city that were designed to meet conditions prevailing at an earlier period in the region's development. The problem of obsolescence is accentuated when there are employment declines *(job erosion)* taking place in production activities.[2] In such cases, older areas may be abandoned as they become dysfunctional. Placing the development of metropolitan areas in the context of qualitative and quantitative changes helps to identify the underlying causes of many urban problems. The nature of solutions becomes more evident once the causes are understood.

UPGRADING: THE QUALITATIVE DIMENSION OF
METROPOLITAN GROWTH PROCESSES

Quality improvements or the upgrading of economic opportunities may occur in either the local or export sector. The nature of change is different, however, and changes in one may affect the other.

Three general types of upgrading in the export sector are readily visualized.

1. The export sector may be upgraded by increased productivity (including product-quality improvements resulting in increased value added per worker) in existing industries. This type of upgrading we shall call *process upgrading*. If productivity increases measured on a per-worker basis exceed increases in demand for the product, this type of upgrading will result in contraction of the work force.

2. Upgrading also occurs when new and higher-order functions are added to the export sector in terms of new products or services. A higher-order function would be one in which value added, skills required, and salaries paid are higher than in existing activities. For example, a long-range planning staff, corporate counsel, or a research-and-development center may be added by a manufacturing firm, or a new production facility may be added that employs more highly paid workers. The term *broadening* is used to describe growth through product innovation and diversification (adding new products), or through production of goods or services previously not produced locally. The latter *(import substitution)* is a major source of broadening.

3. Another source of upgrading, which usually accompanies the other two, is the dropping of lower-order functions—job erosion in the lagging sectors. A low-wage textile mill will not be able to hold on to its work force if a higher-wage electronic or automobile-assembly plant

settles nearby and tries to bid away its workers. If the textile mill is unable to compete by attracting new entrants into the work force, then that function will be dropped from the export sector and the average value added per employee in the export sector will increase.

Upgrading of the local sector may occur in the same three fashions: 1) by increased productivity or greater use of expertise in existing functions; 2) by the addition of new functions (local business services, hospitals, universities, museums, etc.); by the expansion of higher-order functions (lawyers, teachers, architects, etc.); and 3) by the dropping of lower-order functions (local food processing, household help). Import substitution may be the source of upgrading in the local, as well as in the export, sector. Further, local firms that are upgraded may find that they are able to compete in regional and national markets and thus become partly export-oriented.

The level, type, and diversity of activity in the local sector is closely related to the level, type, and diversity of activity in the export sector. If productivity increases in the export sector and, as a result, export earnings flow into the region's economy in the form of increased wages, rents, and taxes, then the level of activity in the local sector increases in some related manner and the local sector is broadened. As the scale of operations in the local sector is increased, possibilities for productivity increases and import substitution are enhanced.

THE EXPORT-BASE MULTIPLIER

The relationship between the export sector and the entire economy, which operates through the effect of the export sector upon the local sector, is called the *export-base multiplier*, and it may be expressed in terms of employment or income. The multiplier is computed by expressing total income or employment as a multiple of income or employment in the export sector.[3] The larger the community and the more diverse the local sector, the less income leaks out to purchase imports and the larger the multiplier. If, as a community grows, the local sector grows disproportionately because of import substitution, then the multiplier increases. In fact, increased activity in the local sector may generate sufficient employment to offset employment declines in the export sector resulting purely from upgrading in that sector.

This is an important observation, since upgrading of the export sector may be accompanied by a decline in the number employed in export activities, even though total earnings of the export base increase. We are thus left with a development scenario where employment in the export sector is declining, but employment in the local sector is increasing.

In order to illustrate how growth occurs through changes in the export and local sectors and, particularly, how qualitative changes in the export sector, even when accompanied by job erosion, may lead to increased total employment, we present in Appendix B, page 204, a series of hypothetical examples of growth dynamics. Our concern in preparing these illustrations is not with direction of causality, or with lags in adjustment, but simply with showing the relationships between the export and local sectors.

URBAN-DEVELOPMENT PROCESSES IDENTIFIED

It is well to observe at this point that we have now identified four major types of urban-development processes:

1. Industry expansion ("more of the same")
2. Job erosion
3. Process upgrading
4. Broadening, (includes export and local-sector diversification, largely through import substitution)

Although the significance of particular types of processes varies considerably from place to place, each occurs in every metropolis. The classification is presented simply for conceptual purposes. No attempt is made at quantification of a given process, although some of the analyses serve to illustrate how processes may be quantified. We believe research designed to bring about such quantification would make an important contribution to urban development.[4]

GROWTH AND CHANGES IN SPATIAL ORGANIZATION

Some activities in the export and local sectors are located in the central city; others in the suburbs. In the export sector, headquarters and administration offices tend to locate centrally, whereas production facilities, research and development, warehousing, and regional sales offices tend to be decentralized in industrial parks and districts, and in research and development and office parks. Many local-sector needs are met in both cities and suburbs by local schools, police, churches, convenience shops, etc.; other service needs of the entire metropolis are met by institutions which may be located in either city or suburb (e.g., stadiums, airports, universities, teaching hospitals, and museums). Certain activities that service both export and local sectors (e.g., legal, financial, accounting, insurance, advertising firms, and communications institutions) tend to cluster in the CBD.

DEVELOPMENT AND SHIFTING OF LOCATION OF FUNCTIONS

With urban development comes changes in the range of functions performed and changes in their spatial organization. As export-oriented firms become organized on a national or multinational basis, export functions are differentiated and specialized. Some functions (e.g., rou-tinized production) become more footloose and decentralize to more efficient sites in smaller, lower-cost communities; others (e.g., administration offices and research and development laboratories) are centralized in larger places in order to take advantage of infrastructure and external economies. Similarly, as the metropolis develops and residents become more affluent, local functions become differentiated and more specialized. Residents, firms, and institutions serving the needs of residents often decentralize to take advantage of a wider range of environments.

This centrifugal movement of people and jobs is called *suburban shift*, a fifth developmental process which must be added to the other four listed on page 13 above.[5] Suburban shift is selective. Only certain functions become suburbanized. Thus, as the urban form loosens up, there is an increasing differentiation between cities and suburbs with many critical functions remaining centralized in the CBD. In general, the larger, older, and more developed a city, the greater the potential for suburbanization. In a large measure suburbanization has been, simply, a loosening up of residential settlements which had developed before low-density spatial organization was feasible.

URBAN DEVELOPMENT—THE MATURING METROPOLITAN ECONOMY

The benefits from relocation within the metropolitan economy are, by no means, distributed evenly. As the functions are reorganized and regrouped into more efficient arrangements, some metropolises, and some communities within metropolises, move ahead while others fall behind. The dualistic nature of development is more evident in the maturing industrial areas where some sectors within the metropolitan economy decline while others expand or upgrade.

Leading and expanding sectors are usually separate, both geographically and socially, from lagging or eroding sectors, and the weakening of linkages between these sectors leads to an ever-widening gap between them. The social inequities that are created lie at the base of many urban problems.

It is easy to overlook the fact that, under conditions of rapid transition, values created in one area are offset by values destroyed in other areas within the same metropolis. The shift of property values, employment opportunities, public services, and amenities from inner city to suburbs triggers powerful economic (and social) forces that tend to be cumulative and difficult to reverse. For example, once neighborhoods begin to deteriorate, mortgage institutions, by restricting or refusing mortgages on homes in "red-lined" neighborhoods, accelerate the process. Similarly, public sector response to suburban shift has been to facilitate it, to subsidize mortgages on suburban homes and to build up the suburban highway system and other physical and social infrastructures.

Just how suburban shift has worked out in practice may be observed in Cuyahoga County (Cleveland), Ohio. An analysis of official records of assessed property values indicates that between 1962 and 1971 there was a shift of investment in properties from the city to the rest of the county amounting to 3.6 billion dollars, which represents 64 percent of the increase in the county area outside the city during the period. The outlying area contained 37 percent of the county's assessed valuation in 1960; 69 percent in 1971 [6]

Disinvestment and loss of employment opportunities for the disadvantaged in the inner city are accompanied by rising costs of commuting, public services, and public financial assistance, by a decline in personal safety and in the quality of urban life generally. Moreover, there is reduced contact with viable sectors and, hence, reduced access to information networks which lead to employment opportunities. Not only do commuting distances increase with urban decay and sprawl, but time, energy, land, and pollution costs increase as well. Not surprisingly, residents of the inner city, working through the political process and observing no advantages accruing to them, tend to resist any change. They may veto development such as the construction of new interstate highways within the city or urban revewal efforts, thus preventing badly needed upgrading of physical and social facilities.

As a result, pressures are generated to shift CBD functions to the suburbs where they are performed sub-optimally or to other metropolises here or abroad that offer a more supportive environment. The final outcome of a failure to cope with central city problems is a decline of the export base of the entire metropolis, a deterioration in its wealth and income, and an out-migration of the young and the highly trained.

The implication of the above is that declining sectors can undermine neighborhoods, creating social inequities and welfare burdens that retard development or bring about decline (e.g., East St. Louis, Newark, Gary). This problem of unequal development has been addressed at the regional level (e.g., backward rural areas versus modern urban areas) through national economic development plans and programs.[7] It demands the same degree of concern at the metropolitan level.

DEVELOPMENTAL PROCESSES WITHIN THE
METROPOLITAN ECONOMY: CITY AND SUBURBS

Treating cities and suburbs separately (as we shall do in the chapters which follow) sheds additional light on metropolitan development. This simplification permits us to focus on certain unique characteristics of city and suburb. In general, cities face a very different set of problems and opportunities than do suburban areas.

The qualitative dimension of metropolitan development—the upgrading of human resources-institutions and infrastructure—is of particular significance to the study of intra-metropolitan development. A few observations will illustrate how upgrading of individuals and institutions affect urban form. The first observation concerns the relationship between the place of work and place of residence; the second, the relationship between place of residence and the local sector, and the third, the location of export activities.

RELATIONSHIP BETWEEN PLACE OF WORK AND PLACE OF RESIDENCE

A number of labor-market studies have noted that the distance between place of work and place of residence increases with income.[8] Among higher-income persons, preference for space tends to outweigh preference for access to place of work, and, thus, homes tend to be purchased in suburbs which generally require longer commutes, but where lots are larger and land is cheaper. Consequently, as real incomes increase, the average journey to work tends to increase. Upgrading of the work force of the city implies a rise in real income and a concomitant upgrading of place of residence, usually in the form of lower-density housing located at greater distance from the city.

Accordingly, the suburbs, to a large extent, have drawn their residents from those who, having achieved affluence, can afford to seek out a higher-quality neighborhood—one which is newer and further from the central city. This has meant that the upgrading of economic activity within the city has generally involved a radial movement of residents outward as they try to upgrade their place of residence in line with the upgrading of their jobs. Thus, city workers who commute daily from the suburbs are actually exporting their services from suburb to city and comprise a "hidden-export sector" of the suburbs. As we shall see in Chapter 4, this export sector accounts for the largest share of suburban export earnings.

RELATIONSHIP BETWEEN PLACE OF RESIDENCE AND THE LOCAL SECTOR

The second observation is that the local sector, which has accounted for a major share of recent job increases, tends to expand in the expanding suburbs. Consumer services tend to locate in proximity to the residences of the above-average-income households which have located there. Since wages in the local sector are generally lower than in the export sector, local-sector workers tend to be recruited from the most-immediately-available supply. (Low-wage workers cannot travel far to work and are particularly hampered by the lack of public transportation which characterizes the suburbs.) Although only indirect evidence is available, this source frequently appears as a secondary labor force, consisting of second and third wage earners of middle-to-high-income households, whose head may be employed in the export sector.

Thus we see that the local sector, which is likely to be the major generator of employment opportunities in a developed metropolis, will become more suburban in its location as some of the older export activities (especially low-value-added manufacturing) are closed out, as upgrading proceeds, and as better-paid workers relocate to the periphery. The local sector will be shifting from the older areas where export sector activities are in decline, and jobs are being destroyed, to the suburbs where new export activities (especially manufacturing) are being located, and where upgraded workers of the city are finding residence.

Changes in the geographic distribution of income by residence tend to amplify the process of development in the suburbs and of decay in the city. The local sector tends to locate in the center of its sales market and is, therefore, pulled towards high-income areas to a greater extent than would be expected in terms of simple demographic shifts. Moreover, the new shopping centers and discount stores in the suburbs serve not only nearby residents that once patronized downtown, but also draw customers from the city. Thus, in addition to loss of export-sector jobs, the older areas of the inner city lose jobs for their remaining residents in their local sectors as such residential activities shift to the suburbs.

It must also be kept in mind that the upgrading of jobs may occur in both the export and local sectors of the city, and that suburban communities may export the services of its residents to either. For example, teachers, policemen, doctors, and administrators employed by the local sector of the inner city may well reside in the suburbs. Thus, paradoxically, what would commonly be regarded as a part of the local sector of the city's economy becomes, to the extent that there is commuting, a part of the export sector of the suburbs. In fact, for many city residents, a good civil-service appointment or promotion will enable their households to move to the suburbs.[9]

The change of residence of high-wage households brings with it, therefore, a redistribution of low-wage jobs. But those low-wage city workers whose jobs are undermined will not know where the jobs are going and will not be able to afford to commute, or be able to move, to the suburbs. Low-wage jobs at their new location will tend to be filled by second and third wage earners from high-income households in the nearby suburbs. Those inner-city workers detached from the work force are likely to become unemployed for periods of varying duration, some falling back on public financial assistance.

There are serious welfare and fiscal implications here. The loss of high-wage households from the city and undermaintenance of property as landlords withdraw their capital, depress property values and tax revenues. The loss of low-wage jobs which supported a low-income household in the inner city may result in the entire household turning to public assistance. On the other hand, the additional income contributed by the second or third wage earner in the suburban household is more likely to be income of a discretionary, rather than of an essential, nature. The poor and disadvantaged become increasingly concentrated in the inner cities; the affluent in the suburbs.[10]

THE LOCATION OF EXPORT ACTIVITIES

Location of export activities depends on the nature of the activity, but for conceptual purposes it is helpful to distinguish two types: centralized and dispersed. Activities which require centrality or extensive face-to-face interaction with other activities (e.g., banks, law firms, courts, government, insurance, advertising) tend to agglomerate at central places, and together they constitute the central business district. Activities not requiring face-to-face contact, such as manufacturing, research and development, and warehousing, have increasingly tended to disperse. Predominantly high-wage manufacturing industries tend to move out to the suburbs where sites are available at more favorable prices than in the center city. Their highly paid workers can afford to commute from all over the metropolitan area, and their lower-paid clerical workers are recruited locally. Low-wage manufacturing industries are more likely to remain at their old locations in the city where they wither on the vine until their plants and equipment are no longer useful, or to move to low-wage labor markets in smaller towns, rural areas, or offshore.

Thus, two locational patterns of *export* activities appear to dominate metropolitan development. First, high-wage jobs in regional firms and in oligopolistic, or protected, activities are located either in the CBD where they are filled largely by suburban commuters, or they are located in the suburbs where they are also filled by commuters (mainly from within the suburbs, but to some extent from the outlying areas and from the city). Secondly, low-wage jobs found in more competitive manufacturing industries that are usually in decline are generally located in the older parts of the metropolis, primarily in the inner city.

The locational pattern of jobs in the *local* sector (largely low-wage) is strongly influenced, in turn, by residential patterns of high-wage workers in the export sector and import sector, although it is often influenced, as well, by considerations of access to major highways.

TRADE BETWEEN CITY AND SUBURBS AND INTERMETROPOLITAN TRADE

Trade between the city and suburbs must be distinguished from trade between metropolitan areas. The suburbs are not highly developed, self-sufficient economies, but depend upon the city for a variety of services and as a market for much of their labor and certain of their goods and services. Cities, in turn, draw upon the suburbs. Accordingly, suburban and city multipliers are considerably smaller than multipliers for the entire metropolitan economy because a relatively smaller proportion of residents' income is spent locally than is true for the metropolitan area taken as a whole. An extreme, but interesting, example is that of a residential suburban neighborhood which has no local sector, and thus would have a multiplier of one since no income is respent within that area. Residents would export their labor and import all goods and services from non-residents.

When examined closely, the relationships between city and suburb are found to be quite complex. Cities provide a variety of goods and services for the entire metropolitan market, including the suburbs (legal, business, cultural, as well as some retail shopping services). Suburbs, in turn, provide a variety of goods and services (certain manufactured goods, back-office services, and a considerable volume of retail services from their large shopping centers). The large flows of labor from suburb to city, and the smaller flows from city to suburb, may also be viewed as a form of intrametropolitan trade.

Thus, suburban exports and imports (or city exports and imports) are not necessarily exports or imports of the entire metropolitan economy. For example, doctors residing in the suburbs but practicing in the city would be classified as "hidden" exports of the suburbs, and suburban purchases of medical services in the city would be classified as imports. Yet, at the metropolitan level of analysis, these medical services would appear as part of the local economy (unless some portion involved patients from outside the metropolis). Accordingly, the metropolitan economy as a whole is seen as more self-sufficient. Its local sector is relatively larger—and so is its multiplier—than is the case for suburban or city components. Appendix C, page 210, presents numerical example illustrating how low multipliers in city and suburb become significantly larger when the city and its suburbs are regarded as a single metropolitan economy.

METROPOLITAN STRATEGIES FOR DEVELOPMENT

Perhaps the major problem of the metropolis is that the city government, which presides over the central work place of the metropolis, must be responsive to the needs of its political constituency—the residents of the city. Since city voters have typically not understood the extent to which their destinies are tied to the economic vitality of the city, municipal government is much less likely to be responsive to the needs of its economic constituency, those highly strategic firms and institutions centralized in the CBD. Consequently, public policies in the central city tend to be based on defensive strategies which are oriented towards propping up lagging sectors (e.g., trying to hold onto a rapidly declining low-wage manufacturing industry). Such strategies have typically not been successful since they are attempting to counteract powerful national economic forces. A greater awareness of the strengths of those industries which comprise the leading sectors of the metropolitan economy, coupled with more effective communication to the public-at-large of the implications of economic development, is required before affirmative—and aggressive—strategies can be formulated.

The distinction between national and local forces is important. Whereas national developments must be taken as given, local development processes can be influenced by local policies. We are arguing that, within the constraints set by national forces, the metropolis can exercise more effective control over its own development than is generally realized. The "managed" or "intentional" city can replace the "unintentional" city.

Failure to distinguish between developments which are beyond control and those which are not has, in the past, resulted in many cities (e.g., New York, Philadelphia, Cleveland) following strategies designed to revitalize manufacturing activity. Not only are the private and social returns on resources spent in this way typically insufficient to justify such investment, but such public investment may have an adverse effect on private investment.

Attention is focused on the region's weakness, and a generalized pessimism develops. As the city loses sight of its strengths, the vision of the city's future becomes blurred; the region turns against itself; the quality of leadership declines; and the lagging sectors exercise their veto power with increasing frequency.

Fortunately, agglomerative forces are strong, and the CBD has tended to develop even while manufacturing-production activity has contracted and some functions have moved to suburban locations. Nevertheless, failure to realize the potential of the central city must have a long-term effect on the metropolis and the nation. Firms will not be able to interface in an optimal fashion, new investment in the CBD will not be realized, private and social costs will increase, and key firms and individuals that value a more cosmopolitan quality of urban life will leave, or will not be attracted to the region.

METROPOLITAN DEVELOPMENT
AND EMPLOYMENT OPPORTUNITY

To conclude, with upgrading of the metropolis, suburbanization is accentuated. The residences of the high-income workers in the CBD become more suburbanized; and economic opportunity for low-skill and low-wage jobs in the local sector is partially shifted away from the city where the disadvantaged reside and where economic opportunity for workers in low-income households is already contracting. The outcome is that older neighborhoods in the inner city become obsolete locations for work and residence; jobs become increasingly scarce; access to labor-market information networks is cut off; unemployment rates increase; quality of public services declines; and, in short, low-income neighborhoods in older parts of the inner city become dysfunctional.

The conceptual framework devised above may be applied to different sizes and types of metropolis. The prominence of a process will depend on the place examined. In a manufacturing metropolis, the shift of high-wage jobs to the suburbs and the contraction of low-wage jobs in the city would be greater than in a service-oriented metropolis where there is little manufacturing employment to be lost. In a service metropolis, however, expansion accompanied consequently by upgrading would energize the suburbanization of residences of the local sector.

An additional observation is that the larger and the younger the metropolis, the greater will be the distance of the expanding local sector from the older declining neighborhoods because of size and the influence of transportation mode on the urban form. Under any given growth conditions, where greater distances obtain, older neighborhoods will, in all likelihood, be characterized by higher unemployment levels and a higher degree of obsolescence.

The suburbanization process appears to be creating a very severe long-range problem as employment opportunities and residences shift to the suburbs. The problem is aggravated by still another development, the loss of low-wage manufacturing jobs which are not going to the suburbs, but are being lost to small towns, rural areas, and foreign countries. The fact that the necessary manpower adjustments are worked out in practice on an intergenerational basis poses problems for both young and old. Blue-collar workers being laid off could perhaps be rehired as low-wage clerk typists or as service workers if they did not have to compete with the large number of women and young workers entering the labor market. On the other hand, as blue-collar employment in the city is phased out, the opening-up of low-wage job vacancies is not adequate to absorb the large flow of persons newly entering the labor force.

In the metropolitan areas today the process of work establishment begins primarily in the local residentiary sector for those who do not go on to college or join the armed forces. These local service jobs have come to be located to a disproportionate extent in peripheral areas, where they are likely to be filled by newly employed persons heavily subsidized by husbands or parents who support the household with a high-wage job. As well as we can observe, it is typically not sufficient to be a resident in the suburbs or to have public transit to gain initial access to employment opportunities. For most, a combination of factors is required: membership in an already viable household that can afford to susidize an initial work period, communication and computational skills attained largely through formal education, and an outlook that derives from a middle-class environment. Once established, a suburban worker has the option of upgrading by commuting to the CBD or to other suburbs, or of moving to other metropolises wherever the good jobs and major career ladders are.

In the analysis that follows, we attempt to provide as accurate a description and quantification of metropolitan development processes that underlie suburbanization today as available data allow. We do not argue that market forces alone must dictate how our cities and suburbs should develop any more than we would argue that floods should be allowed to wreak their damage unhindered by flood-control measures. Rather, we would argue that once we begin to understand the growth processes underlying suburbanization, we can opt either to let market forces continue in the same fashion as in the past, or to intervene and confront the problems implicit in these processes. Our position is that the better we understand the forces and processes underlying metropolitan development today, the more effective we can be in anticipating and guiding future urban development. If we understand our cities and the constraints within which they operate, we can build them to serve our needs. If urban-growth dynamics are understood and society continues, nevertheless, to allow adverse forces to persist unabated, then we must acknowledge that costly dysfunctional urban design exists by choice; that the outcomes are expected; and that we prefer to tolerate dysfunctional institutions and neighborhoods (perhaps by blaming the victims) rather than to "design them out."

REFERENCES

1. For a review of the development of the export-base concept which dates back to Werner Sombart (1916), see Gunter Krumme, "Werner Sombart and the Economic Base Concept," *Land Economies*, XLIV (February, 1968), 112-116, or Richard V. Knight, *Employment Expansion and Metropolitan Trade* (doctoral dissertation, University of London, 1971).

2. The term "job erosion" will be used throughout to describe employment declines for reasons *other than suburban shift*. For example, job erosion may occur through plant closings, reduced activity, mechanization, and increased productivity.

3. Readers who are acquainted with economic concepts will recognize that this is simply an application of the Keynesian multiplier. The formal assumptions and a detailed discussion of the processes involved are found in Charles M. Tiebout, *The Community Export Base Study* (New York: Committee for Economic Development, 1962).

4. For example, see the analysis of sources of job increases and job decreases in Richard

V. Knight, *Employment Expansion and Metropolitan Trade* (New York: Praeger Publishers, Inc., 1974), chap. 5.

5. Several researchers have attempted to identify factors underlying suburban shifts. Their efforts are reviewed by Bennett Harrison. *Urban Economic Development: Suburbanization, Innercity Opportunity and the Condition of the Central City* (Washington: The Urban Institute, 1974), pp. 7-14.

6. For a discussion, see Richard V. Knight, *Regional Development Perspective for Welfare Policy* (working paper, Public Welfare Policy Project, Federation for Community Planning, Cleveland, Ohio, 1975), pp. 47-48.

7. The underlying dynamic of cumulative causation leading to dualistic development has been explored at length for less-developed countries by Gunner Myrdal, *Rich Lands and Poor: The Road to World Prosperity* (New York: Harper and Row Publishers, Inc., 1957). See also Denis Goulet, *The Cruel Choice: A New Concept in the Theory of Development* (New York: Atheneum Publishers, 1971).

8. See, for example, Albert Rees and George Schultz, *Workers and Wages in an Urban Labor Market* (Chicago: University of Chicago Press, 1970). Rees and Schultz note that "the distance variable was found to have a significant positive relationship to wages in ten of twelve occupations examined." Pp. 172-173.

9. A recent survey in Rockland County, more than a half hour's drive from New York City, indicated that more than 3,000 residents were New York City policemen who commuted into the city each day. New York City firemen work 24-hour shifts, and many live in Orange and Monroe counties, 60 miles out, commuting into the city in organized car pools three times a week. These suburban police working in New York City have even formed an organization, the Shields, to promote their interests.

10. For example, Cleveland, which accounted for 45 percent of households in Cuyahoga County in 1972, had 87 percent of the welfare case load. Moreover, areas in the city which accounted for only 18 percent of the county's households accounted for 70 percent of the county's welfare cases. Based on analysis of data compiled by the Federation for Community Planning, *Fact Book* (Cleveland, Ohio, 1974).

Transportation, Institutions, and Other Factors Influencing Suburbanization

The rapid suburbanization which has characterized metropolitan areas during the postwar years finds its roots in a number of causes including the natural tendency for cities to grow beyond their political boundaries, the rise in affluence which has permitted families to purchase automobiles, the high level of family formation coupled with high birth rates (the latter now reversed), the aggressive program of road building, particularly of freeways, and the greatly expanded air-transportation system. In addition, it has been expedited by the invention and refinement of new institutional arrangements which have permitted firms to settle more readily in the outlying areas of the metropolis and to operate more efficiently.

In this chapter, we discuss the importance of the rapidly developed highway and air-transport systems and of certain of these institutions (the industrial park, the office park, and the shopping center). In addition, we examine locational tendencies of office activities as well as certain trends in suburban housing construction.

THE HIGHWAY SYSTEM

It is difficult to overestimate the significance of the development of the highway system in shaping the suburban economy. The program itself has been immense. Moreover, it has acted not only to bring about dramatic increases in the commuter range of metropolitan areas, but also to alter spatial patterns of industrial, commercial, and residential activities.

24

Some notion of the extent of the revolution, which occurred within cities and their outlying areas following the enactment of the Federal Highway Act of 1956, may be gained by observing both the growth in total urban highway mileage from 1956 to 1969 and the extent to which this growth has been accounted for by expansion of the primary system:[1]

	1956	1969
Urban highway mileage, total	36,222	55,980
Percent	100	100
(a) State primary system, 4-lane divided (miles)	2,596	13,112
Percent	7.2	23.4
(b) State primary system, full-access control (no grade crossing)	355	6,247
Percent	1.0	11.2
(c) Remaining urban highway mileage	33,271	36,621
Percent	91.0	65.4

The effect of this dramatic enlargement of highway facilities within metropolitan areas has been to open up large areas for residential use. Workers have gained access to a larger area with no increase, or even a reduction, in travel time. One study has shown that there is an elasticity to reduction in travel time, which is analogous to elasticity of response to reduction in price. Workers have traded off about half of the advantage of reduced travel time in favor of the advantage of increased distance and a less-urban setting.[2]

More than a decade ago, one major real estate executive described the effect of major highway improvements in the greater Boston area as follows:[3]

The extension of the distance that can be covered within 30 minutes driving time from Boston, coupled with the post-war housing demand and industrial development, has transformed sleepy farming towns into populous suburbs and brought them within the influence of Boston. . . .

Without the expressways, most shopping and manufacturing facilities of any size would still be concentrated in and around Boston itself. Land values 10 miles beyond the city would have remained stationary or suffered a decline. As it is, most towns and cities served by the web of highways are finding it difficult to keep up with their phenomenal growth.

Overnight, acres of idle farmland and parcels of tree-studded countryside are being bought up and subdivided into new house lots, as the demand for suburban homes increases. Cities and towns are laying pipelines to extend sewerage, water and gas facilities. Land is at a premium and values are generally high.

At the same time that modern highways have opened up outlying areas for residential purposes, they have rendered them attractive for industrial and commercial development. Of course, firms do not move from the city simply in search of fresh air, trees, and grass. There usually must be economic advantages. These advantages have been found in a combination of factors: lower taxes, opportunities to modernize and to expand (using efficient single-story plants), adequate parking, lower taxes, lower property costs, greater access to suppliers and customers, improved exit from the metropolitan area, and easier recruiting of professionals and managers.

The highway matrix has sharply altered the pattern of accessibility. No longer is it typically the city location which renders the distributor or manufacturer most accessible to the large metropolitan market. More often it is a location outside the city situated minutes away from an interstate thruway. One firm which moved from New York City to Paramus, N.J., reports that it has actually improved its access to customers in Brooklyn.[4]

One aspect of interstate highway development of special significance is the construction of limited-access beltways circumventing all, or a part, of the central city and lying a number of miles outside of the city itself. Although originally designed mainly to facilitate intercity traffic, these beltways, which now at least partially encircle many large cities, have become the major thoroughfares of the suburbs—what *The New York Times* has called "the accidental main streets of the outer cities."[5]

One study conducted by the Federal Highway Administration provides substantial evidence that beltways act to encourage suburban growth.[6] When metropolitan areas with beltways were compared with metropolitan areas without beltways, it was found that the SMSAs with beltways showed larger increases in population, retail establishments, and retail employment in areas lying immediately outside central cities.

Another study relating to the St. Louis metropolitan area revealed not only that industrial-park development was sensitive to the location of the interstate beltway, but that the beltway had encouraged growth on the periphery.[7] From 1965 to 1970, following the construction of the beltway, industrial employment density was found to have risen most sharply in the area outside the beltway. Another well-known example of rapid development is the Capital Beltway around Washington, D.C. According to *Fortune*, "some 800,000 new inhabitants settled along the beltway's borders during the last decade and no less than twelve regional shopping centers vie for their trade."[8]

Thus the role of modern highway transportation in the development of the suburbs is an extremely dynamic one. It involves the creation of access for residential, industrial, and commercial activities on an entirely new and different scale. Suburbanization has also involved the catalytic action of real estate brokers and developers and the creation of virtually new institutional arrangements.

A sense of at least part of this interplay of forces is conveyed by a quotation from another real estate executive, R. P. Nordblum. His remarks on the impact of Massachusetts Route 128 are representative of those of developers and executives from firms in areas outside of New York, Philadelphia, and Baltimore:[9]

> The highways were making it possible for distributors of consumer products to cover a greater road area within a much shorter time than was ever possible before. Instead of having district warehouses, distribution of products from large regional warehouses located at strategic highway intersections was more efficient and economical. Overnight service from regional warehouses became the rule rather than the exception. Distribution patterns were changed throughout the country, and a few regional warehouses requiring a smaller investment in real estate were doing the job that many smaller ones had done previously.
>
> With new techniques of materials-handling and automation, the need for modern, efficient, one-story plants became apparent to manufacturers. This created a demand for land to spread out in a horizontal fashion as contrasted with the vertical type of construction which prevailed in most urban areas prior to the war. Most large cities offered practically no industrial land within city limits; consequently, industry was forced to look further and further into the suburbs to find adequate land. Most of these suburban sites were not accessible by public transportation, but in the postwar period every worker owned an automobile and this became the main form of transportation to and from the new industrial plant. This fact alone put a premium on industrial plant locations served by major highways.
>
> These technological changes together with the widespread ownership of the automobile opened up great opportunities for the realtor. Every company in a multi-story factory in an urban location became a prospect for a new building overnight. . . .

Two additional aspects of the recently constructed highway system need to be emphasized. The first is the creation of strategic nodes for development at interchanges and points of limited access. Older highways with unlimited access and few or no zoning restrictions were characterized by the now well-known "strip" development of commercial and industrial activities stretching for miles with varying densities, both within the city and in outlying areas. New major highways with limited access are characterized, however, by sharply focused agglomerations near intersections, where commercial and industrial firms seek to maximize access to these high-traffic transportation lanes.

One successful developer ventured the opinion that an intersection of two "interstates" was a profitable development opportunity no matter how remote the location. The significance of this is that a spatial organization has been brought about which is logical largely in terms of a single criterion: access to highways. New plants are tightly integrated with neither residential concentrations nor existing agglomerations of a more traditional sort (i.e., towns and cities).

A second aspect is that the major-highway network is now characterized not only by high-speed, heavy-traffic facilities stretching between and around cities, but also by being tied into the central city, typically into the CBD. No one arriving in such cities as Atlanta or Houston by air or car can fail to observe this as a dramatic feature of the skyline: the huge ribbons of highways, frequently elevated, leading into the very heart of the metropolis, with their great spaghetti-like loops of ramps and interchanges. It is this highway complex, coupled in a handful of the largest places with the rapid-transit systems, which permits the inner city to be supplied, and which provides access, especially for firms within the CBD, to the labor supply of the suburbs. Clearly, the highway matrix has opened up the suburbs. But at the same time, it has provided everywhere an improved access to the inner city.

THE AIR-TRANSPORT SYSTEM

The development of an air-transport system—airports, air lanes, commercial airlines, and air-freight services—has caused a major shift of inter-city travel from wheel to wing. As with the development of the interstate highway system, which shifted travel from rail to road, the air-transport system seems destined to effect a major change in urban settlement patterns. Its impact on the location of jobs and residences has, as yet, only begun to be felt. In part this is due to the fact that airport growth has been obscured by the generalized rapid growth of the suburbs as a whole. It is due also to the fact that the building of a new generation of regional airports is only just beginning, and that the locational effects of these new facilities on business activity must await their completion.

As the new generation of airports becomes operational, users will not only alter their travel or shipping patterns to take advantage of the air-transport system, but will also take into account this new cost factor in their location decisions. Once primary adjustments are made, secondary or related activities will follow. Since these adjustments are likely to be very selective, a fuller understanding, not only of the air-transport system but of its relation to the process of the metropolis, is required. Such information is needed by both the public and private sectors if appropriate location decisions and land-use plans are to be made.

Seven aspects of the air-transport system are considered below: (1) The factors underlying the rapid rise of the air-transport system, (2) the effect of the air-transport system on overall metropolitan growth, (3) the effect of technological improvements and environmental considerations on the scale and location of airports, (4) the combined effect of the movement of airports away from the CBD and the shift in patterns of inter-city travel, (5) the effect of changes in the air-transport system on plant and office location, (6) the agglomeration of ancillary activities such as airline maintenance and operations, hotels, car rentals, restaurants, and residential communities in the proximity of airports, (7) scale of investment required in regional airport development and opportunities for planning.

DEVELOPMENT OF THE AIR-TRANSPORTATION SYSTEM

The introduction of air transportation is a new development in the history of metropolitan economies. Although the first commercial flight occurred in 1929, almost a half century ago, the system's growth has occurred primarily during the last twenty-five years. Between 1950 and 1970, the volume of domestic inter-city passenger traffic increased from 10 billion to 119 billion passenger miles, and the number of passengers served, from 19 million to 171 million. In contrast, rail inter-city passenger miles declined from 32 billion to 11 billion during the same period.[10]

The ninefold increase in passengers carried reflects increased seat capacity, increased speed, and higher utilization rates achieved through improved scheduling and night flights. Moreover, improvement in performance is expected to continue. For example, it is anticipated that the average number of passengers per flight, which increased from 18 in 1948 to 58 in 1970, will rise to 250 by the end of the century.[11] The potential development of air freight, which also increased tenfold from 300 million ton-miles in 1950 to 3.4 billion ton-miles in 1970, is also promising but is less important. Air freight accounted for 12 percent of airline revenues but only 0.17 percent of freight-ton miles (all carriers) in 1970.[12]

The basic advantage of air travel over ground travel, and thus the basic reason for the rapid rise in its use, is the saving it offers in time. For example, the new Dallas-Fort Forth Metroplex is less than three hours away from any major United States city and less than fourteen hours away from any country in the world. It is important to note that travel-time reductions by airlines have been even more dramatic than they were with the introduction of railroads. In the 1860's, travel time between Cleveland and New York was cut to one-seventh of stagecoach time (from three and one-half days to one day), whereas by the 1960's, airlines had reduced travel time for the same trip to one twenty-fourth of rail time, or to one hour. The supersonic Concorde (SST) will reduce travel time even further since it travels roughly one-third faster than commercial jet aircraft. The result of these dramatic reductions in travel time and improved accessibility of once faraway places is that our concept of distance has been radically altered. It will probably take a generation for the adjustment to be complete.

An understanding of the interplay between air travel, specialization, and productivity is essential to an understanding of urban development. One cannot unravel all factors that are behind the increased use of air transportation. However, we do know that the decreased time costs of travel and communication have the effect of increasing the reach of companies, i.e., the size of their markets. And as market size increases, further division of labor (increased specialization) becomes feasible, and more expertise is developed and applied to production, marketing, research, and administration. Expertise is costly to maintain. Hence, once developed, there are strong pressures to increase its utilization. And with increased utilization, the value of an expert's time rises and the time savings from air travel become even more important.

THE EFFECT OF THE AIR-TRANSPORT SYSTEM
ON OVERALL METROPOLITAN GROWTH

As noted above, the increased reach of firms, the greater division of labor, and the reduced travel times lead to greater use of highly trained manpower. The location of this highly skilled and highly paid manpower plays a major role in determining which metropolitan areas shall benefit most from these new trends. The separation of skill from physical work being carried out in new industrial plants, the greatly increased accessibility of low-cost rural areas due to improvement in both the highway and air-transport system, the shift of markets to the South and Southwest, improved communications, and the increased ease of using low-skilled workers abroad have resulted in the drawing off of routinized production jobs from major metropolitan areas. In contrast, the highly skilled jobs became more concentrated in those major metropolitan centers which can offer the established transportation, communication, business, cultural, and social infrastructure required to support specialized operations, maintain highly skilled personnel, and bring about further development of human resources.

Finally, with the advent of global markets, there is a tendency for control of once-independent firms to be drawn towards large metropolitan centers through mergers and acquisitions. In short, high-skilled, white-collar jobs are becoming more centralized in major metropolitan centers, while low-skilled, blue-collar jobs are becoming more geographically dispersed.[13]

Although the full impact of the air-transport system on metropolitan development has not been documented, it is of obvious importance. Even the casual observer will note that certain type facilities are relocating to take advantage of the air system that is evolving. What is hard to determine is the extent to which air service or improved access becomes a key element in the growth process. As route structures evolve and usage of the system increases, scale economies and frequency of flights increase and enhance the attractiveness of those areas which are well served. Once a metropolis has a competitive edge, it tends to stay ahead, for places with a superior air-transportation system offer advantages as sites for location of new activities over places offering poorer services (assuming, of course, that congestion and other costs often associated with size do not offset these advantages of access). Atlanta, by mobilizing resources and constructing the first regional jetport in its area, became the airline hub and, as regional offices located to take advantage of air service, developed into the major regional office center in the Southeast.

Thus, major regional airports may serve as growth poles, just as seaports did in an earlier age. It may well be that the new generation of jetports (such as the Dallas-Fort Worth Metroplex discussed below) will be the critical factor in creating major world cities of the future.

It should be noted, however, that there are important exceptions to this generalization where manufacturing is involved. Although air-transportation costs may be higher where an area is not served by a major airport, there may be other savings derived from a favorable labor supply and low costs of living. Cities without regional airports may remain competitive for many production-type activities as long as access is provided by general aviation. There are over 12,000 municipal or private airports that privately owned or leased aircraft may use.[14] And many small communities are building airports with the aid of government subsidies in an effort to attract new industry by improving access, especially for the management of firms which operate private aircraft. The Airport Aid Development Program, enacted in 1960, provided $280 million in one-half matching grants to aid small communities.[15]

EFFECT OF TECHNOLOGICAL IMPROVEMENTS AND ENVIRONMENTAL CONSIDERATIONS ON SCALE AND LOCATION OF AIRPORTS

A new generation of regional jetports is being created to replace those now ill-suited to today's needs. Most of the major airport sites in use today were selected prior to World War II, and they were not originally planned to serve as commercial aviation terminals, but rather to meet the needs of private flying clubs or of the military. These airports are typically outmoded and outgrown.[16]

Four factors have contributed to their obsolescence and thus created a need for new airports which are larger and, hence, more distant from the central city: (a) changes in aircraft technology; (b) increased operations, both in moving people and freight; (c) residential encroachment due to urban growth; and (d) the need to coordinate air- with ground-transportation systems, such as highways and mass transit.

The size of aircraft, frequency of flights, and land area affected by airport operations have increased rapidly. In 1945, propeller planes such as the DC-3 carried 21 passengers. Jets such as the Boeing 707 were introduced in the late 1950's, and jumbo jets such as the Boeing 747, seating 450 passengers, came into commercial use in 1970. Moreover, night flights became more frequent with the growth of air freight. Increased size of aircraft and frequency of flights have created serious environmental problems of noise, air pollution, safety, and ground access. As John R. Wiley, Director of the Port Authority of New York, has stated: "The growth pace of the aviation industry has the effect of rendering obsolete our most sophisticated projects, even while they are still in planning."[17]

Many major airports are already congested, and many more will soon reach capacity if the demand for air travel increases as expected. Air passengers to New York airports, the major hub of the nation's air system, increased from five million in 1950 to thirty-seven million in 1970. Trips per capita increased from .34 to 2.90 during the same twenty-year period.[18] Passenger enplanement in the United States is forecast to more than double according to data released by the Office of Research, Federal Aviation Administration:[19]

	Passengers in Millions	
Type of Flight	1970	1981
Domestic	155.1	417.2
International	16.2	47.3
Total	171.3	464.5

New airports are needed both to accommodate increased traffic and to relieve the social costs imposed on surrounding communities by increased operations, and this need for new or expanded facilities has come to be generally recognized. In addition to heavier and noisier planes and more frequent flights (especially during the night), residential development has encroached on the airport; and community development pressures mount in opposition to airports.[20] The effect of increased scale of projected operations required to service expected demand and the expanded site requirements made necessary by the federal environmental guidelines for noise-impacted areas, along with the sprawled pattern of residential growth, have led most new airports to be constructed even farther from the city centers than the original airports.

Many of the older airports were laid out before the interstate highway system was constructed, and they are not adequately tied into the highway system. Rail connections are rare. Consequently, the new regional airports are being constructed to accommodate projected high levels of traffic and to provide for a variety of airport related activities.[21] The land area required is extensive.[22] The new Dallas-Fort Worth airport is 17,500 acres (27 square miles), of which 8,000 acres are for the airfield, 4,000 for roads, parking and terminal, 2,000 for aircraft maintenance, and 3,000 for cargo sites. The Charles de Gaulle Airport, where even greater environmental precautions were taken, occupies 75,000 acres (one-third as many as the entire city of Paris), and the new Montreal airport has an 88,000-acre buffer zone.

Since airports are land intensive, the required size of the tract dictates a site located at a considerable distance from developed urban areas.[23] Dallas-Fort Worth (10 million enplanements in 1975) is equally distant— 17 miles from both cities; Washington's new Dulles International (10,000 acres) is 25 miles from the city, compared to National Airport, which is 4 miles; Charles de Gaulle Airport is 15 miles from Paris; and the new New York-planned regional airport in Newburgh is 50 miles from Manhattan.

The distance factor will be ameliorated, however, as high-speed ground-transportation systems, such as expressways or direct rail lines, are constructed to link airports with the CBD. The Charles de Gaulle Airport is perhaps the most advanced in this regard. Built directly above the Paris-Brussels Toll Road, it is tied to a new limited-access regional transit system and is also linked to the new core development project, La Defense. The CDG Airport is designed for a planned capacity of 60 million passengers in 1990 (three times the JFK International Airport, New York, in 1973) and 2 million tons of air freight (twice that of JFK in 1973).

THE IMPACT OF SHIFTS IN PATTERNS OF INTER-CITY TRAVEL

Most metropolises in the United States were established during the rail era. Major terminals for inter-city travel were in the heart of the central business districts, with hotels, office complexes, and principal department stores built nearby, if not over the terminals. Similarly, factories were located near freight yards, or on sidings. During the last decade, many manufacturing plants and offices relocated near the new interstate highway system, and now some activities that require use of air freight or inter-city air travel, are beginning to gravitate towards airports. It may well be that the anticipated obsolescence of older airports has delayed major moves until the new jetports are in operation. Once a major long-term investment is made in a regional jetport, the new port will become a key factor in the location decisions of those whose productivity is affected. Airports are already the major employment center outside of the CBD in some metropolitan areas.

Moreover, in the future there is likely to occur a differentiation of activities now agglomerated in the CBD, with many inner-city functions that do not require frequent face-to-face contact with the rest of the CBD moving out to airports. The CBD will be left to specialize in those activities more highly dependent on face-to-face contacts.

Residential patterns of those who use air travel frequently will also be affected. Few air trips originate or terminate in the central city. The Port of New York Authority discovered this in a detailed analysis of airport trips undertaken as part of a feasibility study of a direct rail link to J.F. Kennedy International Airport. The explanation lies in the fact that those who travel frequently to other cities are likely to be the professionals, managers, and technicians who live in the suburbs and commute to city jobs. Their business travel, as well as their personal travel, usually originates at place of residence.

Finally, as the major terminus of inter-city travel has shifted to airports, related activities such as hotels, air freight, car rentals, and various regional offices and manufacturing are relocating in their environs. If, in the future, high-speed ground transportation, such as Amtrak between Boston, New York, Philadelphia, Baltimore, and Washington, is developed, it will draw some inter-city travel back to the CBD. Inter-city air travel will, however, continue to be primarily from suburb to suburb, not CBD-to-CBD, unless new technological breakthroughs, such as vertical takeoff aircraft (VTOL/STOL), coupled with energy shortages, bring about a change in public-transport policy.

EFFECT OF THE CHANGING AIR-TRANSPORT SYSTEM
ON PLANT AND OFFICE LOCATION

Suburban locations for facilities of major corporations are often favored because of the savings in terms of travel time of key corporate management personnel who must commute between cities. Since a considerable proportion of employment expansion in the suburbs has occurred in plants and regional sales offices of national corporations, it is not surprising to find the growth of industrial and office parks close to airports.[24] Although access to airports is only one of many locational factors that favor suburban location, it is important to keep in mind that those who actually select the sites for regional facilities are sensitively aware of the time constraints imposed on corporate managers who will be visiting these sites periodically. And since regional operations are usually truncated operations, dependent on distantly located corporate staff for management and technical matters, rather than upon locally based service firms, the ability of managers and technical personnel to reach the plant quickly is a strategic factor.[25] This means that even the location of some corporate headquarters may be influenced by the proximity of airports. Since the time of senior executives is a scarce corporate resource, the location of headquarters and regional offices of firms whose personnel travel frequently will be pulled toward sites that minimize commuting and travel costs, i.e., toward their suburban residences and airport facilities.[26]

The use of air freight has also increased rapidly in recent years, especially for high-value and light manufactures, perishable goods, and high-fashion merchandise. A continued clustering of industrial parks around airports may be expected; and as new land is developed, new sites will become more distant from the city, remaining on or near the interstate highway system to maximize overall access to airports, CBD, and residential communities.

AGGLOMERATION OF ACTIVITIES IN PROXIMITY TO AIRPORTS

The airport is a major generator of activity, and consequently it creates opportunities for related maintenance, service, and other ancillary activities. Airports are becoming the focus of the second major metropolitan employment concentration outside the CBD. For example, there are about 8,000 hotel rooms near Chicago's O'Hare Airport, port, which is almost half as many as in downtown Chicago.[27] Employment by the airport, the airlines, restaurants, stores, hotels, car-rental agencies, etc., is forming the base of a large employment complex which, when combined with air-freight forwarding, warehousing, and manufacturing office parks, begins to resemble the export base of a major city. If even a modest share of the workers and passengers established residence close to the airport, a major urban settlement would appear. In short, a regional airport acts as a growth pole for the area by increasing access, but at the same time it draws off a certain share of jobs from the city.

It will be interesting to observe how these processes will work out in the years ahead. The creation of new sub-metropolitan hubs around airports, and the drawing off of inner-city related activities from downtown could, by reducing the concentration of functions in the CBD, create a more desirable ambiance in the older downtowns. Land values, density, rents, and congestion will be lower if there are two hubs, and lower rents will, in turn, allow for more residential and commercial activity than would otherwise obtain. With two hubs, a more cosmopolitan environment would be feasible downtown.

Clearly, the air-transportation system will have a significant impact on future development of metropolitan areas. The increased level of operations, the increased scale of airports, and the clustering of airport-related facilities around very large airports located at greater distances from the city will alter patterns of urban settlement and of commercial and industrial location just as the increased dependence on the interstate highway system has done in years past. There is, then, need to coordinate air transportation with the highways and rail systems at the metropolitan level and to coordinate transportation policies with other metropolitan development policies, such as housing, community development, human resources, and economic development. A much more thorough understanding of the interfaces between transportation, jobs, and metropolitan development is required if costs of living are to be held at a reasonable level, and if the quality of life is to be improved. In response to the new environment created by the modern highway and air-transportation systems, many new institutions have evolved. These must also be evaluated in the context of metropolitan development.

SCALE OF INVESTMENT REQUIRED AND OPPORTUNITIES FOR PLANNING

Construction of a new regional jetport requires a direct investment of over one-half billion dollars which, in turn, tends to stimulate indirect investment within the airport's environs amounting to some multiple of the original investment. Some of these investments may not have been made in the region without the construction of the jetport; others may have been made, but at other locations. In short, the new regional jetports will act both as development poles, drawing investments into the region from outside, and as magnets drawing related activities from within the region that will benefit from close proximity to the airport.

For example, the Dallas-Fort Worth airport represents a $700 million direct investment that has already triggered major indirect investment commitments of $2 billion.[28] The initial direct investment of $700 million includes $60 million by the two cities for land, $54 million from the federal government, with the rest being paid by airlines and concessionaires. One half is being spent for airport facilities and the remainder for site developments, including a foreign-trade zone on 3,000 acres, with 200 cargo gates that could each handle a C-5A aircraft and, according to *Engineering News Record*, more freight than any seaport in operation today. Another example is the new Charles de Gaulle Airport which is in operation. It represents a direct investment of $330 million in Phase One, already finished, and a projected $1.6 billion direct investment for completion by 1990.

Indirect investments take many forms and are likely to be many·

times greater than the original direct investment in the airport. According to newspaper reports, about $2 billion of major developments are already committed within a 10-mile radius of the new Dallas-Fort Worth Airport. This does not include numerous small-scale investments that are also expected. Included are new towns—Lewisville Valley, a $500 million residential community being developed by the Hunt Properties for 20,000 people; Flower Mound, a 6,156-acre community development 4 miles north of the airport (21 miles northwest of Dallas, and 21 miles northeast of Fort Worth); Century 21, a $150 million new city on 320 acres being developed 10 miles south of the airport; a $150 million Park Central hotel-office-retail complex; a $250 million Six Flags Business Park; and four major entertainment complexes: Six Flags Over Texas, an amusement park; Seven Seas Marine Life Show; and Lion Country Safari.

Land values rise to reflect the increased accessibility of a location. Three examples will serve to illustrate the effect of an airport on nearby land values.[29] In 1947, land around O'Hare Field in Chicago was valued at about $400 per acre; in 1960, when the airport became fully operational, land was selling at $20,000 per acre; three years later, prices had risen to $50,000 per acre. Land around LAX (Los Angeles) rose from $80,000 per acre in 1960 to $130,000 two years later. Land around Dulles, which is 25 miles from Washington, D.C., rose from $3,000 per acre in 1965 to $15,000 per acre in 1968.

Airports, by generating activity, also create employment opportunities. Jobs are created as new towns and facilities are constructed, new plants are put into production, and local service sectors expand to meet the needs of visitors, workers, and residents in the area.

Clearly, new regional jetports will have a major impact on the patterns of suburban development and will tend to influence public policy regarding the overall growth of the region. Communities in proximity to the Dallas-Fort Worth Airport, such as Southlake and Arlington, have already responded by annexation and have drawn up master plans for development. The mayor of St. Paul argued that every $1,000 in tax money invested in general aviation produces in excess of $2 million per year. The economic evaluation committee for an intercontinental jetport for New Jersey argued that estimated income in the area served would be increased 7 percent by the proposed facility.

Finally, the construction of a new jetport provides a region with an opportunity to plan its development at a level not previously possible. Because of the obvious scale of the changes which are about to unfold, the costs of not planning are clearer than is true when development is piecemeal and projects are smaller. As the experience of more and more metropolitan regions in airport development becomes available, it is likely that planning will become more thorough and more effective.

NEW INSTITUTIONAL ARRANGEMENTS AND REAL ESTATE INNOVATIONS

The history of postwar suburbanization has been a process involving not only the creation of a new transportation matrix, but also of an extensive adaptation of people and firms to the new environment of the outer city. In bringing about such adaptation, major roles have been played by real estate innovations in the form of the industrial park, the office park, and the large shopping center or mall.

INDUSTRIAL PARKS

Until the 1950's, there were probably fewer than 100 industrial parks in the United States. In 1970, the number was estimated to be more than 2,400, of which almost four-fifths had been established since 1960 and more than half since 1965.[30]

The attractiveness of the industrial park arises out of the locational advantages it offers firms, especially medium-sized and small firms. Not only does the industrial park developer assemble land, but he assumes responsibility for securing appropriate zoning arrangements, water, sewerage, utilities, and highway access. Frequently, he constructs roadways within the park itself. All of this eliminates managerial problems, and, frequently, because of economies of scale, reduces costs. In addition, the developer may offer the prospective firm a choice between purchase of land or leasing of existing facilities and may actually design and construct buildings to meet specific needs.

Also, the industrial park is distinguished by several features which give it a special character and which influence the industrial composition of the suburban economy: (1) There is formal planning of the park in terms of subdivision of lots, provision of utilities, establishment of access to highways, railways, or both, and often actual installation of streets, rails, and utilities. (2) There are restrictions on tenants relating to types of construction, minimum lot sizes, grounds maintenance, and types of production (e.g., processes which are accompanied by objectionable odors, by-products, etc., are excluded). (3) There is continuous management of the park to enforce restrictions.

Of course, parks vary in the features that they offer. One park, for example, offers golf club privileges to executives of member firms, as well as athletic facilities for employees, conference facilities, and a management luncheon club. On the other hand, some parks offer few amenities and exercise less stringent restrictions.

Taken as a whole, the development of industrial parks appears as a selective and adaptive process which has probably led to the upgrading of the suburban industrial sector. A major developer of industrial parks' in the Philadelphia area confided that his salesmen regarded as prospects only the more progressive firms, especially those which had moved at least once in the past fifteen years. Firms in antiquated quarters in the center city were considered to be lacking in financial and managerial resources.

It has been widely observed that suburban communities have consistently tried to exclude all but "clean tax-rateables." The industrial park, with its comprehensive planning and enforceable restrictions, goes far to guarantee to a municipality that it will get just that kind of industrial neighbor. It is intriguing to observe that industrial parks have brought about a new kind of agglomeration—an agglomeration based not on traditional considerations of need for firms to be cheek-by-jowl with suppliers or customers, but upon a shared desire for good neighbors, good housekeeping, and access to the best possible highway facilities.

OFFICE PARKS

Office parks closely resemble industrial parks. In each, the developer assembles land, subdivides, arranges for the necessary adjustments in zoning, installation of utilities and access to highways, sets forth restrictions regarding architecture of plants, maintenance, and business function, and provides for continuous supervision. Indeed, many so-called industrial parks house office and other activities as well as manufacturers. For example, one park lists among its seventeen client firms five office-type establishments, one research organization, five wholesaling or distributing establishments, and six manufacturers.

Not all clusterings of office activities in the suburbs have followed the developmental patterns of office parks, however. In some instances, substantial agglomerations of office activities are put together through the independent actions of a number of firms and developers responding more or less concurrently (or in sequence) to the attractions of access, zoning influences, and the externalities each offers the other in terms of rendering the area attractive both as a place to recruit white-collar employees and as a prestige address for doing business. An excellent example is the extensive development of modern office and research quarters in the eastern suburbs of Cleveland.

Thus, office parks and related office developments represent new forms of agglomeration in which firms seek not traditional input linkages, but good access to the highway system, attractive surroundings, and the mutual benefit in terms of increased prestige that accrues from proximity to reputable firms housed in modern facilities.

SHOPPING CENTERS

Three points demand emphasis in discussing shopping centers: that they have evolved slowly from humble beginnings, that they are strongly oriented toward the matrix of major highways in the suburbs, and that the modern regional shopping center represents an important new form of urban agglomeration.

Although shopping centers have prewar origins, their development has occurred largely since 1950. In earlier years, centers were little more than a haphazard cluster of stores combined with parking facilities and access to highways. Bit by bit it was discovered that there were significant economies accruing from scale and from the attraction resulting from a larger choice among stores. A major turning point came when merchants discovered "to their surprise that two department stores could attract more business by sharing a center."[31]

The evolution has continued as developers constructed all-weather enclosed malls, with an ever-greater variety of stores and additional facilities such as restaurants, theaters, swimming pools, skating rinks, and community meeting places. Today there are shopping centers of various shapes and sizes, representing different marketing strategies (ranging from convenience shopping in the simple neighborhood shopping center to the all-purpose regional center), and different stages of evolution (ranging from the poorly designed cluster along a strip highway development to the major enclosed mall).

But everywhere they are oriented toward the highway system. Concerning this orientation to highways, Gurney Breckenfeld has written:[32]

> This new urban form, to be sure, is the outcome of a long process that began with the invention of the automobile and gained momentum with middle-class migration to the suburbs after World War II. But it was the great Interstate Highway program, with its freeways looping around the hearts of big cities, that made the proliferation of huge regional centers economically feasible. The freeway network enabled centers to attract shoppers from much longer distances with no increase in travel time.

Finally, it is the regional shopping center which represents perhaps the most significant development in the institutional adaptation which has marked the whole process of suburbanization. The typical regional shopping center is immense. It includes 3 or 4 department stores, along with 100 to 150 smaller shops. Within its boundaries, or immediately adjacent, there may be office buildings, apartments, medical clinics, banks, motels, stockbrokers, and churches. In recent years, developers have tended to buy larger sites than formerly (often 200 to more than 500 acres) in order to control and profit from subsequent growth.[33]

All this has brought about a new form of agglomeration which is in competition with the downtown areas of suburban towns and cities, as well as with the central business district itself. The result is a splintering of the metropolis—a proliferation of nuclei of economic activities and of centers of employment.[34]

INCREASED SCALE OF DEVELOPMENTS

Perhaps the dominant trend evidenced in most urban areas is the increased scale of these developments, both in the private and in the public and not-for-profit sectors. New institutions, such as airports, shopping centers, industrial and office parks, sports and entertainment complexes, medical and cultural centers, and even planned residential environments, have evolved over relatively short periods into major planned environments. On the one hand, this reflects new opportunities to realize scale economies from serving large metropolitan markets. And on the other, it reflects the emergence of developers and private and public financial mechanisms capable of undertaking such developments. If we inquire into the prospects for the continuance of these trends, we find indications that new institutional investment will account for an increasing share of total metropolitan investment. It is quite likely that the institutional developments will be more coordinated in the future and that the time horizon for planning such developments will be extended.

The past success of commercial developments, the growing influence of developers, the increased affluence of suburban households, and the increased size of local governments suggest that the scale of development is likely to continue to increase or at least to stabilize at present levels. It would be helpful if there were more data on the proportion of new commercial development that falls into the category of major plan developments. Our impression is that this proportion is increasing and that metropolitan development is becoming more planned as a result. Developers representing consortiums of department stores, insurance companies, real estate investment trusts, mutual savings banks, and private investors are now able to create shopping centers—office-apartment complexes that require an investment of a quarter million dollars and over. Randall Mall in Cleveland and Whitfield Mall in Schamburg, Illinois, twenty-five miles northwest of Chicago, are excellent examples of centers with two million square feet of space accommodating two hundred stores or more. Public development of shopping centers may also be observed. The Office of Development, City of New York, is developing a new shopping center in Staten Island with a targeted area of 2.8 million square feet of space.[35] At this writing some 40 percent of this space is completed and in use.

Reorganization of commerce and of industry into increasingly planned, and larger scale, developments acts to undermine smaller establishments in older districts. According to a recent study reported in the *Harvard Business Review*, even supermarkets (which came of age in 1956 and now account for 77 percent of retail grocery stores) are threatened by a new generation of omnicenters. As the size of the markets increases, profit margins are cut (from 1.97 percent to 0.92 percent of sales), and the number of outlets declines. The number of retail food outlets declined from 356,754 to 267,352 from 1958 to 1972. It is the nature of price competition that large outlets, using mass-merchandising techniques, and offering price advantages, draw customers away from smaller establishments.[36]

A related economic principle underlies the predicament of many university teaching hospitals located in cities. As profitable clinics are drawn off to the suburbs, the hospital's ability to subsidize charitable services is undermined. Similar issues underlie public decisions regarding location of new regional facilities such as public colleges or universities, stadiums, museums, and housing for the elderly.

The public sector's recognition of the indirect economic and social benefits to the region from major public projects such as airports, sports stadiums, and convention centers provides a basis for public support of subsidies for construction, renovation, and operation of such facilities. These projects often run at a deficit. Even the Houston Astrodome-sports-convention-hotel and entertainment complex, which draws 7.5 million visitors annually, including almost one-half million tourists, had a deficit of half a million dollars in 1973.[37] The specification of benefits becomes important when public funds are used to subsidize such projects.

Another relatively new dimension of community development in large metropolitan areas concerns planned residential communities for specific population groups. As the elderly seek out communities planned to meet their needs, as the young singles are also drawn off to specialized communities, and as commercial and industrial plants locate increasingly in planned parks, the viability of older residential communities is undermined. Not only is the financial base of school systems—the property tax—eroded, but the social fabric of the metropolis becomes fragmented and torn. Ties between young and old, singles and families, rich and poor are weakened. Since the economic incentives underlying specialized community development and fragmentation are strong, enlightened policies will be required if the traditional communities are to remain viable, or if new and more heterogeneous communities are to be created.

The public has an important lesson to learn from private developers. This lesson is simply that, by increasing the scale of development, and by internalizing the benefits from such scale development, it is possible to provide more desirable environments at lower cost. But planned development as currently practiced does not work entirely in the public interest. Such developments attract not only expansions and new growth, but also viable activities already located in parts of the region, contributing to the decline of these older areas. Relocation of activities has an impact in terms of tax base, utilities, services, traffic, and pollution patterns. It would be highly irresponsible to assume that any development which is financially feasible is socially desirable. Developers with their clearly specified objectives present their case very effectively; the communities are just beginning to develop theirs. It is important that the interests of all parties be clearly set forth. Interventions into complex social and economic systems affect the economic viability of many parts of the system and, hence, the quality of life and growth prospects of the region in general.

OFFICE AND HEADQUARTERS ACTIVITIES

The employment data, which we shall have occasion to examine in chapters 3, 4 and 5, fail to convey as accurate a picture of the extent of office activity in cities and suburbs as we would like. Data are classified either according to broad industrial or occupational classifications, but are not cross-classified, at least for cities and suburban areas. Moreover, we do not have information on employment classified in terms of headquarters or free-standing office activities.

The Regional Plan Association, in its study of the office industry in the New York metropolitan region, has shown that it is useful to classify office activities within three groupings—headquarters, middle market, and local:[38]

... Almost all headquarters jobs are jobs that export their services, from the viewpoint of any one metropolitan area. The market area of headquarters activity is often national or international in scope; the degree of complexity in this type of operation is at its greatest. Included here are the headquarters of the giants of industry, major business concerns in manufacturing, trade, service, financing, and transportation ...

Middle-market activity includes regional, sub-regional, and national back office operations as well as utilities, and headquarters-serving functions such as advertising and public relations. These jobs are found in almost every region for the purpose of serving that region. The category includes few export office-type jobs, although occasionally a branch office may serve more than one region and considerable exporting may occur in indirect ways. ...

Finally, local market office jobs serve areas of roughly under 150,000 population and are located close by the population being served. They are, therefore, the least likely to require the usual benefits of clustering. This category includes local government offices of small municipalities, branch banks, real estate offices, law firms in general practice, and similar establishments.

Regional Plan has also estimated for 1965 the distribution of headquarters, middle-market, and local-market jobs in office buildings among CBD, rest of core, and suburban rings of the New York region as follows:[39]

	Head- quarters	Middle Market	Local Market
Manhattan CBD	80.14	55.46	8.65
Rest of core	6.07	20.37	45.01
Inner ring	6.44	12.00	23.52
Intermediate ring	6.24	10.37	16.08
Outer ring	1.11	1.80	6.74
Region total	100.00	100.00	100.00
% of total jobs in office buildings	29.5%	46.8%	23.7%

Although the above data relate only to the nation's largest metropolitan region, they are strongly suggestive of the general pattern of distribution of office employment. Headquarters activities are very heavily concentrated in the CBD; local-market activities are not. Standing in an intermediate position is the middle-market category. What this means is that local-market office activities, like other activities of the local sector, are oriented to place of residence and will grow with population. Regional headquarters and back-office activity, on the other hand, may locate in either CBD or an outlying area. Presumably these activities are sensitive to shifts in locational advantages of city or suburb. Headquarters (*major* corporate headquarters according to RPA definition) are strongly attracted to the CBD, although one-fifth is found in the outer core and suburban rings of the New York metropolis.

Much has been written in recent years regarding the movement of coporate headquarters from the city. The shift began in the fifties and accelerated in the later sixties. This shift, according to the National Industrial Conference Board, has been largely a New York City phenomenon.[40] Nevertheless, it is intriguing that suburban locations have been increasingly favored in locating major headquarters since it has been traditionally thought that the Central Business District (CBD) offers the special advantages of face-to-face contact and external economies which headquarters require. Interviews indicate several factors which go far to explan this seeming paradox. First, for many headquarters, the orientation of management in its day-to-day contacts, especially at the vice-presidential level, is toward the company itself rather than toward external business services, suppliers, or customers. Executives relate chiefly to operating divisions located in the hinterland and in other areas of the country, to R & D activities located nearby, and to other officials within the company's headquarters. Second, many large companies "internalize" a number of business services (e.g., provide legal, accounting, financial, and engineering expertise within the company's own organization), with the result that it is not necessary to be close to these services in the city. Third, corporations headquartered in the suburbs (at least in the case of New York) typically maintain offices and other facilities in the city so that face-to-face contacts with customers, advertising agents, and other strategic persons are readily made by executives during once- or twice-weekly visits to the city.

When this obtains, the company is free to heed the preferences of its executives for a headquarters location which minimizes commuting and which features the amenities of a campus setting. Many officials claim that such an arrangement improves morale, increases effective work time, and significantly enhances their ability to recruit promising young executives.

This does not mean, of course, that suburban locations are satisfactory for all companies. For many, one or more of the conditions outlined above do not hold. A few firms have moved to the suburbs, only to regret their decisions and to return. Others admit they have gained little.

No data are available to inform us of the spatial distribution of office employment within suburbs. We do have available, however, for the New York region estimates for 1965 of office space in the principal office concentrations located in downtowns of suburban cities and in major suburban clusters.[41] Within the inner ring these subcenters accounted for only 29.8 percent of office space, and within the intermediate ring, for 31.4 percent. These data tell us, at least for the New York metropolis, that although subcenters (largely downtowns of satellite cities) accounted for a significant share of suburban office employment, the largest share is located elsewhere in the suburbs. Research is needed to determine accurately the locational characteristics of this major share of office employment which is located away from major office concentrations and is typically ill served by public transportaion. Observation indicates that these jobs are found in office buildings situated within office parks and industrial parks, adjacent to shopping centers, in free-standing office buildings in open areas, in campus headquarters facilties, and in downtown areas of suburban towns which cannot be classified as major office concentrations. Many of such locations are oriented to major highway arteries, but few are likely to be conveniently located in terms of proximity to the low-income worker.

THE CONTINUED COMMITMENT TO THE CBD

An important observation which will follow from the analysis in Chapter 3 is that employment in the business services has grown in the central cities, although employment in other sectors has tended to decline, or remain virtually unchanged. What is significant in understanding suburban development is that these increases have been paralleled by a great burst of office-building activity which represents a continued commitment to the CBD. Throughout the major cities of the nation, public and private leadership has combined to bring about a physical renewal of the CBD. Aided by federal urban-renewal funding and special incentives (e.g., tax incremental bonding, tax abatements, and eminent domain legislation) archaic structures have been razed and gleaming office towers, hotels, civic- halls, multi-level parking areas, and even parks have taken their place to create renovated, more attractive, centers.

In a recent survey of the growth of office space over the twelve-year period 1960-1972, Gerald Manners found that office space added in the CBD equaled or exceeded office space added in the entire remaining part of the SMSA in five of the nine areas examined (Table 1).[42] According to the survey, only two CBD's (Atlanta, 41% and Minneapolis-St. Paul, 44%) accounted for less than half of the total office space in the SMSA in 1972. Considering the fact that office space is utilized more intensively, e.g., space per employee is lower, in the CBD than in the suburbs, and that local-office activities have grown very rapidly outside the central city, these data appear to us as evidence of a strong and continuing commitment to the CBD as the center of major office activities within the metropolitan economy.

These statistics could very likely be duplicated for any of a large number of other places such as Baltimore, with its highly attractive Charles center, and Louisville, with its ultramodern riverfront renewal project.

The significance of these developments in CBD's is that they have prospered side by side with developments in the suburbs. Since the locational attractions of CBD and suburb differ significantly, it is apparent that we are observing a process of selection and adaptation in which certain types of firms find it advantageous to locate within the CBD, while others seek out a distinctly different environment.

This process of adaptation and the symbiosis which accompanies it is well described by Truman Hartshorn in his examination of the Atlanta office economy:[43]

> . . . There is only minimal competition between surburban and CBD office-areas in Atlanta, and perhaps elsewhere, because each seems to have its own different clientele. The downtown is still a major office service center. Its

facilities are rented to lawyers, barbers, accountants, insurance agents, brokers, advertising agencies, planners, public relations firms, and other professional and service oriented companies. In the office parks are regional and national offices of major corporations. These latter firms typically do not require the face-to-face contact needed by the downtown office activities. The national companies still depend on the CBD offices for services, however, just as they also depend on industrial parks to assemble and distribute their goods. Many firms in Atlanta, for example, have executives in office parks, and distribution centers in industrial parks, with both relying on professional services provided by downtown firms.

HOUSING RESTRICTIONS

While a variety of factors have encouraged growth in suburbs, housing shortages have acted to restrict growth of population during the last decade, at least as regards low and lower-middle income familes. Their impact has been felt not only by blacks and other minorities but by young white families as well.

This housing shortage has been evidenced by sharp increases in prices, which have placed housing outside the income range of all but the affluent. Recent surveys have shown that during the period 1970-74, the median sales price of new single family homes in the U.S. has risen by 53 percent, from $23,400 to $35,400, while the median income of white families advanced by only 30 percent, from $10,236 to $13,356.[44]

These high costs stem from a number of causes: financing, labor and materials, property taxes, land, and zoning practices. While the first three of these sets of causes have contributed to a decline in housing starts throughout the national economy, the last two have acted with a special impact in restricting suburban housing.

Since population increases for the entire postwar period have been greatest in suburban areas, prices of residential property in these areas have been under considerable speculative influence and have risen sharply. NCDH studies have shown that from 1950 to 1967 the cost of site rose from 14.5 percent to 20.5 percent of the sales price of the house in Connecticut, from 16.2 to 18.8 percent in New Jersey, and from 16.0 to 18.8 percent in New York.[45]

An additional factor has been that these higher prices of raw land have been coupled with zoning practices which differ radically from those which obtained in an earlier era. With rapid growth and an increased education, many communities have acted to restrict entry of all but the relatively affluent. The most popular restrictive device has been larger-lot zoning, with minimum-lot sizes for new single-family homes established at multiples set under previous zoning restrictions. For example, in the northern part of Westchester County, where most of the county's available acreage for expansion is located, only 3 percent of vacant land is zoned for lots smaller than 100 feet by 100 or for apartments, and 53 percent is zoned for lots of 2 acres of more.[46]

To some extent, the expense and restrictions involved in building single-family homes have been overcome by construction of multi-family dwellings, but these, too, have faced frequent limitations from community-zoning actions. In many instances, communities refuse to zone for additional multi-family dwellings; in other instances, severe restrictions are placed on the number of units permitted with more than one bedroom.

Finally, in addition to the constraints imposed by high costs and zoning, blacks have encountered special barriers to entry in the form of discriminatory sales practices of realtors and vigorous public opposition to public housing.[47]

It is not our purpose here to inquire deeply into the nature of housing problems in the suburbs. There are critical problems here which involve issues both of equity and efficiency. Suffice it to say that the suburbs as a place to live have been built largely by the settlement of middle- and upper-income families who have sought a way of life featuring spaciousness and a semi-rural environment. As growth has increasingly threatened these conditions through rising costs and congestion, residents have fought to protect the status quo by taking the kinds of actions discussed above.

The result has been a paradoxical development which is examined at some length in chapters 3 and 4. The suburbs have become relatively high-income economies which generate a considerable amount of low-wage local-sector employment, but which tend to be closed to low-income residents. These low-wage jobs do not justify the costs of other than short journeys to work, and, accordingly, as best we can determine from the evidence at hand, are filled to a large extent by secondary workers from within the middle class. On the other hand, better-paying jobs in the manufacturing sector and elsewhere draw increasingly upon commuters from the city and from areas lying outside the suburbs.

SUMMARY

This chapter stands largely as an introduction to the analytical chapters which follow. Its purpose is to place in perspective the importance of several key factors which have influenced, and will influence in the years ahead, the pace and character of suburbanization.

The first of these is the development of the suburban highway system, coupled with widespread automobile ownership. With the advent of the modern-highway matrix, the logic of location has been abruptly altered for many economic activities. Maximum access to markets is no longer dictated by proximity to the center city, but rather by proximity to entry points on major arteries. At the same time, auto-travel speeds have been sharply increased, with resulting enlargement of areas which may be drawn upon for commuting workers. All of this has brought revolutionary changes in terms of growth of suburban employment and residence, and has resulted in markedly different spatial organization of metropolitan areas. Not the least important aspect of the development of the modern highway system has been the recent tying in of the major highways to the central city in such a way that heavy commuter traffic may flow readily between suburb and city.

A second factor, the development of the air-transport system, has been equally dramatic, but its impact on metropolitan spatial organization has not as yet been fully felt. The reason is found in the fact that most airports are both inadequate and obsolescent, and relocation of a variety of economic activities to optimize relationship to air terminals awaits the development of a new generation of extremely large ports. A variety of forces is accelerating this development, and the experience with new regional airports already in operation reveals that both direct and indirect investment is large, and that agglomeration tendencies are strong. Regional airports, such as O'Hare in Chicago, tend to draw off a number of activities from the CBD and to form the nucleus of a secondary node for development within the metropolitan area.

The third factor, the development of new institutions such as industrial parks, office parks, and shopping centers, has also facilitated suburban industrial and commercial growth. These institutions, which are themselves oriented to the highway system, have contributed to the spatial reorganization of metropolitan economic and residential functions.

We have treated as a fourth factor the development of office and headquarters activities. The principal observation is that these activities may be usefully broken down into several categories based on the extent to which services are provided to export to local markets. In general, office activities in suburbs are heavily weighted toward local- and middle-market functions, whereas headquarters functions tend to be concentrated in the CBD. There has been considerable splitting of functions between city and suburb, however; and a general process of adaptation and experimentation is continuously at work. One of the most significant developments has been a renewed commitment to the CBD as a preferred locale for those activities in which face-to-face dealings and business-service external economies play an important role.

Finally, we note that housing restrictions have increasingly acted as a constraint to suburban growth. In recent years, rising costs have been influenced by a number of factors which include not only building and financing costs, but also sharply increasing costs of raw land and large minimum-lot-size zoning. In addition, there is evidence of exclusionary community practices in restricting construction of apartments, and of discriminatory dealer practices where minorities are involved.

REFERENCES

1. U.S. Department of Transportation, Federal Highway Administration, *Economic and Land Development Impacts of Improved Highways, Part II Beneficial Effects of Improved Highways*, 1972 National Highway Needs Study, Background Project E 1 (Washington, D.C.: June, 1971, unpublished), p. 65.

2. *Ibid.*, p. 93.

3. *Ibid.*, pp. 91-92.

4. Interview with data-process service firm.

5. *New York Times*, May 30, 1971.

6. U.S. Department of Transportation, Federal Highway Administration, *Suburbanization and Beltways* (Interim Report on Beltway Impact), Economic and Demographic Forecasting Team (Washington, D.C.: May, 1972, unpublished), pp. 17ff.

7. Peter de Leon and John Enns, *The Effects of Highways Upon Metropolitan Dispersion: St. Louis* (The Rand Corporation, P5061, September, 1973).

8. Gurney Brekenfeld, "'Downtown' Has Fled to the Suburbs," *Fortune*, October, 1972, p. 83.

9. U.S. Department of Transportation, Federal Highway Administration, *Economic and Land Development Impacts* . . . , *op. cit.*, p. 143.

10. U.S. Bureau of the Census, *Statistical Abstract of the United States, 1972* (Washington, D.C.), p. 536.

11. "The Regional Airports," *Regional Plan Association News, No. 89* (New York: July, 1968) p. 12.

12. *Statistical Abstract* . . . , *op. cit.*, p. 536. Air freight currently accounts for less than 1 percent of total freight-ton miles.

13. Richard V. Knight, *Employment Expansion and Metropolitan Trade* (New York: Praeger Publishers, Inc., 1974), p.100.

14. *Statistical Abstract* . . . , *op. cit.*

15. Robert Lindsey, "Towns Building Airports to Lure Jobs," *New York Times*, June 20, 1971.

16. Roy Allen, *Great Airports of the World* (Shepperton, England: Ian Allen, Ltd., 1968).

17. Institution of Civil Engineering, *Airports for the Future* (London: Institute of Civil Engineering, 1967), p. 72.

18. "The Regional Airports," *op. cit.*, p. 8.

19. "Airports Expanding in Size and Traffic," *New York Times*, May 9, 1971.

20. Environmental Studies Board, *Jamaica Bay and Kennedy Airport* (Washington, D.C.: The National Academy of Science, 1971).

21. "The Monstrous New Airport Outside Paris," *Business Week*, March 9, 1974, pp. 171-173; William Borders, "A Big Buffer Area Rings Montreal's New Airport, *New York Times,* January 6, 1975; Robert Lindsey, "Texans Plan Party for Biggest Airport (It's Not)," *New York Times*, April 20, 1973.

22. Calculations based on projected capacity at three major airports indicate that roughly one acre of land is required in all cases for each two enplanements (daily).

23. Environmental impact statements must be prepared to estimate need and impact on the environment, population, and industrial location. Considering the current state of the art, it is not likely that these statements will adequately predict the impact of such a major institution. See U.S. Department of Housing and Urban Development, *Airport*

Environ: Land Use Controls (Washington, D.C.: May, 1970); Richard Witkin, "Governor Seeks Fourth Airport Near Newburgh," *New York Times*, March 22, 1971; "Nixon Pushing Old Plan to Sell Federal Airports Near Capital," *New York Times*, March 1, 1971.

24. David B. Knight and Tatsuo Ito, "Office Parks: The Oak Brook Example," *Land Economics*, February, 1972, 65-69; Truman A. Hartshorn, "Industrial/Office Parks: A New Look for the City," *The Journal of Geography*, March, 1973, 33-45.

25. *Hearings on Industrial Location Policy Before the Committee on Banking and Currency, U.S. House of Representatives, July-December 1970* (Washington, D.C.: U.S. Government Printing Office). See statement of A. L. Bethel, Westinghouse Electric Corporation, pp. 533-545.

26. See "Flight to the Suburbs," *Fortune*, May, 1972; and "Headquarters Move to the Suburbs" (New York City Planning Commission [unpublished study], 1971).

27. "Developments Sprouting Around Major Airports," *Cleveland Plain Dealer*, April 15, 1973, p. 35A. See also Richard Doherty, "The Origin and Development of Chicago's O'Hare International Airport" (Muncie, Ind.: Ball State University, 1970).

28. "Airports and Focal Points of Developers and Debate," *New York Times*, February 14, 1971.

29. The remainder of this section is based on material presented in John A. Nammack, "Airports and the Economic Impact."

30. Linda Liston, "Proliferating Industrial Parks Spark Plant Location Revolution," *Industrial Development*, CXXXIX, ii (March-April, 1970), 7-11.

31. Gurney Brekenfeld, *op. cit.*, p. 83.

32. *Ibid.*

33. *Ibid.*

34. The impact may fall heavily on small-scale city establishments. A survey of inner-city residents in Cleveland found that one-third of retail purchases were made in suburbs. Alpine Group Consultants for the Association of Community Development Corporation.

35. Martin Gansberg, "Staten Island Mall Called Commitment to City's Future," *New York Times*, February 10, 1972, p. 31.

36. Lathrop Douglass, "Tomorrow: Omnicenters on the Landscape?" *Harvard Business Review*, No. 2 (1974) 8 ff.

37. For this and other examples see: Gary Cartwright, "There's More Texas Than Technology," *New York Times*, April 7, 1974, Section 10, p. 1; Roy Reed, "New Orleans Superdome Rises as a Monument to Spectator Sports," *New York Times*, February 3, 1974, p. 40; George P. Rasanen, "New Stadium Sometimes Unprofitable," *New York Times*, March 8, 1973.

38. Regina B. Armstrong, *The Office Industry: Patterns of Growth and Location* (Cambridge, Mass.: Massachusetts Institute of Technology Press, 1972), pp. 18-20.

39. *Op. cit.*, 97.

40. J. Roger O'Meara, *Corporate Moves to the Suburbs: Problems and Opportunities* (New York: The Conference Board, 19), p. 1.

41. Armstrong, *op. cit.*, p. 109.

42. Gerald Manners, *The Office Metropolis* (Cambridge, Mass.: Joint Center for Urban Studies of The Massachusetts Institute of Technology and Harvard University, undated), Working Paper No. 22, Table 1. p. 2. It should be noted that estimates of new buildings in the metropolitan area outside the CBD, but within the metropolitan area, do not distinguish between areas within the city and areas outside the city.

43. Truman Hartshorn, "Industrial/Office Parks: A New Look for the City,"*Journal of Geography*, March, 1973, p. 44.

44. U.S. Bureau of Census CPR Series P60 No. 101, "Money Income in 1974: Families and Persons in U.S.,"; U.S. Department of Housing and Urban Development, *Housing and Urban Development Trends*, September, 1975.

45. *Ibid.*, p. 48

46. "The Future of Westchester County, A Supplement to the Second Regional Plan" (New York: Regional Plan Association, March, 1971), p. 36.

47. *Jobs and Housing: A Study of Employment and Housing Opportunities for Racial Minorities in the Suburban Areas of the New York Metropolitan Region* (New York: National Commission Against Discrimination in Housing, March, 1970), Parts II and III, pp. 36 ff.

[3

Industrial Characteristics

This chapter addresses itself to three questions: To what extent do cities and suburbs differ in the industrial composition of their employment? What were the industrial patterns of change in employment in cities and suburbs during the decade of the sixties? What qualitative differences may be observed between industry employment in cities and suburbs?

These questions are covered within four sections, the first three of which deal with selected metropolitan areas. The first highlights the postwar experience in terms of population and of employment in two key industrial classifications—manufacturing and retailing. The second examines in some detail industrial composition of employment by place of work in 1970 and change during the period 1960-1970. The third surveys relevant qualitative data—wages, value added, and size of establishment. Finally, the fourth comments on the importance of government employment.

THREE DECADES OF CHANGE:
POPULATION, MANUFACTURING, AND RETAILING

Though most of the literature relating to suburban growth has emphasized the postwar period, considerable growth occurred in the prewar years, particularly in the older, and larger, cities of the nation. This was true, for instance, in the case of the New York metropolitan area, where very high rates of suburban growth were recorded in the first two decades of the present century.[1] Nevertheless, our interest lies mainly with the postwar period when a rise of incomes, combined with

increased automobile ownership and an acceleration of highway construction, resulted in a simultaneous increase in population and industry
in areas contiguous to the city. Suburbs boomed as major constraints on
spatial expansion were removed.

The processes by which the suburbs developed during the most
recent three decades are highlighted in three time series: the first,
population, which shows the settlement of the suburbs and growth
through natural increase; the second, manufacturing employment,
which represents the growth of an important part (goods producing) of
the export sector; the third, retailing employment, illustrates the expansion that has taken place in the local sector. Annual rates of increase
for each of these series are shown in Table 3.1 for eight cities and
suburbs. The data cover three periods, each approximately a decade in
duration, which are roughly comparable for the three series.[2]

Manufacturing employment in the suburbs, influenced largely by
wartime demand, grew most rapidly during the first period, the forties,
in every suburban area but Denver. Growth rates were significantly
lower in subsequent decades, but were, nevertheless, quite substantial
in most suburbs.

The most striking observation is that the fifties was the decade of
most rapid growth in suburban population, influenced by high birthrates and migration rates (not shown in Table 3.1). The sixties saw a
decline in rates of population change with reductions in both birthrates
and rates of migration.

In general, retailing employment rates of increase were substantial in
each decade. In the three decades as a whole, annual growth rates for
retailing were well in excess of population growth. Moreover, the last
period brought an acceleration in retail employment growth in six of
eight places, with rates of growth well above those for population. The
figures reflect the development of the local sector in response to the
influence of rising affluence and larger markets. In part, increased retail
employment is the result of a shift of retailing from city to suburb—a
process of import substitution in which suburban residents buy locally
what they had previously journeyed to the city to purchase.

The data for the city reflect a history consistent with the above.
Manufacturing-employment growth was also highest during the forties
under the impact of wartime demand. Population increased everywhere, but rates were well under those for suburbs, indicating that
significant suburbanization of populations was already under way.

The most significant data for the city relate to the last two decades.
This period is characterized by declines, or low rates of growth, in
population, manufacturing employment, and retailing employment.
However, the figures do not reflect the transition occurring within the
cities' economies as shifts are made toward increased specialization in

other service activities. These matters are examined in the next section.

EMPLOYMENT STRUCTURE AND RECENT TRANSITION

INDUSTRIAL SPECIALIZATION

Of all the available data which relate to suburbs and cities, those covering employment tell the most about the nature of economic specialization. Figures describing the industrial composition of employment within both city and suburb provide: (1) a means of identifying the sectors which account for the major exports, (2) a measure of the proportion of the work force involved in essentially local-sector activities, and (3) a guide to the form industrial growth and development are taking. Analysis of industrial employment data permits a fuller understanding of the labor markets of cities and suburbs, of the manpower problems which they face, and of the essential nature of metropolitan economic systems.

In an earlier study, the authors examined the industrial composition of employment and changes in employment of 368 metropolitan areas and classified them on the basis of employment size and principal economic function.[3] An important finding was that metropolitan economies tended to fall into two general groups: those specializing in rendering services (called nodal, or service, centers) and those specializing in a narrower range of economic functions (e.g., manufacturing, government, and medical education). This distinction was found to be of critical importance in analyzing employment change.

Comparisons of distributions of employment among industrial classifications for the cities and suburbs of the ten metropolitan areas studied (Table 3.2) give rise to two observations.[4] The first is that industrial composition of employment in central cities is in substantial agreement with earlier findings regarding total metropolitan-area classification. The second is that the composition of suburban employment is greatly influenced by the composition of the cities which they adjoin.

The distinction between different types of economic specialization of cities is clear. Cleveland and St. Louis rank first and second in shares of employment engaged in manufacturing, with shares of 42.7 and 38.1 percent, indicating their roles as leading exporters of industrial goods. Their ranks in the combined business-services-grouping (MBS-TCU), however, are tenth and ninth, with shares of employment of 23.4 and 30.8 percent.[5] In contrast, New York, Boston, and Atlanta—important service centers—rank first, second, and third in the combined MBS-TCU categories (shares of employment, 44.4, 43.8, and 41.5

Table 3.1. Growth Rates (Annual Basis) Three Decades, Population by Place of Residence, Manufacturing and Retailing, Employment by Place of Work, Eight Metropolitan Areas, 1940–70[a]

		Balti-more	Boston	Cleve-land	Denver	New Orleans	New York	Phila-delphia	St. Louis	Modified[b] Average
Cities										
Forties										
Population	1940–50	1.05	0.40	0.42	2.90	1.53	0.59	0.73	0.50	0.80
Employment										
Manufacturing	1939–47	7.25	9.51	12.44	21.13	9.89	10.43	8.42	11.65	10.39
Retailing	1939–48	5.53	1.69	4.14	5.18	5.08	3.56	4.96	5.50	4.74
Fifties										
Population	1950–60	−0.11	−1.30	−0.42	1.88	1.00	−0.14	−0.33	−1.25	−0.21
Employment										
Manufacturing	1947–58	−0.69	−1.03	−1.99	1.10	−1.55	−0.43	−1.15	−1.93	−1.13
Retailing	1948–58	−0.09	−0.87	−1.01	1.37	1.25	−1.12	−1.46	−1.26	−0.52
Sixties										
Population	1960–70	−0.35	−0.81	−1.43	0.42	−0.54	0.14	−0.27	−1.70	−0.54
Employment										
Manufacturing	1958–67	−0.51	−1.31	−0.21	1.89	1.71	−0.01	−0.89	−0.35	−0.04
Retailing	1958–67	−1.97	−1.68	−2.63	0.13	−0.20	−0.54	−0.96	−3.10	−1.33

Suburbs

Forties										
Population	1940–50	6.09	1.18	4.00	5.99	7.45	3.29	2.61	3.18	4.19
Employment										
Manufacturing	1939–47	7.70	4.53	18.96	20.07	8.59	22.32	7.83	9.82	12.16
Retailing	1939–48	9.96	4.48	10.34	10.39	13.66	4.26	6.60	8.60	8.40
Fifties										
Population	1950–60	7.04	1.77	6.73	12.18	9.70	7.50	4.63	5.08	6.78
Employment										
Manufacturing	1947–58	5.36	1.92	5.94	27.75	4.89	8.30	1.08	3.71	5.02
Retailing	1948–58	12.44	1.94	4.94	11.51	11.00	9.58	4.38	4.70	7.69
Sixties										
Population	1960–70	3.47	1.13	2.71	6.37	6.18	2.62	2.26	2.85	3.35
Employment										
Manufacturing	1958–67	1.98	1.32	6.69	10.29	3.05	4.56	3.98	5.01	4.21
Retailing	1958–67	7.92	2.79	8.96	12.91	12.51	4.53	5.22	5.73	7.48

[a] Periods are not completely comparable, since *Census of Manufactures* and *Census of Business* (Retailing) were not taken at same dates as *Census of Population*. Houston city and suburb data were omitted because of frequent city annexations. Atlanta data omitted because of annexations between 1950–60. There were no other annexations of significance during the three-decade period. Suburbs have been adjusted for change in SMSA definitions.

[b] Highest and lowest values among eight places omitted in computing modified average.

Source: Department of Commerce, Bureau of the Census; *1970 Census of Population*, PC (1) D Series, Table 138.
Department of Commerce, Bureau of the Census; 1939, 1947, 1958 and 1967 *Census of Manufactures*, Volume III, Area Statistics.
Department of Commerce, Bureau of the Census; 1939, 1948, 1958 and 1967 *Census of Business*, Volume II, Retail Trade-Area Statistics.

Table 3.2. Percentages of Employment in Selected Industrial Classifications and Rates of Change in Employment, Ten Metropolitan Areas, 1970[a]

	Cleveland	St. Louis	Philadelphia	Baltimore	New York	Houston	Boston	Atlanta	Denver	New Orleans	Comparisons C>S	S>C	Modified Average[b]
Manufacturing:													
City %	42.7	38.1	33.0	32.2	26.9	22.5	20.2	19.5	18.8	18.1	1		26.4
Rank	1	2	3	4	5	6	7	8	9	10			
Suburb %	47.8	34.8	45.6	41.1	30.9	30.5	42.6	37.1	28.9	25.8		9	36.4
Rank	1	6	2	4	7–8	7–8	3	5	9	10			
Business and Allied Services (MBS-TCU)													
City %	23.4	30.8	33.8	31.1	44.4	32.6	43.8	41.5	37.2	36.9	10		36.0
Rank	10	9	6	8	1	7	2	3	4	5			
Suburb %	12.4	17.4	19.0	18.5	26.0	12.8	20.5	24.2	15.5	20.5		0	18.6
Rank	9–10	7	5	6	1	9–10	3–4	2	8	3–4			
Consumer Services (MCS)													
City	29.0	26.6	28.4	31.3	25.4	29.3	30.4	30.1	35.1	33.4	0		29.8
Suburb	33.3	39.6	29.2	32.9	35.6	31.2	32.4	34.5	43.2	38.0		10	34.7

Construction:												
City	4.6	3.4	4.7	5.3	3.2	11.1	5.4	8.0	7.1	7.2	0	5.7
Suburb	5.1	7.1	5.4	6.8	6.7	15.6	4.7	13.6	10.9	9.3	9[d]	8.1
Other[c]												
City	0.4	0.1	0.1	0.2	0.1	4.4	0.3	0.4	1.8	4.5	e	1.0
Suburb	1.3	1.0	0.9	0.7	0.9	9.3	0.5	5.9	1.5	6.4	e	2.3
Net change employment 1960–1970												
City	17.2	−4.6	−1.8	4.5	6.5	66.4	11.0	42.7	31.7	22.8	e	16.8
Suburb	60.0	56.0	40.0	44.9	46.6	68.2	26.5	138.5	106.4	79.9	e	62.8

[a] Percentages add to 100%. Data are for covered employment at place of work. See footnotes 5 and 6, page 77, for definitions of industry groups.
[b] Highest and lowest values among ten places omitted in computing modified average.
[c] Includes primary.
[d] When differences are ≤ 0.5, as in the case of Cleveland, the comparison is scored as a tie.
[e] No comparisons made.

Source: *Social Security Administration, Continuous Work History Files.*

percent, respectively), but fifth, seventh, and eighth in manufacturing (shares of employment, 26.9, 20.2, and 19.5 percent).

A city tends to specialize in one or another function, while at the same time providing appropriate residentiary (local-sector) goods and services. However, where consumer-service (MCS) employment is relatively large in a city, there is evidence of important export activity in provision of such services to nonresidents from the hinterland and to tourists from other cities and regions of the country, for not all residentiary-type services are purchased by residents of a city or even of its suburbs.[6] Such appears to be the case for New Orleans, an important port and business center, and for Denver, a focal point in the Rocky Mountain region for business and for consumer services for hinterland residents and tourists.

Suburbs take on, to a degree, the industrial coloration of the cities they surround. This similarity derives from the fact that the suburban economic activity, to a significant degree, derives from that of the city. Suburban firms, especially in the case of manufacturing, have frequently been transplanted from the city, or are branch facilities. Suburbs share with the city, in part, a common pool of business services, technical know-how, and regional markets. Thus, Cleveland's suburban ring and central city have the top position in manufacturing, while New Orlean's ring and city rank last. New York's suburbs and central city rank first in MBS-TCU. This clear general tendency is reflected in coefficients of rank correlation between cities and suburbs which are .75 for shares of employment in manufacturing and .78 for shares of employment in MBS-TCU.

Nevertheless, differences in the industrial composition of cities and their suburbs are substantial, and an understanding of these differences is important to the analysis of suburban labor markets. City-suburban differences in industrial structure may be explained by two of the major processes which have accounted for the revolutionary growth of the suburbs: (a) the separation of residential location and local-sector activities from place of work, particularly for middle- and upper-income suburban families whose principal source of employment is within the city's economy, and (b) the strong tendency for growth in manufacturing to take place in the suburbs and, somewhat less important in recent years, the actual transfer of manufacturing activity from city to suburb. Accordingly, the major sources of growth of suburbs have been local-sector and manufacturing activities, the former supported by income generated by commuters (the hidden export discussed previously).

On the other hand, the percentage of employment devoted to business services is considerably smaller in suburbs, reflecting the continued locational advantages of the CBD for most of these activities. Finally, construction employment has tended to be relatively larger in suburbs, reflecting the very rapid growth and need for new structures of all kinds.

INDUSTRY GROWTH AND CHANGE, 1960-1970

The basic differences in city-suburb industrial specialization in 1970 represent the cumulative effect of past development. Suburbanization is a process which, as we have seen, extends back over many decades for most cities. Its current significance lies in the fact that for well over two decades of recent history, growth in population and employment has been sustained in most suburbs at very high rates. The effect of this continuous suburban employment growth, coupled with declining rates of growth (or actual declines) in employment in cities, has brought about a sharp rise in the role of the suburb within the metropolitan area. Significant shifts in industrial composition of both cities and suburbs have occurred.

During the period 1960-1970, both city and suburban economies were moving toward decreased shares of their employment accounted for by manufacturing and increased shares by services (Table 3.3).[7]

Number of cities or suburbs with changes in percentage of employment accounted for by manufacturing and services, 1960–70[a]

	Cities		Suburbs	
	Increases	Decreases	Increases	Decreases
Manufacturing	1	9[b]	0	10
Services, business and consumer	9	1	9	1

[a] Measures are for covered employment at place of work.
[b] Actual declines in manufacturing employment occurred in Baltimore, Boston, New York, Philadelphia, and St. Louis.

The transition differed between cities and suburbs, however. In cities, which for the most part show low rates of growth, or actual declines in total employment, expansion of shares of employment in business services had been accompanied by a decline of shares of employment in manufacturing. At the same time, the local sector has been following population movements to the suburbs, with the result that shares of employment accounted for by consumer services declined in seven out of ten cities, with actual declines noted in two (Baltimore and St. Louis). On the other hand, in the rapidly growing

Table 3.3. Employment Change, All Industries
Related Data, Manufacturing, Mainly Business Services

	All Industries			Manufacturing				
	Rates of		Net	Shares of Employment		Shares of		Rates of Net
	JI	JD	Change	1960	1970	JI[c]	JD[c]	Change[b]
City								
Atlanta	49.8	7.1	42.7	22.8	19.9	14.9	26.1	24.5
Baltimore	15.6	11.1	4.5	34.7	32.2[d]	22.3	40.5	−3.0
Boston	22.4	11.4	11.0	23.8	20.2[d]	19.8	51.2	−5.9
Cleveland	23.6	6.4	17.2	48.8	42.7	20.1	54.5	2.6
Denver	37.0	5.3	31.7	18.9	18.8	26.4	73.5	30.7
Houston	67.9	1.5	66.4	26.7	22.5	16.5	27.1	39.7
New Orleans	28.7	5.9	22.8	16.6	18.1	26.1	31.8	34.0
New York	13.3	6.8	6.5	32.5	26.9[d]	7.1	70.4	−11.9
Philadelphia	11.6	13.4	−1.8	42.8	33.0[d]	0.1	78.2	−24.4
St. Louis	8.2	12.8	−4.6	39.8	38.1[d]	37.8	50.7	−8.5
Modified Average[e]	25.3	8.4	16.8	30.3	26.5	19.2	50.0	7.8
Suburb								
Atlanta	142.2	3.7	138.5	26.3	21.8	19.4	47.4	98.5
Baltimore	60.5	15.6	44.9	63.8	41.1	16.8	92.9	6.8
Boston	35.2	8.7	26.5	53.5	42.0	21.2	89.3	0.5
Cleveland	69.6	9.6	60.0	53.6	47.8	42.4	68.8	42.7
Denver	127.1	20.7	106.4	40.6	28.9	29.4	88.7	46.9
Houston	77.6	9.4	68.2	38.0	30.5	19.2	16.7	35.1
New Orleans	88.7	8.8	79.9	36.8	25.8	20.2	92.3	26.5
New York	52.1	5.5	46.6	34.8	30.9	28.5	80.4	29.9
Philadelphia	43.0	3.0	40.0	52.9	45.6	32.0	90.5	21.0
St. Louis	65.0	9.0	56.0	45.4	34.8	24.4	77.0	19.7
Modified Average[e]	73.0	8.8	62.8	44.5	35.0	25.5	79.3	27.7

[a] All data are percentages. Data are based on covered employment at place of work. The number of job increases (job decreases) were computed by segregating those industries (two-digit classifications) with increases (decreases) and totaling increases (decreases).

[b] Rates of JI, JD, Net change were computed as a percentage of 1960 employment for all industries and for each industry category. Note: the rate of job increase less the rate of job decrease equals the rate of net change.

Changes in Composition of Employment and
Mainly Consumer Services, Ten Metropolitan Areas, 1960–1970[a].

Mainly Business Services					Mainly Consumer Services				
Shares of Employment[c]		Shares of	Rates of		Shares of Employment		Shares	of	Rates of
1960	1970	JI[c]	JD[c]	Net Change	1960	1970	JI[c]	JD[c]	Net Change[b]
26.5	29.4	31.4	2.0	58.6	33.3	30.1	27.0	53.1	29.1
18.2	21.4	31.2	6.7	22.7	32.8	31.3[d]	24.8	35.9	−0.3
29.2	33.0	37.8	8.9	25.5	31.6	30.4	23.7	27.6	6.8
14.7	18.5	31.7	7.5	47.7	25.0	29.0	38.7	3.4	35.7
24.7	27.2	30.2	0.0	45.2	35.7	35.1	29.3	6.9	29.3
19.2	23.7	29.7	0.0	104.9	31.1	29.3	26.8	33.3	56.9
24.5	23.3	15.9	8.2	16.6	34.2	33.4	30.7	34.5	19.7
29.5	33.2	48.7	8.8	19.9	24.3	25.4	24.6	9.1	10.9
21.1	25.3	39.6	5.9	18.0	25.3	28.4	39.3	14.7	10.2
20.4	21.5	22.2	13.6	0.4	27.5	26.6[d]	16.3	26.7	−7.5
23.0	25.6	31.7	[e]	31.8	30.1	29.8	28.2	23.6	17.7
14.6	18.8	21.2	0.0	206.8	36.5	34.5	32.3	5.3	125.4
5.3	12.4	21.3	1.7	238.3	21.2	32.9	43.9	0.8	124.7
10.9	16.4	28.1	1.6	89.3	26.2	32.4	43.7	6.5	56.5
9.0	9.8	11.3	12.5	73.3	29.2	33.3	36.4	12.5	82.5
10.1	12.6	12.7	0.8	158.3	32.2	43.2	45.2	1.6	177.5
5.5	9.8	14.1	0.0	200.0	35.7	31.7	29.3	54.2	49.5
10.2	12.9	14.8	2.6	126m7	32.2	38.0	40.9	2.6	112.0
15.2	19.8	26.8	1.0	91.9	34.1	35.6	34.9	0.6	53.3
10.1	14.2	22.8	0.0	97.4	25.2	29.2	36.4	0.0	62.1
11.3	12.3	12.9	5.0	70.1	27.9	39.6	52.6	3.0	121.5
10.2	13.7	18.3	[e]	130.5	30.3	34.8	39.2	4.1	92.3

[c] Employment, job increases, job decreases were distributed among industrial classifications.
[d] Decline in share accompanied by actual decline in employment.
[e] Highest and lowest values among ten places omitted in computing modified average.

Source: Tabulations from Social Security Administration, *Continuous Work History Files*.

suburbs, both consumer services and business services are increasing in importance.

Number of cities or suburbs with changes
in percentage of employment accounted for
by business and consumer services, 1960–70[a]

	Cities		Suburbs	
	Increase	Decrease	Increase	Decrease
Mainly business services	9	1	10	0
Mainly consumer services	3	7[b]	8	2

[a] Measures are for covered employment at place of work.
[b] Actual declines occurred in mainly consumer services in Baltimore and St. Louis.

It is important, however, not to overemphasize the role that the business services have played in the economies of suburbs thus far. Among cities, the share of job increases accounted for by business services during the sixties averaged 31.7 percent, and the share of employment in 1970, 25.6 percent (Table 3.3). Among suburbs, however, the share of 1960-1970 job increases averaged only 18.3 percent, and the share of 1970 employment, 13.7 percent. Business services are developing in both city and suburbs, but their importance is far greater in the cities. Moreover, as we shall observe below, a larger share of business services in suburbs than in cities is partially devoted to the needs of residents (e.g., lawyers, banks, real estate agencies), and is properly regarded as partly within the local sector.

Manufacturing. The decline in the relative importance of manufacturing as a source of employment expansion in cities and suburbs is clearly one of the most important trends under way in metropolitan places today, even though manufacturing continues to be the principal source of employment in many places (Table 3.3). In the cities studied, manufacturing employment was marked by actual declines in a number of places (Baltimore, Boston, New York, Philadelphia, and St. Louis), and rates of growth in most of the others which were low relative to growth rates for total employment.

What appears to be taking place in the manufacturing sectors of most cities is that, on the one hand, the low-wage activities are declining in importance as these industries shift to other parts of the country and of the world, and, on the other hand, remaining manufacturing activities are finding opportunities for no more than modest employment expansion. In Atlanta, Baltimore, Boston, New Orleans, New York, and St. Louis all or most of the decline in the share of employment in manufacturing, and in Philadelphia well over a third was accounted for by the low-wage segment (not shown in Table 3.3).[8]

In the suburbs, manufacturing has continued to grow in most places, but with rates of growth that have fallen well short of rates of overall employment increases. The results have been declines in manufacturing's share of total employment of more than 10 percent in half the suburbs, and of 4 percent or more in the remainder. Relative declines in shares have, in most instances, been greatest in low-wage manufacturing classifications.

Manpower problems faced in connection with this transition are much more serious in cities because of the slow rate of overall employment expansion, coupled with changes in the type of labor hired (see Chapter 4). Manufacturing continues to account for a significant share of employment in cities, but it is unlikely that recent declines, or low rates of increase, can be turned into substantial employment increases in the years ahead. To the contrary, there is considerable reason to fear that, with suburbanization of high-wage manufacturing and with physical obsolescence, congestion, and rising costs, there will be further manufacturing employment losses in the cities. In the suburbs, however, manufacturing is a relatively more important source of employment and continues to show, in most places, some growth as well. There is little reason to expect that the manufacturing sectors of the suburban economies will soon fall into decay. What is at issue is whether they can continue to contribute as much as in the past to the needs of a burgeoning population for increased employment.

Business Services. Growth of the sector classified as "mainly business services" involves problems of interpretation. Some of these services are essentially residentiary in orientation and overlap the local sector. Banks, lawyers, real-estate agents, repair services, and a variety of related activities provide jointly for the needs of families and of tradesmen who, in turn, serve these families. On the other hand, certain service activities are essentially export in character. For example, the growing, but still relatively small, wholesaling-warehousing-trucking sector, as well as those suburban-based business services which provide for the needs of these activities and of manufacturing concerns may be regarded as exports, along with manufacturing.

Table 3.3 makes clear just how important the business services have been as a source of new jobs in cities. Only in New Orleans and St. Louis did business services account for less than 29 percent of job increases, and only in St. Louis for more than 9 percent of job decreases.

In Philadelphia, substantial gains were made in business services at the same time that heavy losses of employment were being experienced in manufacturing. In Houston, business services accounted for 30 percent of job increases under conditions of extremely rapid employment growth. The result was a rise in business-service employment of 74,900 jobs (second only to that of New York City) and an increase in share of total employment of 4.5 percentage points during the decade. In Cleveland, a city heavily specialized in manufacturing, business services accounted for 32 percent of job increases (but only 7.5 percent of job decreases), resulting in a net gain of 43,200 jobs in this category and an increased share of total employment of 3.8 percentage points. Baltimore's net increases in business services were somewhat less impressive in relative terms and occurred under conditions of slower growth. Nevertheless, business services did increase as a share of employment by 3.2 percentage points.

Of the two remaining cities, one, New Orleans, experienced relatively strong growth in manufacturing, primary activities, and consumer services, but more modest growth in business services. Its share of total employment accounted for by business services declined slightly (by 1.2 percentage points from 1960 to 1970). Finally, the city of St. Louis experienced a very small growth in business services (only 3,000 jobs) in the face of larger declines elsewhere within its economy. The net result was a small increase (1.1 percentage points) in the size of its business-service sector.

In the suburbs, there was considerable variation in the role played by business services as a source of additional employment. In five suburbs, New York, Boston, Atlanta, Philadelphia, and Baltimore, business services accounted for more than one-fifth of all job increase, but in the remaining suburbs, the sector accounted for shares of job increase ranging only from 11 to 14 percent.

Consumer Services. Rapid growth of suburban employment in the consumer services reflects principally growth in local-sector activities: retailing, personal services, medical services, and recreation. If government and education were included in the data, the increases in employment in these categories would, doubtless, be similar. In part, such growth stems from rising affluence in the suburbs, but, to an important extent, it represents import substitution of services formerly purchased by suburbanites in the central city.

Suburban import substitution represents a shift of function from city to suburb, and the logic of such a process is that it cannot continue indefinitely. At some point the relative size of the sector must stabilize in both city and suburb in recognition of the local needs which must be met. The "equilibrium" share of employment in consumer services may be expected to be larger for suburbs as long as there is a net balance of commuting from suburb to city and a higher average income, but the increases in shares which characterized the postwar decades should be regarded as transitional.[9]

Just how job increases contribute to change in industrial composition is illustrated in Table 3.3, which shows shares of total employment in 1960 and 1970 and of job increases 1960 to 1970 which were accounted for by the consumer services sector. It will be seen that substantial shares of job increases are necessary to bring about significant changes in shares of employment over the decade. Thus, the share of total job increases is found to be larger than the percentage of employment in 1960 in those places where business services increased in importance over the decade.[10]

There is, of course, no way of knowing what is the ideal proportion of consumer services to total employment. In the suburbs this proportion depends on tendencies to purchase in the city, on the relative size and affluence of the commuting segment of the population, the affluence of the noncommuting population, the productivity (i.e., output per employee) in the various consumer industrial classes, and the extent, if any, to which sales by the consumer-service sector are made to persons living in the city or outside the metropolitan area. Just as suburbanites once traveled to the city for certain services, the advent of widespread auto ownership and the large shopping mall has brought about an increase of shopping by city residents in the suburbs.

Thus, we cannot account for the relative size of the consumer sectors which are observed in Table 3.3. The above parameters are not known; nor do we know that, in any instance, the "system" was in equilibrium in 1970. It is interesting to note, however, that where shares declined between 1960 and 1970 (Atlanta, Houston), they were relatively large in the initial year. In such cases, 1960-70 growth took place disproportionately in other sectors than consumer services.

The implication of this discussion is that the consumer-services sector is likely to remain a major sector in the suburban economy in the years ahead and, to the extent that the suburban economies grow, a correspondingly important source of employment expansion. It is unlikely, however, that consumer services will play quite as important a role as a source of growth once the opportunities for import substitution in this sector are exhausted, although it may grow as a result of upgrading in the other sectors. Conversely, when the period of suburban import-substitution is largely over, this source of weakness will be removed from the cities' economies.

Construction-Related Activities. Perhaps the most important characteristic of construction-related activities is that they are sustained by the growth processes within the economy. Thus, the size of the contract-construction industry is determined largely by the amount of building that is carried out each year: as long as the demand for additional structures is increasing (i.e., the increment is increasing), the demand for construction services will rise.[11]

Thus, in a rapidly growing economy there will be a whole segment of that economy—the construction-related activities—whose function is principally to provide for the growth process. In a suburban economy, this segment will include not only the contract-construction industry, but also some fraction of the employment of wholesaling firms and manufacturing firms that take care of its needs. On the other hand, any diminution in the amount of growth will tend to lower the absolute level of demand for employment by the industry.

There is little doubt that, under the conditions of growth which have characterized suburbs during the past two decades or more, these construction-related activities have been of considerable importance. Their growth has provided a significant portion of the increased demand for employment and, to the extent that their employees live within the suburbs, has fed the demand for sevices of the local sector as well.

It is not our task here to project growth trends for the suburbs. It should be noted, however, that the share of covered employment in contract construction declined in six out of ten suburbs (not shown), reflecting, presumably, the tendency for population growth to be slower in the sixties than in the fifties. Although the relationship between growth and shares of employment is not so close in practice as in theory, it has been shown to be significant. Clearly, it has been an important source of strength in the suburbs in the past. More important, it could be a source of weakness in the years ahead, since the extremely high-growth momentum of the fifties and sixties is not likely to be sustained.

CITY-SUBURB COMPARISONS BY INDUSTRY: QUALITATIVE ASPECTS[12]

VALUE ADDED: WAGES AND SALARIES[12]

While it is not possible to account fully for the qualitative dimension of industrial composition, value-added data for manufacturing and wage and salary payments for all industrial classifications can be examined. When these data are compared (Table 3.4), two major patterns are observed: (1) in manufacturing, value added per worker is higher in eight out of ten suburbs; (2) in the trade and services categories, average annual earnings are higher in cities than in suburbs in virtually every comparison.

Do these measures reflect greater productivity, the performance of higher-order (i.e. skilled) functions, or do they reflect simply higher pay scales for similar tasks and/or full rather than part-time work schedules?

For manufacturing, the evidence seems clear. In nine comparisons out of ten, suburban workers receive higher rates of remuneration than do city workers. Moreover, value added per worker, excluding wages, indicates more capital-intensive production in suburbs and, since suburban plants are typically more modern, a more advanced technology.

This does not mean that all manufacturing in the suburbs is modern and highly productive. There are many firms that have located in poorer areas of the suburbs in search of cheaper space, lower taxes, and favorable wage rates for unskilled labor. Many such firms have been a part of the suburban economy for decades.

Moreover, it is interesting to observe that, in the period since the mid-fifties, value added per worker, though typically higher in the suburbs, has failed to grow as rapidly as in the city. This was true during the period 1954 to 1968 in every area but Houston (not shown in Table 3.4). Presumably, this was the result, largely, of a weeding out within the cities of those firms in lower-wage industries, which was observed above.

Nevertheless, the evidence does indicate that suburban manufacturing firms are, on the average, more productive (more capital-intensive), and that the sector plays a more important role than the employment data suggest. Suburban manufacturing generates a large flow of income from the outside world which is passed on, in part, to feed the demand for suburban residentiary services.[13] At the same time, suburban manufacturing requires sizeable inputs of goods and services from local firms and from the public sectors (e.g., fuel, grounds maintenance, certain business services, utilities, police protection).

Turning to the business services, there is less direct evidence, but considerable indirect evidence, that the higher average wages of the city do, indeed, represent payment for more sophisticated and productive activity than in suburbs. For example, in considering the FIRE classification, where average earnings are higher in the city in every comparison, it must be kept in mind that these higher averages obtain in spite of a higher proportion of low-wage female clerical workers in the city (see Table 4.1). Central-city banking, insurance, and real-estate activities require a higher level of professional expertise than is true in suburban activities bearing the same industrial classification. Although there is much routine banking, insurance activity, and real-estate brokerage carried out in both areas, the city is typically headquarters for these firms, and planning and major transactions are typically carried out in the city. Similarly, legal services (included but not presented separately in "Services" in Table 3.4) show higher wages in the city in every case. Once again general observation suggests a higher average output per person, for leading city law firms are known to handle the most complicated and most remunerative cases.

There are exceptions, of course. Some trucking, warehousing, and wholesaling operations are larger, more modern, and more remunera-

Table 3.4. Qualitative Aspects of Employment: Earnings, Value Added, Hours Worked Selected Industries 1967 or 1970, Ten Metropolitan Areas[a]

		Atlanta	Balti-more	Boston	Cleve-land	Denver	Houston	New Orleans	New York	Phila-delphia	St. Louis	Comparisons C>S	S>C
					Earnings per employee (January–March Quarter) 1970								
Total Employment	C	1,690	1,600	1,756	1,898	1,689	1,716	1,509	1,959	1,720	1,771	8	
	S	1,688	1,663	1,676	1,600	1,603	1,622	1,574	1,768	1,708	1,726		2
Manufacturing	C	1,820	1,870	1,890	2,190	1,890	2,150	1,790	1,981	1,850	1,980	1	
	S	2,210	2,140	1,960	1,870	2,330	2,220	1,930	2,127	2,080	2,180		9
FIRE	C	1,856	1,652	1,846	1,767	1,705	1,695	1,658	2,058	1,806	1,575	9	
	S	1,651	1,460	1,615	1,640	1,510	1,313	1,478	1,810	1,587	1,601		1
Wholesaling	C	2,126	1,979	2,178	2,286	2,050	2,051	1,892	2,406	2,120	2,124	7	
	S	2,110	2,091	2,111	2,005	1,867	1,654	1,900	2,400	2,134	2,085		3
Retailing	C	1,193	1,099	1,120	1,128	1,117	1,110	1,060	1,343	1,198	1,235	10	
	S	1,075	993	1,044	1,038	1,005	935	1,036	1,213	1,080	1,087		0
Services	C	1,312	1,304	1,540	1,404	1,297	1,286	1,178	1,840	1,470	1,342	10	
	S	1,254	771	1,466	1,028	1,075	970	1,162	1,435	1,259	1,152		0

Manufacturing: Selected Data (1967)

Manufacturing Value added per worker	C	12,839	14,255	14,649	13,839	13,296	15,839	13,734	11,444	12,391	13,597	2
	S	14,410	12,988	12,635	14,217	17,351	32,896	18,244	14,113	15,130	14,458	8
Aver. hourly income per prod. worker	C	2.58	3.04	2.80	3.36	3.02	2.99	2.86	2.69	2.93	4.07	1
	S	3.00	3.21	2.98	3.53	3.58	3.64	3.08	3.05	3.20	2.62	9
Hours worked per prod. worker	C	2,011	1,972	1,894	2,051	1,982	2,111	1,925	1,896	1,954	1,974	2
	S	2,033	1,994	1,972	2,027	2,051	2,040	2,143	1,987	1,980	2,002	8

[a]All data are in dollars except hours worked per production worker.

Source: Earnings per employee from *County Business Patterns, 1970* (Tables 2 and 3). Selected manufacturing data from *Census of Manufactures, 1967*, MC67(3) Tables 6 and 7.

71

tive in the suburbs. Still another interesting exception is that of the small, but rapidly growing, service classification, "miscellaneous business services" (included in "Services" Table 3.4), which is comprised of firms delivering a variety of "out-of-house" services, such as office temporaries, public accounting, and custodial services. Comparisons for this classification show higher average earnings in suburbs per worker in six out of nine comparisons for which data were available.

Nevertheless, on balance, business services in the cities appear to be characterized by a higher proportion of professionals, by a greater sophistication, and by higher earnings per worker than those of the suburbs. Accordingly, employment data examined alone tend to understate the importance of this sector as an export base and as a source of competitive strength in cities.

In comparing consumer-services sectors, the evidence is not conclusive as to whether or not consumer services of the city are qualitatively of higher order than those of the suburbs. Worker incomes in the suburbs are lower for retailing and for the various other consumer services included in the overall category. But these differentials are explained, at least in part, by a greater tendency to use part-time employees (see Chapter 5, page 124). Where this is true, workers are frequently performing as second or third wage earners in a family. The result is that their wages, though perhaps lower than those of the city, will serve to raise average family income above the level for the city.

City and suburban consumer services do differ in important respects, however. Cities, especially large service centers, demonstrate a greater degree of specialization in many services. Hospitals, colleges, theaters, and sports arenas are likely to be larger and staffed by better trained and more talented personnel and performers. Many city specialty stores and restaurants offer superior and more varied goods and services than are available in the suburbs. On the other hand, over a considerable range, consumer services in the suburbs are probably of equal quality, since the sector caters mainly to a middle-and upper-income clientele. The suburbs' shopping centers frequently offer goods comparable to the best in the city; their primary and secondary educational institutions are manned by well-trained and well-compensated staffs and frequently offer an augmented curriculum; and their restaurants and places of recreation and amusement are usually attractive (if not exciting).

SIZE OF ESTABLISHMENTS

It is important in examining the fundamental characteristics of suburban economies to determine whether or not firms are relatively small or relatively large. While large firms are not necessarily the most productive within a given industrial class, there is a presumption that small firms in an industry will, on an average, be less well-financed and will experience higher rates of mortality. Moreover, employees of small firms will be more likely to work under arrangements in which there are fewer fringe benefits and poorer opportunities for promotion than in large firms. An additional consideration is that the search for employment is rendered more difficult when there are many small firms than a few large ones. The would-be employee is likely to be less familiar with job openings and to find it more difficult and time-consuming to contac all potential employers.

The available data relate to establishments rather than to firms. Establishments are simply physical facilities (e.g., plants, warehouses, retail outlets), whereas firms are complete business organizations—in most instances, corporations. For most purposes, information on establishments is quite satisfactory, but where the firm has many separate facilities, such information conveys an impression of a greater importance of small business activity than is justified.

County data giving the number of establishments within each of a number of employer-size categories (1-3 employees, 4-7 employees, etc.) are available for separate industry-classifications, however, and these data shed some light on size characteristics by permitting us to determine what percentage of establishments are in each size grouping.

It is not possible to estimate the amount (or share) of employment found in each size category. Distribution of establishment sizes within size categories is unknown, and size intervals of categories are variable. Even crude estimates are out of the question for the largest (500 employees and over) category, which is open-ended.

The data (Table 3.5) do make it clear, however, that in both cities and suburbs there are relatively large numbers of small establishments in each industry category: on an average, close to 90 percent of establishments are found in small- (1-19 employees) size class in services and in retailing; 79 percent or more in wholesaling, and roughly 60 percent in manufacturing.

In general, there is a tendency for the suburbs to have larger proportions of establishments in the small- (1-19 employees) size class, but for the cities to have larger shares in the 20-99 and 100-499 employee-size classes. This is true for wholesaling, services, and manufacturing, but in retailing there is no clear-cut tendency.

The largest-size class (500 or more employees) does not figure importantly in the analysis, except in manufacturing, where it accounts for small, but significant, shares of establishments (ranging from 2.1 to 2.4 percent) in both cities and suburbs. In this size class, shares of manufacturing establishments are larger in suburbs in eight out of ten comparisons, but the average share is not significantly larger for the suburbs. Since this category is open-ended, the data tell us nothing

Table 3.5. Size of Establishments in Selected Industries, Ten Metropolitan Areas, 1970 (Percent Distribution)

	NUMBER OF EMPLOYEES							
	0–19		20–99		100–499		500 and above	
	Cities	Suburbs	Cities	Suburbs	Cities	Suburbs	Cities	Suburbs
Manufacturing								
Average %[a]	58.7	60.9	29.4	27.7	10.7	9.6	2.1	2.4
C>S	3		8		6		2	
S>C		7		2		4		8
C=S								
Wholesaling								
Average %[a]	78.7	85.9	18.9	13.1	2.4	1.0	0.2	b
C>S	0		9		10		6	
S>C		10		1		0		0
C=S							4	
Service								
Average %[a]	88.7	92.4	9.1	6.5	1.9	0.9	0.4	b
C>S	0		10		10		10	
S>C		10		0		0		0
C=S								
Retail								
Average %[a]	87.9	88.3	10.3	10.2	1.5	1.3	0.3	b
C>S	5		5		7		8	
S>C		5		5		3		1
C=S							1	

[a] Modified average of percentages for ten places. Lowest and highest values have been dropped except, where two, or more, places show no establishments in a given-size category. Average percentages will not necessarily add to 100.
[b] Two or more places with no employment in indicated category.
Source: Department of Commerce, Bureau of the Census; *County Business Patterns, 1970.*

about where the very large firms (say, 1,000 or more employees) are located. On the basis of general observation, we might expect them to be found in the suburbs, but we cannot confirm this from the evidence at hand.

A NOTE ON PUBLIC EMPLOYMENT

It is unfortunate that the previous analysis cannot be extended to include the public sector, but data are not available for federal, state, and local employment on a basis which permits city-suburb comparisons for all the metropolitan areas in the years under study.

Estimates of public-sector jobs in selected metropolitan areas for

1966, prepared by Bennett Harrison, indicate the division of such employment between cities and suburbs.[14] Table 3.6 presents for 12 places estimates of each city's share of public employment in its metropolitan area, as compared with its corresponding share of total metropolitan employment in the nearest census date (1970).

The analysis reveals that the cities' shares of metropolitan public-sector employment are larger than corresponding shares of total metropolitan employment in 9 out of 12 comparisons. It is interesting that these relatively large shares of government employment are due, in part, to the abnormally large shares of federal jobs. Shares of federal jobs are larger in 11 out of 12 comparisons. On the other hand, shares of state and local jobs (the two are combined) are larger than shares of total employment in less than half (5) of the 12 comparisons.

We have prepared for the New York metropolitan area 1965 and 1970 estimates of shares of city and of suburban jobs accounted for by public-sector employment as follows:[15]

	City		Suburbs	
	1965	1970	1965	1970
	%	%	%	%
Total government	12.9	14.1	18.0	18.6
Federal	(3.2)	(2.6)	(2.0)	(2.0)
State and Local	(9.7)	(11.5)	(16.0)	(16.6)

These estimates differ somewhat from those of Harrison in that they indicate that public-sector employment is relatively larger (not smaller) in suburbs than in cities. In spite of this lack of comparability, they are useful in that they provide a measure of the importance of public-sector employment within one major city and its suburbs. What we observe is that the public sector accounts for more than a seventh of total city employment in 1970 and more than a sixth of total suburban jobs.

These findings are hardly definitive, but they are helpful in putting the role of government employment in perspective. They indicate that such employment is important in cities and in suburbs, but that it plays a role which is clearly secondary to that of the private sector. There is nothing here that contradicts, in any way, the general findings of this chapter, which have been based on private-sector employment data.

It is, of course, interesting that the importance of the public sector increased significantly from 1965 to 1970 in New York City. This confirms the general observation that in those years city government played a more important role in the job market than formerly. It would be useful to delve more deeply into this matter since such employment provides an important means of securing initial work attachment for low-income job seekers.

Table 3.6. Intrametropolitan Location of Public-Sector Jobs (1966)
and Total Employment (1970), Twelve Metropolitan Areas

Metropolitan[a] Area (1)	Central City as % of Total				
	Federal[b] (2)	State[b] and Local (3)	All[b] Public Employment (4)	Total[c] Employment (5)	Ratio (4)÷(5)
Baltimore	72.2	59.3	61.7	51.3	1.20
Boston	64.4	35.6	44.4	36.7	1.21
Denver	72.4	45.2	53.1	60.1	0.88
Houston	97.0	87.2	88.9	74.7	1.19
Memphis	99.1	94.9	95.9	86.3	1.11
New Orleans	94.9	62.0	69.4	66.3	1.05
New York	85.2	71.1	73.7	75.7	0.97
Omaha	73.5	76.5	75.8	74.9	1.01
Philadelphia	79.0	48.8	58.6	49.1	1.19
Richmond	98.1	56.7	64.6	71.6	0.90
San Antonio	99.8	96.4	98.2	84.0	1.17
St. Louis	75.6	37.6	48.1	41.9	1.15

[a] Except for Baltimore (Harford County was added), there have been no changes in definitions of metropolitan areas 1966–1970.

[b] Bennet Harrison, "Public Employment and Urban Poverty." *Urban Institute Paper,* (Washington, D.C.: The Urban Institute, 1971).

[c] *Census of Population, 1970.*

SUMMARY

Although there are differences among cities in terms of industrial composition of employment, and suburbs tend to take on their industrial coloration, suburbs are basically different from cities and have certain common traits. Specifically, suburbs have larger manufacturing sectors, larger consumer-services sectors, and more construction employment than cities, but smaller business-service sectors.

Suburbs have grown rapidly in recent times. Manufacturing has played an important role, but employment in manufacturing has grown less rapidly than total employment. The leading edge of growth has been in consumer and business services; the former, larger and more important; the latter, dynamic, but thus far of secondary importance (also to a large extent a part of the local sector, e.g., local lawyers, real-estate firms, etc.). Past growth in the consumer services has, however, been, in a considerable measure, due to import substitution, which is a one-shot source of increased employment, and to increases in construction employment, which relies on continued rapid growth. In these activities growth opportunities could narrow sharply in the years ahead.

In cities, total employment has grown more slowly and, in some instances, has declined. There has been considerable transition, however. Employment increased at substantially higher rates in business services than in consumer services, where there were even declines in two instances (Baltimore and St. Louis).

When qualitative aspects are examined, we find manufacturing has higher wages and value added per worker in suburbs than in cities, but that the cities have higher levels of productivity in the business services than do suburbs. In general, wages are higher in cities in service activities. In addition, suburbs tend to have slightly larger percentages of very small establishments in most industrial categories and smaller proportions of medium-sized establishments. It is not unlikely—though the rather sketchy evidence at hand does not prove it—that the suburbs typically have a larger proportion of very large manufacturing establishments.

Finally, there is some evidence that government jobs are somewhat more important in cities than in suburbs. Although public employment is clearly important, it does not appear to be of sufficient size that its omission from the analysis invalidates the findings of this chapter.

REFERENCES

1. Thomas M. Stanback, Jr., "Suburbanization," in Eli Ginzberg *et al.*, *New York is Very Much Alive* (New York, N.Y.: McGraw-Hill, Inc., 1973).

2. Throughout this study, employment data are examined in terms of the worker's place of employment, not his place of residence.

3. Thomas M. Stanback, Jr. and Richard V. Knight, *The Metropolitan Economy* (New York, N.Y.: Columbia University Press, 1970).

4. The analysis in this section is based on the *Social Security Continuous Work History* materials. Data are based on employment at place of work and include only employees covered by Social Security. County definitions of central cities are used throughout; see Appendix A.

5. Mainly business services (MBS) consists of these classifications: wholesaling, finance-insurance-real estate (FIRE), miscellaneous business services, and legal services. The TCU group includes all transportation, utilities, and communications services covered by Social Security.

6. Mainly consumer services (MCS) consists of the classifications: retailing, hotels, personal services, auto repairs, miscellaneous repairs, motion pictures, amusement and recreation services, medical services, museums and similar institutions, and non-profit organizations.

7. In the analysis of service employment which follows, only MBS and MCS are treated. These two categories reflect more clearly trends in services than does the TCU category, which includes a considerable amount of blue-collar employment.

8. In analyzing employment change, manufacturing-industrial classifications were

grouped into two categories—low wage and high wage—based on national averages for earnings per worker.

9. Of course, the city might have a larger share of employment in consumer services than its suburbs if it is a heavy exporter of retailing and entertainment to transients because of its role as a tourist, government, or regional service center.

10. In most instances, the share of job increases is also larger than the 1970 share, where the share of employment has increased. This need not be the case, however, where there are substantial job decreases as well as job increases occurring within subclasses. See, for example, the New York suburbs.

11. This relationship was examined for 368 metropolitan areas in Stanback and Knight, *op. cit.*, pp. 179-184.

12. The special characteristics of the data employed in this and the following section (i.e. *County Business Patterns, Census of Manufacturing*) are described in Appendix A.

13. Of course, to the extent that workers commute from the city to jobs in the suburbs, this effect is dampened.

14. Bennett Harrison, "Public Employment and Urban Poverty" (URI-30008, The Urban Institute [Washington, D.C., 1971]).

15. Thomas M. Stanback, Jr., "Suburbanization," in Eli Ginzberg, *op. cit.*, pp. 48-49.

[4

Occupation Characteristics and Commuter Flows

The growth and restructuring of cities and suburbs involves not only changes in the industrial composition of employment, but also changes in occupational composition and in patterns of commuting as well. The first section examines, for cities and suburbs, work-force composition and growth and change in terms of occupation and analyzes evidence of upgrading. The second section not only looks into the size and recent trends in commuter flows, but also presents estimates of the amounts of suburban income attributable directly and indirectly to earnings of suburb-to-city commuters and of city earnings attributable to noncommuting (resident) workers. A final section examines the role of suburban towns and cities.

OCCUPATIONAL COMPOSITION AND CHANGE AND THE UPGRADING OF EMPLOYMENT

OCCUPATIONAL COMPOSITION

The basic city-suburb differences in industrial composition of employment noted in the previous chapter find their counterpart, to some extent, in differences in the occupational composition of employment (Table 4.1). The relative importance of white-collar occupations (professional, managerial, administration, and clerical) in cities tends to reflect emphasis on office and other CBD-type activities, while the relative importance of blue-collar occupations (craftsmen, operatives, and laborers) in suburbs reflects emphasis on manufacturing and construction.

This relationship is by no means clear-cut, of course, for published

Table 4.1. Percent Distribution of Employment by Occupation, by Sex,[a] Ten Metropolitan Areas, 1960 and 1970

	City			Suburb			Comparisons			Averages of
	Average Percentage[a]			Average Percentage[a]			Cities-Suburbs 1970			Median SMSA Earnings, 1970[a]
	1960	1970	Change	1960	1970	Change	C>S	S>C	C=S[b]	
Male										
White-collar	44.3	48.7	4.4	38.2	43.1	4.9	10	0	0	
Professional-Tech.	12.0	16.5	4.5	13.4	16.4	3.0	5	4	1	11,192
Man. & Admin.	12.5	12.4	-0.1	11.4	11.7	0.3	5	0	5	12,199
Sales workers	8.8	8.3	-0.5	6.7	7.5	0.8	6	1	3	9,087
Clerical	10.9	11.0	0.1	7.0	7.7	0.7	10	0	0	7,300
Blue-collar	45.1	41.3	-3.8	50.5	45.2	-5.3	1	7	2	
Craftsmen	19.1	19.0	-0.1	23.2	21.7	-1.5	0	9	1	8,522
Operatives[c]	19.0	16.8	-2.2	20.3	17.1	-3.2	4	6	0	6,989
Laborers	6.7	5.4	-1.3	6.8	6.0	-0.8	1	7	2	5,141
Service[d]	8.2	8.9	0.7	6.6	8.0	1.4	8	2	0	5,106
Other[e]	2.4	0.8	-1.6	4.5	3.1	-1.4	0	7	3	3,884

Female

White-collar	61.2	69.8	8.6	60.3	67.6	7.3	7	3	0	
Professional-Tech.	11.5	15.2	3.7	16.6	18.2	1.6	0	10	0	6,094
Man. & Admin.	3.5	3.7	0.2	3.7	3.6	0.1	3	2	5	5,894
Sales workers	7.5	6.3	−1.2	9.3	9.3	0.0	0	10	0	2,463
Clerical	38.8	44.7	5.9	30.9	36.9	6.0	10	0	0	4,429
Blue-collar	15.8	13.0	−2.8	12.1	11.9	−0.2	7	1	2	
Craftsmen	1.4	1.7	0.3	1.1	1.6	0.5	0	0	10	4,605
Operatives	14.5	10.4	−3.9	11.1	9.5	1.6	7	1	2	3,642
Service	20.1	16.4	−3.7	24.6	20.0	4.6	0	9	1	2,498
Other^f	2.6	0.9	−1.7	2.7	1.4	1.3	0	5	5	3,022

[a] Modified averages. Highest and lowest values among ten places omitted in computing average. Employment reported at place of work.
[b] Cities and suburbs are equal when the difference is less than 0.5.
[c] Includes transport workers.
[d] Service workers consist of service workers and private household workers.
[e] Includes farm workers and 'occupational not reported' in 1960, while in 1970 it includes farm workers and armed forces.
[f] Includes farm workers, laborers and 'occupational not reported' in 1960, while in 1970 it includes farmworkers, laborers, and armed forces.

Source: *U.S. Census of Population, 1960*, PC(1) 37D, Table 131; *U.S. Census of Population, 1970*, PC(1) D37, Tables 175, 190.

employment data for cities and suburbs are grouped within a limited number of broad occupational classifications, each of which extends across industry lines and includes a wide range of skill levels. For example, the classification clerical workers is important both in the non-production side of manufacturing and in FIRE and retailing, and includes specific occupations ranging from relatively skilled warehousing operatives to low-skilled file clerks. The professional-technical classification embraces public, private, and not-for-profit sectors, and includes a wide range of skills—public school teachers, medical technicians, lawyers, doctors, computer programmers, college professors, and even the clergy. Transportation operatives (a blue-collar occupation) are largely employed in railway and trucking activities but, again, there is considerable variation in skill and pay levels.

Such wide variation in industry categories and in skill levels represented tends to blur city-suburb differences, yet the differences in occupational structures of cities and suburbs are large enough to indicate fairly consistent variations between the types of demand for labor: There are relatively more white-collar jobs in cities; relatively more blue-collar jobs in suburbs (Table 4.1).

Among males, the percentage of white-collar employment is larger for cities in every comparison, and percentage of blue-collar employment is larger in suburbs in seven out of ten comparisons (with two ties). If transportation operatives (a largely city-oriented occupation comprised disproportionately of rail and/or water-transport workers and truck drivers) are omitted from this grouping, the average percentage of male employment is larger in suburbs than in cities in all ten SMSA's. Service workers, a classification which does not fit well into either the white- or blue-collar grouping, account for a larger percentage of male employment in cities than in suburbs in eight out of ten comparisons, although the average for cities (8.9 percent) is not markedly greater than for suburbs (8.0 percent).

Among females, the share of white-collar employment is again larger in cities than in suburbs (in seven out of ten comparisons), but in contrast to males, blue-collar female employment tends, also, to be relatively larger in cities than in suburbs (seven out of ten comparisons with two ties). Service employment, which is a larger share of total employment for females than for males, is relatively smaller (nine out of ten with one tie) in cities than suburbs.

When occupational classifications are examined in more detail, further insights are gained. Among males, it is chiefly the clerical and sales workers, both strongly oriented to office activities and the business-service sector, who cause the white-collar occupations to comprise a larger share of employment in cities than in suburbs. The professional-technical and managerial-administration classifications are larger in only half the cities, indicating that in the suburbs there is substantial employment in a variety of professional, technical, and managerial jobs ranging from local-sector activities in education, government, medicine and retailing, to export activities which include research and corporate branch offices, and even headquarters operations. In blue-collar employment, all levels of occupations—craftsmen, operatives, and laborers —are more heavily represented in the suburban work forces than in those of the cities.

Although white-collar employment tends to account for larger shares of female jobs in cities than in suburbs, it is relatively large in both: on an average, 70 percent of female employment in cities, 68 percent in suburbs. The largest white-collar classification by far is clerical, comprising 45 percent of total women employed in the city, 37 percent in suburbs. Service workers are a somewhat less important occupation for women in cities than in suburbs (16 compared to 20 percent), but more than twice as important for women as for men in both parts of the metropolitan economy. Finally, operatives are the most important category of blue-collar, accounting for about ten percent of female employment, on an average, in both cities and suburbs.

The important difference between city and suburban labor markets for women is that the former are characterized by a relatively larger share of clerical workers (45 percent of total women employees compared to 37 percent); the latter by a relatively larger share of professional-technical workers (18 percent versus 15 percent), and by a larger share of sales workers (9 percent versus 6 percent) and of service workers (20 percent versus 16 percent). The service worker classification includes domestic servants as well as waitresses in restaurants and bars, cleaning persons in retail stores, motels, and so on.

OCCUPATIONAL GROWTH AND CHANGE 1960-1970[1]

Occupational-growth trends differ between cities and suburbs. The two principal observations relating to occupational change in city employment are (Table 4.2): (1) White-collar occupations (male and female combined) are principal sources of growth. They have accounted for well over 90 percent of all job increases and less than a third of job decreases in eight out of ten cities. (2) In terms of employment, women have gained most from economic change in cities. Female employment accounted for 69 percent or more of job increases in 7 out of 10 cities and 27 percent or less of job decreases in 9 out of 10 cities.

These trends were, of course, not confined to cities, and it is important to place them in perspective by comparing them to similar computations for the national economy. When job increases are computed on a similar basis for the United States between 1960 and 1970, we find that

Table 4.2. Percent Distribution of Job Increases and Decreases, by Occupation, by Sex in Ten Cities, 1960–1970[a]

	Atlanta	Baltimore	Boston	Cleveland	Denver	Houston	New Orleans	New York	Philadelphia	St. Louis	Modified Average[b]
Job Increase:											
Total											
White-collar	93.3	92.0	94.7	97.5	81.7	68.9	96.6	99.5	98.0	95.4	93.7
Blue-collar	6.8	2.5	–	2.5	5.0	24.1	2.9	0.4	0.3	4.6	3.1
Service	–	5.5	5.3	–	13.3	7.0	0.6	–	1.8	–	c
Male											
White-collar Prof-Tech.	37.9 (18.8)	20.9 (20.9)	26.1 (26.1)	30.8 (30.8)	34.9 (23.7)	32.8 (15.3)	29.3 (29.3)	23.5 (23.5)	22.7 (22.7)	25.2 (25.2)	28.2 (23.8)
Blue collar	5.0	–	–	–	1.9	21.0	–	–	–	–	c
Service	–	5.5	–	–	7.2	2.5	0.6	–	1.8	–	c
Total	42.9	26.4	26.1	30.8	44.0	56.3	29.9	23.5	24.5	25.2	31.2
Female											
White collar Prof-Tech.	55.4 (13.7)	71.1 (26.9)	68.6 (30.5)	66.7 (28.4)	46.8 (12.8)	36.1 (8.5)	67.3 (21.3)	76.0 (31.6)	75.3 (28.7)	70.2 (31.3)	65.2 (24.2)
Clerical	(35.8)	(42.3)	(34.3)	(37.1)	(31.3)	(22.3)	(44.3)	(44.4)	(43.0)	(38.9)	(38.4)
Blue-collar	1.8	2.5	–	2.5	3.1	3.1	2.9	0.4	0.3	4.6	2.1
Service	–	–	5.3	–	6.1	4.5	–	–	–	–	c
Total	57.2	73.6	73.9	69.2	56.0	43.7	.70.2	76.4	75.6	74.8	68.8

Job
Decrease:
Total

White-collar	–	37.4	31.0	19.5	–	–	19.5	24.2	27.5	37.4	c
Blue-collar	43.7	54.9	68.4	70.9	100.0	–	68.2	70.3	64.3	59.6	62.5
Service	56.3	7.6	0.6	9.5	–	–	12.4	5.5	8.3	3.0	c
Male											
White-collar	36.7	32.8	29.1	14.9	–	–	19.0	22.8	24.6	31.7	c
Blue-collar	13.1	46.9	52.7	63.9	100.0	–	62.2	50.4	51.5	48.5	51.6
Service	–	–	0.6	1.3	–	–	–	0.2	–	0.6	c
Total	49.8	79.7	82.4	80.1	100.0	–	81.2	73.4	76.1	80.8	75.4
Female											
White-collar	–	4.6	1.9	4.6	–	–	0.5	1.4	2.9	5.7	c
Blue-collar	7.0	8.0	15.7	7.0	–	–	6.0	19.9	12.8	11.1	c
Service	43.2	7.6	–	8.2	–	–	12.4	5.3	8.3	2.4	c
Total	50.2	20.2	17.6	19.8	–	–	18.9	26.6	24.0	19.2	c
Rates:											
JI	20.4	6.3	8.1	4.3	22.0	51.5	8.0	5.1	4.0	3.4	9.8
JD	4.9	10.3	13.5	17.8	0.5	–	9.2	13.3	13.9	16.4	10.3
Net Change	15.5	–4.0	–5.4	–13.5	–21.5	51.5	–1.2	–8.2	–9.9	–13.0	–5.0

[a] Job increases and decreases computed from 1960 and 1970 data for employment reported at place of work. Method of computing is same as described in Footnote a, Table 3.3, except that occupational classifications are used.
[b] Highest and lowest values among ten places omitted in computing modified average.
[c] Not computed.

Source: U.S. Census of Population, 1960, Pc(1) 37D, Table 131, U.S. Census of Population, 1970, Pc(1) D37, Table 190.

white-collar occupations (male and female combined) were responsible for 61 percent of the total and female employment for 73 percent.[2] Thus white-collar employment was decidedly more important as a source of employment gains in the cities studied than it was in the nation as a whole. On the other hand, the share of city job increases accounted for by female employment was roughly in line with the overall national experience.

Patterns of job increase during the sixties are remarkably uniform among the ten cities studied. Job increases among males are found entirely in the professional-technical occupational class in all but the most rapidly growing cities (Atlanta, Denver, Houston) and in Baltimore, where there was a small increase in service employment. In these three fastest-growing cities, there were job increases among males in other white-collar occupations as well, but only in Houston was there any significant share accounted for by blue-collar increases. At the same time, increases in female employment occurred principally (or entirely) in two categories—professional-technical and clerical—with the latter category's share being considerably larger.

These figures reflect the growth of medical, education, and business services and the widespread increase in office activity. Job increases in the male professional-technical category represent increasing numbers of doctors, lawyers, engineers, accountants, teachers, as well as technicians (including, especially, computer technicians). Job increases in the female professional-technical and clerical categories represent largely growth of employment in nursing and paramedical activities, teaching, and a host of supportive activities in both the public and private sectors.

Patterns of job change in the suburbs are significantly different (Table 4.3). Although white-collar employment gains remain the major source of job increase, and employment increases accounted for by women are disproportionately large (relative to women's share of jobs at the beginning of the decade), blue-collar and service-worker occupations play a much more important role than in cities. In general, the fast-growing suburbs have witnessed growth on a much broader spectrum of industrial activities and occupational classes.

UPGRADING OF CITY AND SUBURBAN WORK FORCES

There is considerable evidence that both city and suburban work forces have been upgraded by shifts in occupational composition. In cities, among males there has been a substantial increase in the share accounted for by the relatively well-paid professional-technical group; declines, or virtually no change, in the remaining white-collar classes; and declines in blue-collar shares (Table 4.1). Among females, there has also been a significant increase in the share of employment found in the professional-technical classification; as well as in the clerical group, where earnings are lower than professional-technical, but above average. At the same time, there have been declines in lower-paid blue-collar and service shares. In suburbs, male employment again shows a significant increased percentage within the professional-technical group, with declines, or only small changes, in shares accounted for by other classifications; and among females we observe, once again, increases of some importance in professional-technical and clerical.

It is important to keep in mind that, in a large measure, changes within city economies have involved a very different sort of transition from changes occurring in suburbs. The former have occurred as a result of difficult adjustments involving simultaneous job increases and job decreases. The occupations in which job increases have occurred have tended to be above average income for the sex category, whereas those in which job decreases have taken place have been largely low income. Using 1970 SMSA median male or female earnings for occupational classes to compute average (weighted) earnings for job increases and for job decreases in each of the 10 cities, the following were determined:[3]

	Male	Female
Job increases	$10,747	$5,161
Job decreases	7,410	3,174

On the other hand, there were virtually no job decreases among the fast-growing suburbs (Table 4.3). The changes which occurred in the suburban occupational composition were almost entirely the results of differences in rates of increase in employment among the various occupations.

Additional evidence of upgrading is available from Social Security data which show 1960-70 percentage increases of earnings for sex-race categories in cities and suburbs (Table 4.4). Cities are found to have experienced greater improvement than suburbs during the 1960-70 period.[4] This was true in virtually all comparisons of average earnings for white males and females, and in eight out of ten comparisons of average earnings for black females. For black males, however, the pattern was less well established. In six out of ten metropolitan areas, average earnings of black males in the city increased more rapidly than for those in the suburbs; but in four (Atlanta, Cleveland, Denver, and New Orleans), gains were greater in the suburbs.

These data help put the upgrading of employment in cities and suburbs into perspective: Both cities and suburbs have experienced recent transition in which there has been a shift toward higher-paying occupations for both males and females. In cities the transition has been more

Table 4.3. Distribution of Job Increases by Occupation and by Sex, and Rates of Employment Change in Ten Suburbs, 1960–70[a]

	Atlanta	Baltimore	Boston	Cleveland	Denver	Houston	New Orleans	New York	Philadelphia	St. Louis	Modified Average[b]
Job Increase:[c]											
Total											
White-collar	64.6	65.4	83.5	45.6	64.0	47.2	58.9	82.2	75.2	63.5	65.1
Blue-collar	27.2	21.4	0.7	40.9	22.7	40.1	29.7	9.2	13.8	22.8	23.4
Service	8.1	13.1	15.7	13.5	13.1	12.9	11.4	8.7	11.1	13.7	12.2
Male											
White-collar	31.9	30.9	33.9	20.1	30.9	23.8	29.7	31.6	34.1	28.7	30.2
Prof.-Tech.	(10.9)	(12.5)	(18.4)	(7.1)	(14.5)	(12.3)	(9.7)	(14.1)	(15.5)	(13.0)	(12.8)
Blue-collar	23.4	16.1	–	33.8	17.6	37.3	28.3	4.9	8.8	18.1	18.9
Service	2.7	5.9	8.7	5.5	6.6	3.6	4.4	7.1	6.8	6.3	5.8
Total	58.0	52.9	42.6	59.4	55.1	64.7	62.4	43.6	49.7	53.1	54.3
Female											
White-collar	32.7	34.5	49.6	25.5	33.1	23.4	29.2	50.6	41.1	34.8	35.1
Prof.-Tech.	(9.2)	(8.4)	(14.2)	(4.2)	(10.1)	(6.9)	(7.7)	(12.9)	(9.3)	(8.7)	(9.2)
Clerical	(18.8)	(21.3)	(28.4)	(16.2)	(17.1)	(11.2)	(15.8)	(30.7)	(25.3)	(20.4)	(20.4)
Blue-collar	3.8	5.3	0.7	7.1	5.1	2.8	1.4	4.3	5.0	4.7	4.1
Service	5.4	7.2	7.0	8.0	6.5	9.3	7.0	1.6	4.3	7.4	6.6
Total	41.9	47.0	57.3	40.6	44.7	35.5	37.6	56.5	50.4	46.9	45.7
Rates:											
JI	125.1	83.1	24.9	85.6	88.8	171.6	115.0	34.6	32.6	61.9	78.3
JD	–	–	3.3	–	–	–	–	0.2	–	–	[d]
Net change	125.1	83.1	21.6	85.6	88.8	171.6	115.0	34.4	32.6	61.9	78.3

[a] Job increases and decreases computed from 1960 and 1970 data for employment reported at place of work.
[b] Highest and lowest values among ten places omitted in computing modified average.
[c] Job decreases not distributed. In most suburbs, there were no job decreases.
[d] Not computed.

Source: *U.S. Census of Population, 1960*, PC(1) 37D, Table 131; *U.S. Census of Population, 1970*, PC(1) D37, Table 190.

88

Table 4.4. Percentage Increases in Average Earnings of Workers by Sex and Race in Ten Metropolitan Areas, 1960–1970[a]

	CITIES					SUBURBS				
	Male		Female			Male		Female		
	White	Black	White	Black	Total	White	Black	White	Black	Total
Atlanta	70.1	91.5	67.3	134.5	69.6	68.1	143.6	64.4	105.8	68.1
Baltimore	60.9	74.7	59.3	138.4	59.6	51.4	48.2	52.8	93.2	46.9
Boston	70.9	81.1	67.8	62.4	65.6	61.8	44.2	49.3	47.8	56.7
Cleveland	50.5	47.9	40.6	59.3	45.9	49.0	53.1	48.7	6.1	39.2
Denver	50.4	51.0	55.2	92.0	49.1	33.9	80.1	30.5	90.2	28.2
Houston	61.0	82.3	54.1	91.4	60.8	61.5	76.2	18.9	114.7	51.5
New Orleans	73.3	71.1	70.3	91.1	72.7	72.3	82.8	51.4	93.8	63.6
New York	66.0	80.6	60.8	94.0	61.2	58.3	71.2	55.2	74.6	61.9
Philadelphia	59.8	72.2	61.2	91.4	56.6	58.3	65.8	54.9	77.6	53.0
St. Louis	67.9	73.6	65.2	102.7	65.5	56.2	54.3	39.1	85.5	44.7
Modified Average[b]	63.4	73.3	61.4	94.9	61.0	58.1	66.5	47.7	83.6	52.2
C>S	10	6	9	8	9					
S>C						0	4	1	2	1

[a] Covered employment at place of work.
[b] Highest and lowest values among ten places omitted in computing modified average.

Source: Tabulations from Social Security Administration, *Continuous Work History Files.*

difficult, occurring under conditions of slow growth or decline, and involving job decreases as well as increases, whereas in suburbs there has been rapid growth with differential rates of increase among the various occupations favoring certain of the higher-paid groups. Nevertheless, it is in the cities that incomes are highest, and it is in the cities that the greatest improvement both relative and actual has occurred for the average employed worker.

COMMUTER FLOWS IN SUBURBS AND CITIES

SIZE OF COMMUTER FLOWS AND RECENT TRENDS

A distinguishing characteristic of the suburbs is that they "export" a large number of commuters to the city daily. The earnings of these commuters may be regarded as returns from a "hidden-export sector." Put differently, a major source of personal income in the suburbs is the earnings of individuals who work in the city, but who live in the suburbs, and whose needs, along with the needs of their families, must be provided for largely by the local sector within the suburbs.

Suburb-to-city commuters comprised from 23 to 47 percent of all workers residing in the suburbs in 1970, and averaged 36 percent (Table 4.5). The importance of this group declined from 1960, when suburb-to-city commuters accounted for from 26 to 52 percent and averaged 40 percent. As the suburbs have grown and their local-sector activities have become more important, these activities have provided employment for a larger share of suburban resident workers.

Of course, these estimates omit an offsetting flow of commuters who come to the suburbs from the city.[5] This latter flow is not unimportant, ranging from 23 percent of suburb-to-city commuters in the St. Louis area to 53 percent in Baltimore, and averaging 30 percent. Moreover, this reverse flow was substantially larger in 1970 than in 1960, when it averaged 24 percent of suburb-to-city commuting.

The size of commuter flows understates the importance of the hidden-export sector, for commuters from suburb to city tend to earn substantially more than commuters from city to suburb. On an average, 36 percent of the males commuting to the city are in the occupational groups with the highest incomes—professional-technical and managerial-administrative—compared to only 23 percent of male commuters to the suburbs.[6] Only 8 percent of male suburb-to-city commuters are in the low-paying occupations—laborers and service workers—compared to 16 percent of the male city-to-suburb commuters. Among females, there is little difference between shares of city-to-suburb and suburb-to-city commuters classified in professional-technical and managerial-administrative occupations (roughly a fifth in each case), but considerable difference in the percentages classified as laborers and service workers: 9 percent of female suburb-to-city commuters; 26 percent of female city-to-suburb commuters.

Also of importance is the fact that the racial composition of city-to-suburb and suburb-to-city commuter flows is different, the former being more heavily weighted with blacks, whose income is typically below average within each occupational group. Blacks make up a very substantial part of city-to-suburban commuters—28 percent—but only 4 percent of suburb-to-city flows.

When commuter flows are reexamined in terms of their role in the cities' economies, their significance is seen in a quite different light. Commuters from the suburbs comprise a much larger portion of the city work force in each of the 10 SMSA's, on average 41 percent in 1970 compared to 27 percent in 1960 (Table 4.5). Suburb-to-city commuting is relatively greatest in the occupations which are increasing and least important in the occupations which are declining, but has shown significant increases in all occupations.

Average Shares of City Employment Accounted for by
In-Commuters from the Suburbs, by Occupation:
Males and Females, 1960 and 1970[a]

	Males		Females	
	1960	1970	1960	1970
Professional-Technical	40.9	51.4	21.6	33.4
Managers	42.5	55.0	24.5	36.2
Sales Workers	38.1	50.8	22.0	31.1
Clerical	29.7	40.3	28.9	38.4
Craftsmen	33.1	47.7	24.4	34.6
Operatives	25.1	34.8	19.2	25.4
Laborers	14.3	25.0	[b]	[b]
Service	12.7	23.2	18.0	24.8
White-Collar	37.8	49.6	26.4	36.7
Blue-Collar	27.8	39.6	19.6	26.3

[a]Modified Averages. Highest and lowest values have been dropped in computing averages.
[b] This category is of negligible importance.

This means that the cities face an even more difficult situation than simple employment figures reveal. Not only are many engaged in a painful transition in which blue-collar jobs are being lost in manufacturing, along with jobs in the local-sector, with replacements generated only through expansion of professional and white-collar activities, but the growth in these expanding occupations is largely accounted for by suburban commuters. Either the suburban labor

Table 4.5. Selected Measures of Major Commuter Flows, Ten Metropolitan Areas, 1960–1970[a]

	Atlanta	Balti-more	Boston	Cleve-land	Denver	Houston	New York	New Orleans	Phila-delphia	St. Louis	Modified[b] Average
Suburb-to-city commuters as % of suburban resident workers											
1960	49.0	40.8	29.3	52.4	43.3	46.2	44.6	31.6	26.0	35.1	40.0
1970	42.8	34.6	26.3	43.5	42.3	46.9	42.3	28.0	23.4	30.2	36.3
Suburb-to-city commuters as % of total city employment[c]											
1960	38.7	27.7	50.9	40.8	28.8	14.6	17.2	15.1	23.7	41.2	29.2
1970	55.2	38.2	56.7	54.7	41.6	24.0	30.3	18.6	29.0	54.7	41.0
City-to-suburb commuters as % of suburb-to-city commuters											
1960	15.6	35.7	23.5	13.8	27.4	31.9	27.1	26.9	26.1	13.6	24.0
1970	25.1	52.8	24.4	29.0	27.8	33.0	38.3	29.0	34.1	23.3	30.1

[a] Additional measures of major commuter flows are presented in Appendix Table D.
[b] Highest and lowest values among ten places omitted in computing modified average.
[c] Total city employment includes workers from outside SMSA.

Source: *Census of Population, Journey to Work. PC(2) 1960, 1970.*

market is being drawn upon for these additional workers, or such workers move to the suburbs when they secure such employment. The extent to which this occurred during the 1960s can best be seen by expressing increases in suburb-to-city commuters as a percentage of job increases in those occupations in which employment expansion in the cities was concentrated—professional-technical (male and female) and clerical (female):

| | Professional-Technical | | Clerical |
| | Male | Female | Female |
	%	%	%
Atlanta	88.0	64.6	87.1
Baltimore	114.5	66.7	72.5
Boston	88.7	64.5	44.3
Cleveland	146.0	100.9	136.8
Denver	77.0	58.6	72.3
Houston	38.6	22.6	31.7
New Orleans	81.8	52.4	75.8
New York	28.8	9.5	5.9
Philadelphia	79.7	38.0	40.0
St. Louis	187.3	116.1	173.5
Average (modified)	89.3	58.5	70.1

Note: The relatively low percentages for New York City are due to the fact that commuters from New Jersey are not included.

Indeed, in some places the increase in in-commuters actually exceeded the number of additional jobs, indicating that there was a decline in the *number* of city residents who were employed in these expanding occupations.

Furthermore, the share of city employment in poorly paid occupations which is accounted for by in-commuters is substantial, e.g., for males: laborers, 25 percent, and service workers, 23 percent (see above) and has risen sharply since 1960. Since suburban incomes are typically higher and low-paid workers have difficulty commuting, the implication of this finding seems clear: better-paid jobs within these occupational classifications, as well as in the more highly-paid occupations, are going to suburban residents, workers are moving to the suburbs when they secure such jobs, or both. Here, again, cities are placed at a disadvantage in terms of retaining a balanced cross-section of the metropolitan populace for community enrichment and in terms of retaining their tax base.

DIRECT. AND INDIRECT INCOME ATTRIBUTABLE TO COMMUTERS[7]

Earnings of suburb-to-city commuters are of major importance in all places, ranging from 26 to 49 percent of total suburban earnings and averaging 39 percent (Table 4.6). These figures alone seriously understate the overall impact of commuter income, however. As stressed in Chapter 1, earnings of the export sector provide the demand which underwrites the local sector. To estimate the total impact of commuter income, the size of the income multiplier must be determined and commuter earnings multiplied by this factor to determine total earnings attributable to the "hidden export sector." (See Appendix E for procedure.)

When the income multipliers are computed, these multiplier values are found to range from 1.5 to 2.1 and to average 1.8 (Table 4.6).[8] In other words, every dollar earned by a commuter yields an additional 50 cents to $1.10 in local-sector earnings. When these multipliers are applied to (suburb-to-city) commuter earnings, total income associated with commuter earnings (both directly and indirectly through the local sector) account for from 51 percent to 77 percent of total suburban resident earnings, with an average of 67 percent (Table 4.6).

It will be recalled that the percentage of suburban workers accounted for by suburb-to-city commuters fell, on an average, from 40 to 36 percent from 1960 to 1970. Yet total income associated with commuter earnings as a percentage of total suburban earnings declined only slightly, from 68 to 67 percent. This paradox is explained largely by the fact that the local sector increased in importance in the suburbs, thereby increasing the size of the multiplier in every suburban area except Houston (where many suburban areas were annexed by the city). Accordingly, the indirect effect of each dollar of total export-sector earnings (regular and hidden) was larger.

Although these estimates are admittedly crude, the findings seem sufficiently strong to justify the conclusion that the often-mentioned "increasing independence of the suburbs" is a misinterpretation of employment and income trends. The principal growth-sector in the suburbs in recent years has been local services, which have grown largely as a result of rising incomes and consequent import substitution. In the final analysis, these local-sector activities derive their demand from earnings which rest, fundamentally, upon the export sector. The estimates indicate that the most important export sector continues to be the hidden sector of exports—the earnings of suburb-to-city commuters.

Three observations must be added to place the development of the suburbs in proper focus. First, the local sector is not linked to the export sector in a simple dependent fashion; it is also a source of growth. Its development increases the attractiveness of an area for additional firms, which, in turn, may become a part of the export sector. Second, many growing suburban business services such as legal, insurance, and real-estate offices originate, in considerable measure, as local-sector functions. Third, in business services, the focal point of activity continues to be the city, and this principal export sector of the city tends to be manned predominately by suburban commuters.

CITY EARNINGS ATTRIBUTABLE TO RESIDENTS

The same technique used to estimate suburb-to-city commuter earn-earnings (Appendix D) was used to shed light on the relative magnitude of these earnings within the city's economy. For example, in 1970, suburb-to-city commuter-earnings comprised an estimated 56 percent of total earnings paid to those workers employed in the city of Atlanta, leaving an estimated 44 percent paid to city residents. Estimates of the percentages of total earnings generated by city jobs which were accounted for by city-resident workers in 1960 and 1970 were as follows:

	1960	1970
Atlanta	60.3	44.4
Baltimore	69.9	59.0
Boston	47.1	42.3
Cleveland	57.9	42.3
Denver	69.5	56.6
Houston	87.2	76.4
New Orleans	83.2	69.4
New York	87.8	85.5
Philadelphia	73.0	67.7
St. Louis	54.9	41.2
Average (modified)	69.5	52.3

It is important to note, as we did earlier, that suburban commuters tend to hold jobs paying higher than the median income for the SMSA in each of these occupational classes. Because estimates do not reflect these differences, the share of city work-force earnings accounted for by resident workers is probably overstated here.

In any event, the principal finding is that residents' share declined in every city between 1960 and 1970, in most cases to a very substantial extent. It is especially interesting that in Houston there was a sharp decline (from 87 to 76 percent) in spite of sizable annexations of suburban territory into the city's boundaries. The implication is that the city's position as an earnings base for its residents has eroded sharply.

Table 4.6. Sources of Suburban Earnings, 1960 and 1970[a]

		A[b] Total Suburban Earnings ($ Millions)	B[c] Earnings Suburban Commuters ($ Millions)	C Commuter Earnings as % of Total	D[d] Earnings, Sub. Mfg. (working and living in sub.)
Atlanta	1960	1,187.4	643.8	54.2	208.9
	1970	2,418.2	1,079.2	44.6	369.5
Baltimore	1960	1,739.1	766.8	44.0	376.9
	1970	2,742.3	995.1	36.2	517.8
Boston	1960	4,600.8	1,457.1	31.6	1,075.4
	1970	5,320.1	1,489.6	27.9	994.7
Cleveland	1960	2,594.4	1,420.8	54.7	379.7
	1970	3,633.1	1,688.6	46.4	676.6
Denver	1960	971.8	453.9	46.7	146.0
	1970	1,755.7	780.6	44.4	239.8
Houston	1960	649.5	302.8	46.6	130.9
	1970	1,749.2	854.8	48.8	345.2
New Orleans	1960	456.9	219.1	47.9	90.1
	1970	894.9	398.3	44.5	166.0
New York	1960	7,673.2	2,866.9	37.3	1,418.7
	1970	9,640.8	3,127.5	32.4	1,519.2
Philadelphia	1960	5,420.6	1,604.2	29.5	1,555.4
	1970	6,665.6	1,725.9	25.8	1,673.3
St. Louis	1960	3,088.5	1,227.4	39.7	758.6
	1970	4,285.1	1,373.8	32.0	988.4
Modified average[f]	1960	2,531.5	984.6	43.5	561.9
	1970	3,571.2	1,248.5	38.6	706.4

[a] Both 1960 and 1970 earnings are estimated by multiplying relevant employment data by 1970 median SMSA earnings for each occupational class for males and for females residing in suburbs.
[b] Column A equals earnings of persons living in suburbs, working in suburbs or in city.
[c] Column B equals earnings of persons living in suburbs working in city.

E Suburban Mfg. Earnings as % of Total	F Total Suburban Export Sector Earnings (B+D)	G Suburban Income Multiplier (A÷F)	H Commuter- Related Sub- urban Income (B×G)	I Commuter-related Income as % of Suburban Income (H÷A)	J[e] Adjusted Estimate Commuter-related Income as % of Suburban Income
17.6	852.7	1.39	894.9	75.4	
15.3	1,448.7	1.67	1,802.3	74.5	70.1
21.7	1,143.7	1.52	1,165.5	67.0	
18.9	1,512.9	1.81	1,801.1	65.7	60.6
23.4	2,532.5	1.82	2,651.9	57.6	
18.7	2,484.3	2.14	3,187.7	59.9	54.6
14.6	1,800.5	1.44	2,046.0	78.9	
18.6	2,365.2	1.54	2,600.4	71.6	66.5
15.0	599.9	1.62	735.3	75.7	
13.7	1,020.4	1.72	1,342.6	76.5	72.5
20.2	433.7	1.50	454.2	69.9	
19.7	1,200.0	1.46	1,248.0	71.3	66.5
19.7	309.2	1.48	324.3	71.0	
18.5	564.3	1.59	633.3	70.8	65.9
18.5	4,285.6	1.79	5,131.8	66.9	
15.8	4,646.7	2.08	6,505.2	67.5	62.3
28.7	3,159.6	1.72	2,759.2	50.9	
25.1	3,399.2	1.96	3,382.8	50.8	45.3
24.6	1,986.0	1.56	1,914.7	62.0	
23.1	2,362.2	1.81	2,486.6	58.0	52.6
20.1	1,563.6	1.58	1,577.7	68.2	
18.6	1,974.1	1.77	2,231.4	67.4	62.4

[d] Column D equals earnings of persons classified as craftsmen or operatives living and working in suburbs.

[e] Column J was prepared by increasing column D by 25% and recomputing column I.

[f] Highest and lowest values among ten places omitted in computing modified average.

Source: Department of Commerce, Bureau of the Census, *1970 Census of Population,* PC(1) D Series, Tables 131, 175 and 190.

INCOME DISTRIBUTION AND THE IMPORTANCE
OF SUBURBAN CITIES AND TOWNS

DISTRIBUTION OF INCOME BY CENSUS TRACTS

Perhaps the characteristic which is most important in distinguishing suburbs and cities is the level and distribution of income. Because of their substantial flows of relatively well-paid commuters to the city, their relatively highly capitalized and well-paying industrial sector, and their exclusion of low-income housing, suburbs have higher median family incomes than cities (Table 4.7). These higher incomes determine the level and quality of local-sector demand (i.e., the quantity and quality of merchandise and personal services that are offered by the private sector, and the quantity and quality of educational and other services provided by the public sector).

City and suburban income-averages alone do not suffice to describe income characteristics. How this income is distributed is equally important. Accordingly, frequency distributions of census tracts based on average resident family-incomes were prepared (Table 4.7). These distributions provide a basis for comparing between city and suburb the proportions of all residential areas that are inhabited principally by low-, middle-, and upper-income families. The measures of income used are relative. The lowest income category is comprised of tracts in which the median family income is less than half of that of the median family income for the entire SMSA.[10] Remaining tracts are distributed in five categories (each category designated in terms of a range of median family incomes in individual tracts, expressed as percentages of the SMSA median family income: 50 to 74.9 percent, 75 to 99.9 percent, 100 to 124.9 percent, 125 to 149.9 percent, and 150 percent or greater).

The measures reveal more than that suburban residents tend to have higher family incomes than city residents. They reveal something about the spatial arrangement of people in terms of typical income within each tract: the city is comprised of a disproportionately large number of low-income areas, the suburbs of a disproportionately large number of higher-income areas.[11] Perhaps the most striking finding is that there are virtually no "poverty" tracts (i.e., tracts with median family income below 50 percent of metropolitan median family income) in the suburbs and relatively few tracts in the "greater-than-150-percent" category in the city.[12] Further, residential space in the city is characterized by a wider distribution among areas: median family-income levels of city tracts range from poverty to affluence. In the suburbs, the range is, with few exceptions, from levels above the poverty line to levels of affluence.

What is the significance of this dispersed spatial arrangement by which low- and high-income families are separated? The location of the individual's residence affects his access to labor markets and his ability to determine what employment opportunities are available. In addition, it affects the time and out-of-pocket cost of traveling to and from the job. In the city, the problem may be mitigated for the poor by public transportation, particularly where rapid transit is available, as in New York City.[13] In the suburbs, public transportation is poor or nonexistent, and spatial organization is extremely loose. Spatial segregation of lower-income groups works a hardship unless the individual has access to private or public transportation, or unless he lives in close proximity to employment opportunities.

Moreover, these findings support the view that the city's local sector is likely to be undernourished, whereas the suburb's is relatively vigorous, at least in respect to those local-service activities which are in the private sector. Demand for workers in the residentiary activities of the city is reduced by lower income of residents, while similar demand in the suburbs tends to flourish. If residentiary activities of the suburbs tend to be spatially oriented toward the residences of higher-income groups, the poorer groups will be disadvantaged in securing and holding employment. In affluent communities of the suburbs, such employment demands are likely to be filled by drawing on the secondary labor force—second or third workers frequently employed on a part-time basis. At the same time, job seekers in the lower-income groups, those most in need of jobs in the residentiary sector, are located largely in the city.

THE IMPORTANCE OF SUBURBAN CITIES AND TOWNS

The discussion has proceeded thus far without explicit recognition that the suburban economy is organized to a considerable extent around towns and small cities. These places often provide schools, medical services, police, fire protection, and utilities, as well as a variety of business and consumer services. Moreover, some suburban places are actually satellite cities of considerable size, which have served in years prior to rapid suburbanization as important service or industrial centers.

Towns and cities represent, of course, a greater clustering of residential economic functions than is found elsewhere. There is a greater tendency for rich and poor to live in relative proximity to one another and to share residentiary services in both the public and private sectors. Such spatial and economic organization, in turn, tends to favor the poor by increasing the choice of employment and by reducing the journey to work. To what extent, then, does the existence of towns and small cities within suburban areas tend to reduce the problems of sprawl and to ameliorate labor-market conditions?

Table 4.7. Spatial Distribution of Families by Income: Cities and Suburbs, Ten Metropolitan Areas, 1970

	Percentage of Tracts with Median Family-Income in Categories Indicated[a]								Median Family Income (dollars)[b]
	Less than Median	Less than 50% of Median	50–74.9% of Median	75–99.9% of Median	100% or more of Median	100–124.9% of Median	125–149.9% of Median	150% or More of Median	
City									
Atlanta	76.1	43.6	6.0	26.5	23.9	12.0	5.1	6.8	$8,418
Baltimore	80.0	11.5	25.0	43.5	20.0	14.0	3.0	3.0	$8,815
Boston	89.2	10.2	39.5	39.5	10.9	8.2	0.7	2.0	$9,133
Cleveland	93.3	13.9	28.4	51.0	6.7	6.2	0.5	0.0	$9,107
Denver	63.5	5.1	23.7	34.7	36.4	16.9	11.9	7.6	$9,654
Houston	60.8	6.3	20.3	34.2	39.3	22.2	8.9	8.2	$9,876
New Orleans	68.2	11.9	25.0	31.3	31.9	15.0	11.3	5.6	$7,445
New York	58.0	6.2	19.5	32.3	42.0	31.2	6.2	4.5	$9,753
Philadelphia	69.6	6.9	21.1	41.6	30.4	20.8	6.1	3.5	$9,366
St. Louis	87.8	8.1	37.4	42.3	12.2	10.6	0.8	0.8	$8,182
Suburb									
Atlanta	35.8	0.0	4.0	31.8	64.3	39.1	12.6	12.6	$11,827
Baltimore	25.5	0.0	1.6	23.9	74.5	47.7	15.3	11.5	$11,793
Boston	42.3	0.0	5.3	37.1	57.7	37.9	9.9	9.9	$12,094
Cleveland	29.9	0.0	0.8	29.1	70.0	49.6	11.0	9.4	$12,649
Denver	42.4	0.0	7.1	35.3	57.5	33.8	14.3	9.4	$11,549
Houston	49.6	1.5	10.0	38.1	50.4	34.2	10.0	6.2	$10,522
New Orleans	29.3	0.0	8.5	20.8	70.8	43.4	21.7	5.7	$ 9,989
New York	15.7	0.0	1.4	14.3	84.3	36.0	25.5	22.8	$13,579
Philadelphia	38.7	0.1	4.5	34.1	61.2	38.2	12.3	10.7	$11,776
St. Louis	37.6	1.9	4.8	30.9	62.5	42.0	12.8	7.7	$11,150

[a] Frequency distribution of census tracts, based on tract median family-income.
[b] Median family-income for cities is from *Census of Population*. Median family-income expressed as percentage of SMSA median family-income. Median family-income for suburbs has been estimated by computing an average of median family-incomes of census tracts, weighted by population.

Source: Department of Commerce, Bureau of the Census, 1970 *Census of Population,* Census Tract Reports, PCH(1) Series.

From such evidence as is available, it would appear that such agglomerations within suburbs do not significantly alter previous generalizations. A first reason is that these places play a secondary role in terms of total population housed and served. Among the ten suburban rings, only three (Boston, Denver, and New Orleans) show more than 23 percent of total population residing in suburban cities of 50,000 or more, and only two (Cleveland and Denver) show more than 45 percent of total population residing in cities of 25,000 or more (Table 4.8). In short, a large majority of suburbanites reside in small towns or outside of town or city limits.

Secondly, individual suburban towns and cities tend to vary widely in terms of the typical income of residents (Table 4.8). Some places, such as Shaker Heights (Cleveland) [average incomes of $19,900], and Garden City (New York) [$21,200], are predominantly high-income suburbs, while others such as East St. Louis (St. Louis) [$6,600], and Lynn (Boston) [$8,973] and Essex (Baltimore) [$9,937] are disproportionately low income. Spatial organization tends to limit job opportunities for members of low-income households to those areas in which they reside and in which employment opportunities created by the private and public sectors are limited. Second and third wage earners in middle and high income households are not similarly constrained.

A third reason is that suburban towns and cities are themselves very loosely organized spatially, and they are served by inadequate public transportation. The percentages of workers using private cars in the journey to work differ little between most suburban cities or towns and the remainder of the counties in which they are located (Table 4.8).

Finally, cities and towns serve as the focal points of only a fraction of suburban economic activity. To be sure, local public services, as well as downtown and neighborhood shopping, are located within these places. In some instances, as in White Plains, N.Y., the heart of the city is a major shopping center. In other places, such as Valley Stream, N.Y., the growth of large retail centers, located away from the center of town and poorly served by public transportation, has gone far to reduce the role of the suburban city's downtown shopping area, which was formerly a major part of its income and tax base. *Census of Business* data show that in 1967 major retail centers (with rare exceptions—shopping centers located away from downtown areas) accounted for from 24 to 36 percent of total retail sales in eight of the ten suburban areas studied.[14] In addition, office activities, hospitals, and colleges, as well as manufacturing, have tended to locate outside of towns and cities and close to major highways. Such changes have altered the character and function of suburban cities by destroying previous patterns of access and by altering the locational strategy of economic activities.

Table 4.8. Selected Information Relating to Suburbs, 1970

SMSA	% of Population in Towns:[a]		Income (Median) of Towns:		Percentage of Workers Commuting by Auto[b]	
	25,000+	50,000+	Highest	Lowest	Highest	Lowest
Atlanta	7.4 (2)	0 (0)	East Point $10,662	Marietta $9,602	94.3	87.2
Baltimore	38.3 (10)	18.7 (3)	Pikesville $16,899	Essex $9,937	92.1	76.9
Boston	45.2 (16)	30.3 (8)	Newton $15,381	Chelsea $8,973	88.3	41.9
Cleveland	46.7 (13)	23.1 (4)	Shaker Heights $19,928	East Cleveland $9,819	94.1	66.9
Denver	56.0 (8)	32.9 (3)	Littleton $12,740	Englewood $9,999	93.8	78.1
Houston	17.7 (2)	11.9 (1)	Pasadena $11,062	Baytown $10,906	93.7	84.0
New Orleans	43.0 (2)	30.0 (1)	Metaire $11,448	Marrero $8,900	86.8	81.1
New York	34.2 (29)	12.7 (5)	Garden City $21,221	Port Chester $10,727	89.6	54.9
Philadelphia	8.7 (5)	5.5 (2)	Pottstown $9,968	Fort Dix $7,288	86.5	15.5
St. Louis	26.6 (11)	7.8 (2)	Kirkwood $13,854	East St. Louis $6,654	93.5	74.5

[a] Figures in parentheses indicate numbers of towns.
[b] Highest or lowest percentage in suburban towns or remaining parts of counties.

Source: Department of Commerce, Bureau of the Census; *1970 Census of Population*, Census Tract Reports, PHC(1) Series.

SUMMARY AND CONCLUSIONS

Analysis of occupational data confirms the important role of business services and office activity generally in cities: virtually all job increases (90 percent, on an average) have been in white-collar employment, and over two-thirds of all job increases have gone to women. In the suburbs, there is again emphasis on white-collar and female-employment growth, but a greater tendency for jobs to open up across the board. Changes which have occurred have served to upgrade both city and suburban employment, with gains in average wages being somewhat higher in cities.

Analysis of commuter flows indicates that city-to-suburb commuting was larger in 1970 than 1960 relative to total employment in cities, although it was smaller relative to total employment in the burgeoning suburbs where local-sector employment was growing rapidly. Commuting was also found to be more important in the very occupations in which job increases were significant within cities—the professional and white-collar occupations.

Estimates of earnings of suburb-to-city commuters indicated that this "hidden export-sector" was a major source of income of suburban residents, averaging close to two-fifths of such income when measured directly, and roughly two-thirds when measured in terms of combined direct and indirect effects (i.e., including the effect on local-sector earnings).

Income distribution is skewed in favor of higher incomes for suburban residents when measured in terms of median family incomes in census tracts. This has important implications as to where consumer-service jobs are located, since such activities tend to be oriented toward purchasing power. In short, a large share of suburban local-service jobs appear to be poorly situated in relation to the residence of low income households, but favorably located in relation to second and third wage earners in middle- and high-income suburban households.

To the extent that there are cities and towns in the suburbs, agglomeration of low- and high-income families is possible, but this is of secondary importance because (a) only a fraction of suburban populations is located in cities and towns; (b) these urban places themselves tend to be homogeneous in terms of income (i.e., do not contain a broad cross section of income classes); (c) shopping centers have drawn local-service employment away from suburban cities and towns.

A central theme clearly emerges from this and the previous chapter: patterns of change within metropolitan economies are similar everywhere. They involve a restructuring of the city which favors business services and involves an upgrading of activities—an expansion of business services, and a decline of manufacturing and local-sector employment. At the same time, they involve a growth and restructuring of the suburbs which favor high value-added manufacturing and the buildup of a disproportionately large consumer sector to service a populace which is on balance much more affluent than that of the city.

But if these trends are similar in different metropolitan areas, they are not necessarily of the same strength everywhere, nor do they act upon the same base. In some places, such as Atlanta, the development of the central city has proceeded vigorously. In others, such as St. Louis, it has not. Although there appears to be a striking similarity in the processes at work, the pace at which these developments occur varies, and the base from which these changes are occurring varies even more.

Moreover, in cities, the process is one in which restructuring comes about through job creation and job destruction against a background in which the positive forces (evident in the expanding business services) are often obscured by the more dramatic loss of blue-collar jobs in manufacturing. The city tends to drift into obsolescence and decay.

This affects the suburbs, since the relationship of the suburbs to the city is symbiotic. Its local sector depends heavily upon the welfare of its "hidden-export" sector. Its export sector in manufacturing and even back-office activities requires a strong city-service base, nearby urban amenities, a thriving market within the general metropolis region, and the availability of first-rate metropolitan transportation facilities.

REFERENCES

1. Here we have measured job increases and job decreases in terms of occupation-sex differences, using *Census of Population* data. In the employment change analysis in Chapter 3, job increases and job decreases were measured in terms of industrial categories using Social Security data. The two analyses lack complete comparability, not only because job increases and decreases are measured on a different basis, but because the data are different (Appendix A): (1) coverage of employment in the preceding analysis includes, roughly, those individuals covered by Social Security, whereas present analysis includes all persons employed, both covered and noncovered, as reported by the *Census of Population*; (2) employment in "cities" and "suburbs" in the preceding analysis is defined on a county basis, whereas city definitions in the present analysis make use of actual city boundaries with suburbs comprising the remaining areas of SMSA's.

2. When job increases and job decreases 1960-70 are computed separately on an occupational basis for the nation as a whole, there are no job decreases except in the two categories—laborers and farmers.

3. The data presented are modified averages of the weighted average earnings computed in each of the ten cities for job increases and for job decreases. In preparing these estimates, SMSA average earnings in each occupational class were utilized, since city earnings data by occupation were not available.

4. This analysis is based on Social Security materials in which county definitions of cities and suburbs are used. See Appendix A.

5. We also fail to treat flows of commuters to and from areas lying outside the SMSA's boundaries. The importance of these flows is considered in Chapter 5.

6. Data presented in this and the following paragraph are presented in Chapter 5, Tables 5.6–5.9.

7. See Appendix E for a description of the method used in estimating direct and indirect suburban income attributable to commuters.

8. The multiplier mechanism is discussed in greater detail in Chapter 1, pp. 12-14.

9. Total earnings in the city economy were estimated by multiplying city employment in each occupational class by median SMSA earnings for that class and summing up the results. Suburban commuter earnings estimated by the same method were subtracted, leaving estimated city-resident earnings.

10. This analysis makes use of relative income measures similar to the one introduced by Victor Fuchs, in which family income was considered as being beneath the poverty level if it were less than 50 percent of the median. Additional categories have been constructed as indicated. Census tracts are not identical in either size or population or size of area, but there appears to be no consistent bias in size of population within cities or suburbs. Size of tract area does, however, reflect concentration of population: tract areas are smaller in densely populated areas than in lightly populated ones.

11. It is important to recognize what the data tell us and what they do not. They provide a statement of distribution of census tracts according to median family income of census tracts and serve only as a proxy measure of the distribution of family incomes. If there were perfect integration of families in terms of income within each tract, there would be no apparent income distributions in Table 4.10, for each tract would be a replica of every other, and all would have the same median income. On the other hand, if there were perfect income segregation by tracts, the data shown in Table 4.10 would provide completely reliable information on the distribution of family-income.

12. In interpreting these measures, it must be recognized that the median metropolitan family-income which is used as a standard is influenced by how large or small the city is relative to total SMSA population. Where the city's population, with its smaller median income, is large relative to that of the SMSA, the standard is biased downward, and both city's and suburb's distribution appears more favorable. New York is a case in point. Since its New Jersey suburbs are not included in the SMSA, the suburbs are under-represented, and the median metropolitan family-income is lower than it would otherwise have been. New York City's relatively modest low-income bunching and its suburbs' quite strongly skewed distribution favoring the upper-income group are, doubtless, due in part to this distortion.

13. Even within areas served by mass transit, location is a critical factor. Some years ago Columbia University, in a study of the location of residence of its maintenance and service personnel, discovered that workers' homes were located largely in areas contiguous to the Broadway-Seventh Avenue subway system, whose 116th Street exit serves the campus even into Brooklyn.

14. Based on tabulations from U.S. Bureau of the Census, "Major Retail Centers in Standard Metropolitan Statistical Areas," *1967 Census of Business*.

Labor-Market Characteristics

At this point, it is useful to review briefly what has been learned regarding demand-and-supply forces at work in city and suburban labor markets.[1] In the city, there has typically been considerable transition, with manufacturing employment declining in importance, business services increasing, and local-service employment declining or remaining constant at least within the private sector. On the supply side, jobs have been increasingly filled by commuters, especially in the growing sectors and in the better paying jobs.

In the suburbs, there has been rapid overall growth, with growth rates varying somewhat among sectors. Of first importance, however, is the composition of employment. Demand stems from two principal sources: (1) the local-service sector which, aside from government, includes consumer services, plus part of activities classified as business services (e.g., local banking, legal, real estate, and insurance services). This sector, though extremely diverse in terms of specific functions, is characterized by a tendency toward lower-than-average pay scales, which act to restrict distances over which workers typically search for work and commute; (2) the manufacturing sector, in which plants are likely to be newer and more capital intensive than in cities—more frequently the branch plants of national companies in the more oligopolistic and growing sectors of manufacturing. Workers in manufacturing typically receive higher wages than in the local services, and may travel considerable distances to work.

Thus, the two major sources of demand for labor within suburbs stand in contrast—on one hand, offering relatively low wages and the constraint of short commutes; on the other, relatively high wages and the possibility of long commutes.

Of course, there are other sources of demand, but they play a lesser role. The business services (which, as we have seen, may be partly

106

within the local sector), though growing rapidly, are still small in suburbs relative to cities. Combined MBS and TCU accounted for 13 to 26 percent of suburban-covered employment as compared to 23 to 44 percent of city employment. Construction, on the other hand, is somewhat larger for suburbs than for cities because of the higher growth rates in the former. Nevertheless, in eight out of ten suburbs it accounted for less than 11 percent of covered employment in 1970.

When we turn to the supply side, we note that both the mass movement of middle-class Americans away from cities (some away from, some toward, their work), and the expansion of selected economic activity in suburbs, has influenced the suburban labor market in at least three important ways. In the first place, it has created a community in which an important (relatively high-wage) segment of the labor force—the daily commuter—participates in the metropolitan or regional labor market and is likely to work at some distance from his place of residence. Under such conditions, the suburban employer must: (a) look to the remainder of the eligible labor force in the community for his workers; (b) draw upon in-commuters; or (c) compete with city employers for suburban residents who are currently out-commuters. Accordingly, we might expect a different final mix within the work force in terms of sex and age than exists in the city, as well as different participation rates and levels of employment stability.

A second way the suburbanization of residents and of certain economic activities has influenced suburban labor markets is by affecting the supply of female labor. If the suburban society is characterized by a disproportionately large share of middle-class women who are engaged in responsibilities of the home during the years of childbearing and raising a family, and who are typically not available for employment except during their pre- and post-child-rearing years, then the supply and characteristics of labor will differ between city and suburb.

A third way, closely associated with the first and second, is that suburbanization creates a relatively larger supply of qualified secondary workers: wives and young adult sons and daughters in middle-income families. Though many wives do not seek employment and many young people enter the labor market only after college, and then in the city or elsewhere, there are many who enter the suburban labor market as second or third wage earners within the family unit. These workers are willing to accept lower wages than required to support a household and also to accept (in some instances even to prefer) part-time employment. Such workers may be said to be "subsidized" by the family unit. Put differently, they have lower "overhead" costs. For them, the process of work establishment is greatly facilitated: first, because low wages are "acceptable" to them, and second because, as members of families of established households, they are more likely to live in reasonable proximity to firms which are oriented to provide for expanding needs of this major segment of the suburban population than are low-income workers who seek such jobs as primary employment.

These general observations regarding demand and supply suggest the need for examining in greater detail the characteristics of suburban labor markets, contrasting these characteristics with those of labor markets of cities. Such an analysis follows, organized under four general heads: (1) Labor Force Participation and Unemployment; (2) Composition of the Work Force; (3) Stability of Employment; (4) Commuter Flows Within the Metropolitan Area.

PARTICIPATION AND UNEMPLOYMENT RATES

WHITE MALES

Among white males, participation rates are systematically higher and unemployment rates lower in suburbs than in cities (Table 5.1). These rates are, of course, measured in terms of place of residence and relate to persons 16-64 years of age. The higher participation rates and lower unemployment rates of white males reflect principally the basic nature of the suburbs—that they have been settled largely by white, middle- and high-income families whose breadwinners have stable and established employment. Indeed, such employment has been virtually a precondition to settlement in the suburbs. Moreover, since jobs are predominantly white-collar, these employees are less likely to be victimized by work-associated disabilities prior to retirement age.

There is reason to suspect that there is still another process at work which raises levels of white male labor-force participation. Young people in middle-income homes may find entry into the secondary labor market relatively easy. Since they are, in a sense, "subsidized," and are likely to be more favorably located relative to local-sector employment than poor minority youth, they are in a better position to find and to accept low-wage, and often intermittent, employment.

BLACK MALES

The situation regarding black males in suburbs is considerably different. Black males living in the suburbs enjoy neither the same opportunities for white-collar primary employment in city and suburban labor markets as white men, nor the same opportunities for white-collar secondary employment in the burgeoning suburban local-sector activities. Their advantage relative to black males residing in the city is principally that they live within a rapidly growing economy where they have somewhat better access to jobs as blue-collar and service workers.

The data support this interpretation. Participation rates for black males are higher in the suburbs than in cities in only one-half the comparisons, but unemployment rates are lower in almost every comparison. This suggests that, although a substantial portion of the potential black labor force does not participate, employment opportunities are better in suburbs than in cities for that part which does.

On the other hand, participation rates for black males are sharply lower than for white males in all suburban labor markets, with differentials in excess of 7 percentage points in every place but Cleveland. Differences between black and white males residing in the city are typically much smaller. If the suburban black worker's position is, typically, somewhat better than his black counterpart's in the city, it is sharply inferior to that of his white counterpart in the suburbs.

WHITE FEMALES

White women have lower participation rates in suburbs than in cities, reflecting, presumably, the significantly large number of women who perform roles as housewives outside the labor force. Unemployment rates are roughly the same in city and suburb, indicating a general tendency for jobs to be more or less equally available to white women seeking employment in one area as in the other. This would seem to indicate the existence of a hidden supply of female labor in male-headed households. Women take employment, even in affluent households, when pleasant work environment or appropriate work status can be found. Hence the sizeable commuter force of female workers which characterizes the suburbs.

BLACK FEMALES

Significantly, city-suburb differences in participation rates and unemployment rates of black women are not apparent. On the other hand, both participation rates and unemployment rates are higher for blacks in almost every comparison between black women and white in cities and in suburbs. Black women everywhere find it necessary to enter the labor markets in relatively larger numbers than do white women, and they experience greater difficulties in finding and holding employment once they have entered. Moreover, when they are out of work, it is less likely to be from choice. Unlike white women, they tend to remain in the labor force and to be counted as unemployed. White women move out of the labor force much more freely when acceptable work is not available.

COMPOSITION OF THE WORK FORCE

AGE COMPOSITION OF EMPLOYMENT

Age composition of employment is an important characteristic of any labor market. It indicates the extent to which the work force is distribu-

Table 5.1. Participation and Unemployment Rates, 1970, Cities and Suburbs, Ten Metropolitan Areas[a]

	White Males		Black Males		White Females		Black Females	
	Partic.	Unemp.	Partic.	Unemp.	Partic.	Unemp.	Partic.	Unemp.
Central Cities:								
Atlanta	75.5	2.9	75.0	3.9	47.4	3.1	55.2	6.1
Baltimore	75.2	3.1	73.0	5.8	41.4	3.8	51.4	6.6
Boston	71.9	4.6	73.0	6.7	48.0	3.4	46.1	6.0
Cleveland	76.0	4.2	73.2	7.7	40.8	3.8	47.0	6.7
Denver	77.1	4.3	77.6	6.5	46.0	3.6	56.1	5.9
Houston	84.6	2.2	76.7	3.8	42.9	3.3	53.3	6.2
New Orleans	73.7	4.2	67.1	7.8	38.8	4.0	41.8	9.1
New York	74.6	4.4	71.8	5.1	41.3	4.5	46.1	5.0
Philadelphia	74.9	3.5	72.2	6.8	41.0	4.0	48.6	6.2
St. Louis	72.0	4.6	67.4	10.0	41.5	4.7	49.0	8.7
Suburbs:								
Atlanta	86.1	1.8	74.4	3.5	46.7	3.5	57.8	4.8
Baltimore	83.9	2.1	66.7	3.0	41.7	3.5	51.1	4.5
Boston	79.5	3.2	69.0	4.4	44.4	3.4	55.7	3.4
Cleveland	83.1	2.1	80.0	4.6	41.1	3.3	59.7	5.5
Denver	84.1	3.0	72.7	2.5	45.4	4.0	42.86	6.7
Houston	78.5	1.8	53.3	5.3	33.4	3.9	40.8	7.5
New Orleans	82.6	3.2	70.9	7.4	35.1	4.5	41.5	9.7
New York	79.9	0.9	72.5	3.9	38.6	3.7	54.8	3.5
Philadelphia	82.0	2.3	73.1	5.2	40.1	3.7	50.6	7.3
St. Louis	87.0	3.6	69.4	9.1	40.9	4.9	45.0	10.1
Modified	74.9	3.9	72.8	6.3	42.8	3.8	49.6	6.6
Average:[b]	82.7	2.4	71.1	4.7	40.9	3.8	49.9	6.2
City-Suburb Comparisons								
C≥S	1	10	5	8	8	2	3	5
S≥C	9	–	5	1	–	2	5	5
No Significant Difference (within ±.5%)	–	–	–	1	2	6	2	–

[a] Labor-force participation and unemployment are expressed as percentages of the resident labor force in cities and suburbs.

[b] Highest and lowest values among ten places omitted in computing modified averages.

Source: *U.S. Census of Population, 1970*, PCH(1)-45 Census Tracts, Tables P-3, P-6.

ted among young persons whose attachment to the labor force is, typically, not yet firm, among workers within the most productive age cohorts (the young through middle-aged groups), and among older workers, soon to retire from the labor force.

In examining age composition of employment it should be noted at the outset that the suburban population tends to be younger than the city population. In order to adjust for this bias the share of employment in each age bracket from 16 to 64 has been normalized by expressing it as a ratio of the corresponding share of population in the respective age bracket. The adjustment is by no means ideal, since data sources vary (employment data are from Social Security sources, population data from the Census of Population) as do the bases of reporting (employment is on a place of work basis; population on a place of residence basis). Nevertheless, the adjustment does permit us to observe in both suburbs and cities the extent to which employment age composition (16-64 years of age) differs from that of residents within the same age range.

Ratios: Share of Employment to Share of
Population, Males, by Age Bracket, 1970.

	City		Suburbs	
Ages	Whites	Blacks	Whites	Blacks
Less than 20	.50	.57	.78	.46
20–24	.88	1.16	1.20	.94
25–34	1.24	1.24	1.11	1.30
35–44	1.22	1.04	.95	1.10
45–64	.97	.96	.96	1.05

Ratios are modified averages. Highest and lowest values have been dropped.

Source: Employment from Social Security Administration, *Continuous Work History Files*; Population from *Census of Population*.

The principal conclusion regarding white males is that employment is relatively larger in suburbs in the less-than-25 year classes. The average ratios of percentages of employment to percentages of resident population in the two under-25 age brackets are higher in the suburb than in the city. Similar ratios for the 25-44 brackets are lower in suburb than city, and for the 45-64 bracket, roughly the same. These findings are affected by commutation. However, percentages of jobs held by young men are biased upward and percentages of jobs held by men 25 and older are depressed because of the effect of large commuter flows to the city of males 25 and older on the suburban labor supply. Thus we see that, although the evidence supports the argument that suburban labor markets offer better employment opportunities to the young white males than do city economies, this evidence alone is not conclusive. It is, however, supported by the analysis of industrial composition which shows that the share of white male employment accounted for by consumer services is consistently bigger in suburbs than in cities (see Table 5.3 below). It is in the consumer services that the greatest number of low-paid, entry-level-type jobs for young people is found (see Chapter 6).

Among black males, the ratios of employment to population in the under-25-year brackets are significantly smaller in the suburbs than in the city, and slightly larger in the remaining brackets. Two explanations can be offered, neither of which necessarily excludes the other. First, it may be that the substantial flows of black commuters from city to suburb serve to swell disproportionately the ranks of employed blacks over 25 years of age, thereby reducing the percentage of workers under 25 employed in the suburbs and (to a much lesser extent) increasing the percentage of black workers under 25 employed in the city.

Second, young black males fare less well in suburbs than in cities, possibly because low-level jobs in the consumer services are difficult to reach from suburban ghettos or because they compete with young whites in a setting which is overwhelmingly white and in which they are simply not welcome.

The ratios for white females shown below give evidence that young suburban women tend to leave the work force during the years when children are being raised (the 25-34 and 35-44 age brackets) and to return in considerable force in the years that follow. In the suburbs, the ratios are low for the less than 20, 25-34, and 35-44 cohorts—the years of school and the years of family responsibility—but high for the 20-24 and 45-64 years, indicating the two periods when white women are most likely to be participating in the labor force. On the other hand, in the cities the ratio rises sharply in the 20-24-year bracket and remains relatively high until the 45-64-year period. Clearly, in the city employment, it is more customary for white women to continue work during the 25-44-year periods.

Ratios: Share of Employment to Share of Population,
White Females, by Age Bracket, 1970.

	City[a]	Suburb[a]
Less than 20	.70	.89
20–24	1.35	1.32
25–34	1.10	.77
35–44	1.03	.91
45–64	.90	1.12

[a] Modified averages (ten cities or suburbs). Highest and lowest values have been dropped.

The analysis for black females indicates that percentages in the several age brackets do not differ significantly from city to suburb. Patterns of employment by age in both city and suburb are well established: lowest ratio of employment percentage to population percentage in the under-20 bracket; highest ratio in the 20-25-age bracket, with ratios progressively lower in each of the higher-age brackets. In neither city nor suburb do we observe the tendency shown by white suburban women to leave the work force and return in middle life.

SEX CHARACTERISTICS OF EMPLOYMENT

In nine of the ten metropolitan areas studied, the percentage of total covered employment represented by females (measured at place of work) is larger in cities than in suburbs (Table 5.2). The analysis below shows that the dominant reason for this is the difference in industrial composition of employment between cities and suburbs.

How industrial composition may alter the percentage of women employed is easily understood when it is observed that: (1) different industries èmploy widely different percentages of women and (2) industrial composition of cities and suburbs varies significantly. Some sense of the variation among industries in percentages of employment accounted for by women may be gained by inspection of the following average (weighted) percentages of female employment for all SMSA's (1970) in selected industrial classifications:

Industry Classification	Average %	Industry Classification	Average %
Total	37.0	Mainly Business Services	39.3
		Wholesale	25.3
Primary	20.1	FIRE	51.8
Construction	6.6	Other Business Services	43.1
Manufacturing	28.0	Mainly Consumer Services	53.7
Low-wage group	43.4	Retail durable	16.6
High-wage group	22.2	Retail nondurable	54.9
TCU	23.3	Recreation, hotel, etc.	46.0
Transportation	15.4	Medical, educ., etc.	81.9
Communication	51.1	Other consumer services	51.4
Utilities	15.7		

From the previous evidence (Chapter 3, page 68) of differences between cities and their suburbs in the industrial composition of employment, it is to be expected that significant differences in demand for female labor will arise as a result of variations in industry mix.

Accordingly, the issue is: To what extent are variations among cities and suburbs in shares of employment accounted for by females due to

Table 5.2. Effect of Industrial Structure on Female Share of Employment
Ten Metropolitan Areas, 1970[a]

Total Industries	Actual Female Employment %		Expected[b] Female Employment %		Ratio: Actual to Expected	
	City	Suburb	City	Suburb	City	Suburb
	(1)	(2)	(3)	(4)	(5)	(6)
Atlanta	36.0	34.1	37.6	33.3	95.7	102.4
Baltimore	37.3	31.3	38.0	32.6	98.2	96.0
Boston	41.6	39.2	43.5	39.4	95.6	99.5
Cleveland	32.8	39.2	32.7	35.8	100.3	109.5
Denver	37.1	36.3	38.8	37.0	95.6	98.1
Houston	31.3	25.9	32.6	29.6	96.0	87.5
New Orleans	35.8	27.2	36.8	30.1	97.3	91.4
New York	39.2	38.4	42.8	38.6	91.4	99.5
Philadelphia	39.1	35.0	40.6	34.3	96.3	102.0
St. Louis	35.9	36.8	37.1	36.2	96.8	101.7
Modified Average[c]	36.7	34.8	38.1	34.7	96.4	98.8

Comparisons: City vs. Suburb

	Actual Female Employment %			Expected Female Employment %			Ratio: Actual to Expected	
	C>S	S>C	Equal[d]	C>S	S>C	Equal[d]	C>S	S>C
Total Industries	9	1	–	9	1	–	3	7
Manufacturing	8	2	–	9	1	–	2	8
TCU	4	5	1	4	6	–	7	3
MBS	5	5	–	6	4	–	5	5
MCS	5	3	2	8	1	1	–	10

[a] Based on covered employment at place of work.
[b] Expected female percent is computed as described in footnote 3, page 00.
[c] Highest and lowest values among ten places omitted in computing modified average.

Source: Tabulations from Social Security Administration, *Continuous Work History Files.*

industry mix alone? This issue may be explored by estimating female employment in each city and suburb as it would be if percentages of females within each 2-digit industry classification were the same everywhere, but the industrial composition of total employment (male plus female) in the various cities and suburbs remained unaltered. In other words, standardized percentages of employment accounted for by females in each industrial class were used to compute the "expected" number of females in the light of actual industrial composition of total employment, which were summed to compute an "expected" overall female employment percentage for each place.

The expected percentages are presented in Table 5.2, alongside actual female employment percentages.[3] It is immediately apparent that expected female employment does not deviate greatly from actual female employment in most instances. Correlation analysis indicated that the following coefficients of determination (R^2's), for comparisons between the actual and expected estimates of female employment percentages shown in Table 5.2 are:

$$R^2$$
Comparisons for cities .... .95
Comparisons for suburbs .... .88

The degree of correlation is quite high. Among cities, 95 percent of variance in actual female employment percentages is accounted for by variations in expected female employment percentages. Among suburbs, 88 percent of variance is accounted for . Clearly, industrial composition goes far to explain the share of females employed in cities and suburbs.

Table 5.2 also reveals a strong characteristic difference between cities and suburbs. The industrial structure of cities favors the employment of women. The expected estimates of female employment percentages are larger for cities. This is true in every comparison but one, Cleveland. Cleveland's relatively low percentage is due to the concentration of heavy manufacturing in Cuyahoga, the central city county.

In general, the principal structural characteristics which contribute to this basic difference between city and suburb are the relatively high proportion of total employment in manufacturing and construction in suburbs and the relatively high proportion of business services in the cities. Manufacturing and construction employ, on the average, a relatively small percentage of women; business services a relatively large percentage. The resulting tendency for cities to employ relatively more women is only partially offset by the fact that the consumer-services category, which is more important in the suburbs, employs a relatively large number of women.

In addition, employment distribution among sub-categories within industrial groupings acts to bring about city-suburban differences. In order to investigate this aspect, expected female employment percentages were computed separately for manufacturing, TCU, MBS, and MCS.[4] A larger expected female employment percentage in city than in suburb indicates that internal composition of the given industrial grouping favors female employment in the city.

One of the most interesting observations to be made from this latter analysis is that expected female employment percentages in manufacturing are smaller for suburbs (larger for cities) in nine comparisons out of ten. The explanation clearly must lie in a finding presented in Chapter 3. The manufacturing industries which flourish in the suburbs tend to be those with relatively large inputs of capital, high-skill levels, and high wages. Such industries do not typically employ large numbers of women. For example, the expected female percentage for manufacturing in the city of New York is 44.3, which is larger than the corresponding percentage of 30.6 for its suburbs. This reflects, mainly, the importance to the city of the apparel industry (standard female employment percentage of 75.5), an industry which plays virtually no role in the suburban manufacturing sector.

We must conclude that the structure of the manufacturing sector of suburbs, at least among most of the metropolitan areas studied, does not favor employment of females, although the larger relative size of the manufacturing sector does act *ceteris paribus* to enlarge such employment.

Within the TCU and MBS categories there is no clear-cut tendency for industrial composition of the category to favor female employment in either suburb or city. For the former group, expected female employment percentages are greater in four cities, six suburbs; for the latter, in six cities, and four suburbs. For the consumer-services (MCS) group, however, there is a fairly well-defined tendency. Expected female employment percentages are greater in cities than suburbs. This means, of course, that cities tend to have relatively large shares of consumer-service employment in activities for which standard female employment percentages are large. There is no single explanation for this tendency. In three cities (Boston, Baltimore, Houston), it is due, in part, to a relatively large employment in medical services (standard female employment, 81.9 percent). In eight cities (all but Baltimore and St. Louis) there is relatively large employment in a category "other consumer services," which includes, among other classifications, personal services and nonprofit membership organizations (standard female employment percentages of 65.8 and 58.3 percent, respectively). Finally, it is due, partially, to a tendency for most cities to have a retail structure more heavily weighted toward general merchandise and apparel and accessory stores (standard female employment percentages 67.9 and 65.6 percent, respectively).

A related issue is whether or not there are tendencies in cities or suburbs to hire relatively large, or relatively small, numbers of females after controlling for industry mix. Essentially the question for each city and suburb is: "Does this economy have more female employees than the "expected" number (i.e., than it would have if the ratio of female employees in each industry group were the same as the average for all SMSAs)?" Comparisons between actual and expected female employment percentages are presented separately for city and suburb in Table 5.2 (columns 5 and 6) in the form of ratios of actual to expected female percentages.[5] The higher the ratio, the greater is actual female employment relative to that which would be expected on the basis of industrial composition, assuming standard female employment percentage in each industry component.

Ratios of actual to expected female percentages are greater for suburbs in seven out of ten comparisons. Clearly, there is a tendency for actual female employment to be higher relative to expected levels in suburbs than in cities, i.e., there is a tendency for suburbs to "overemploy" female labor. Table 5.2 indicates that this tendency is found in manufacturing and consumer services, but not in TCU and MBS. In manufacturing, ratios of actual to expected female employment percentages are larger for suburbs in eight out of ten comparisons, and in MCS, in all ten comparisons.

The importance of this last finding should not be exaggerated, however. The tendency to "overemploy" women in suburbs by no means fully offsets the opposing tendency in cities to employ a higher percentage of women because of industrial-composition characteristics, even in the manufacturing and MCS groups. When actual female employment percentages are compared, they are found to be larger for cities in eight comparisons out of ten for manufacturing; in five cases out of ten (two ties) for consumer services; and in nine out of ten comparisons for total employment.

INDUSTRIAL COMPOSITION OF EMPLOYMENT BY SEX AND RACE

In this section, the labor market is approached from a different perspective. Comparisons are made of the industrial composition of the major sex-race segments of covered employment both between cities and suburbs and blacks and whites (Table 5.3). Although, in a general way, the industrial composition of employment in each sex-race category reflects the industrial composition of total employment of any given city or suburb, there are important differences among categories. The general finding is that, within sex groupings, blacks and whites have

Table 5.3. Percentage of Employment in Selected Industry Categories by Sex–Race Classifications, Cities and Suburbs, Ten Metropolitan Areas, 1970[a]

	Manufacturing[b]				Mainly Business Services[b]				Mainly Consumer Services[b]			
	Male		Female		Male		Female		Male		Female	
	White	Black	White	Black	White	Black	White	Black	White	Black	White	Black
Central Cities												
Atlanta	21.4	22.8	16.9	16.5	31.0	24.8	32.2	17.4	20.0	30.3	39.2	62.2
Baltimore	38.3	38.8	23.2	18.0	21.3	16.8	27.0	14.6	21.0	22.2	43.4	60.3
Boston	22.2	28.2	16.4	19.9	32.8	26.3	35.0	22.2	22.2	32.1	40.0	51.1
Cleveland	49.2	54.6	29.0	22.7	18.5	12.6	20.9	16.3	19.1	22.6	46.2	59.1
Denver	22.5	25.0	12.0	16.7	25.3	16.7	31.8	16.7	27.0	46.7	46.7	62.5
Houston	27.6	26.8	11.8	9.8	22.5	20.0	29.3	15.0	18.4	24.1	48.0	69.6
New Orleans	21.2	19.3	12.5	15.4	24.0	21.5	28.4	9.2	21.8	27.2	44.2	71.5
New York	25.5	23.3	30.7	24.7	33.9	29.1	34.0	29.6	22.0	26.0	28.4	36.4
Philadelphia	35.5	33.6	27.1	36.9	26.4	20.4	28.7	14.6	19.8	26.9	38.2	45.1
St. Louis	41.7	51.5	31.4	19.7	21.6	17.2	24.5	13.8	18.2	19.1	37.0	60.6
Average (modified)	29.3	31.3	21.1	19.2	25.6	20.5	29.5	16.3	20.5	28.3	41.9	58.8
Comparisons:												
Male: White>Black	4[c]				10				0			
Male: Black>White	5[c]				0				10			
Female: White>Black	5[c]				10				0			
Female: Black>White	4[c]				0				10			

118

Suburbs												
Atlanta	22.3	25.8	19.8	20.4	20.1	17.5	17.4	14.3	27.3	20.8	48.8	61.2
Baltimore	46.4	55.0	27.1	22.0	12.2	8.7	14.4	11.0	24.0	22.7	51.8	61.0
Boston	46.1	57.0	35.0	50.0	17.4	15.0	14.8	14.6	23.5	23.0	46.5	33.3
Cleveland	57.6	64.3	31.8	42.9	6.2	7.1	15.9	d	23.6	14.3	48.8	57.1
Denver	36.2	38.1	15.5	50.0	10.4	9.5	16.9	d	31.8	19.1	64.0	50.0
Houston	37.0	37.8	12.8	5.9	6.8	10.8	19.2	5.9	19.6	18.9	63.8	88.2
New Orleans	30.4	41.3	3.5	15.6	13.8	9.3	15.2	6.7	23.7	26.7	73.7	75.6
New York	33.5	37.1	25.2	34.7	19.3	17.9	21.4	16.2	29.5	29.3	45.9	42.2
Philadelphia	52.1	52.7	33.5	33.8	13.6	10.4	16.2	10.8	20.3	22.0	44.6	51.5
St. Louis	41.7	45.4	23.2	16.3	12.2	9.7	13.9	5.2	27.5	30.1	58.3	74.8
Average (modified)	40.4	45.8	23.6	29.5	13.2	11.3	16.2	d	24.9	22.8	47.4	59.2

Comparisons:

Male: White>Black	0				8				5[c]			
Male: Black>White	10				2				3[c]			
Female: White>Black			3[c]				e			3[c]		
Female: Black>White			6									
C>S	0[c]	1	3	2[c]	10	10	10	e	0	6[c]	0	7
S>C	9[c]	9	7	7[c]	0	0	0	e	10	2[c]	10	4

[a] Data indicate percentage of employment in each race-sex group accounted for by indicated industrial group. Averages are modified (lowest and highest values dropped). Measures are based on covered employment at place of work.

[b] Employment in each sex-race-industry group equals 100%.

[c] Does not include tie(s): within plus or minus .5. Computations not made because of a small sample size.

[d] Comparison not made.

[e] Comparisons not made.

Source: Tabulations from Social Security Administration, *Continuous Work History Files*.

119

different distributions of employment among industries, and that distributions vary between city and suburb.

In cities, black males have a larger proportion of their work force in manufacturing than do white males in six out of ten observations, and a larger percentage in the consumer services in every instance. In suburbs, black males again have higher percentages of their numbers in manufacturing than white males in every comparison, but lower percentages in consumer services in five out of ten comparisons (with two ties). In business services, black males have a lower percentage of employment than white males in almost every comparison in both city and suburb.

The main point is that a larger proportion of black males are employed in manufacturing than of white males (though not necessarily in the best manufacturing jobs) in both cities and suburbs, but that black males appear to have poorer access to consumer-service jobs in suburbs. The earlier evidence regarding age structure of employment suggests that this inferior access to the expanding consumer sector of the suburbs involves principally young suburban blacks. Unfortunately, these are the very persons most in need of the kind of entry-level jobs so common to retailing and other consumer services.

This explanation is also consistent with the earlier observation that labor-force participation rates among black males tend to be lower in suburbs than in cities, even though unemployment rates are somewhat lower. Apparently, participation of black males in suburbs is reduced by lack of employment opportunities for the young, but among those black males who do participate, unemployment rates are lower.

Comparisons between white females and black females indicate that, in both cities and suburbs, shares of white female employment in MBS are relatively larger than shares of black female employment; shares of white female employment in MCS, relatively smaller. Comparisons for manufacturing, however, fail to indicate strong tendencies. Shares of white women are larger than shares of blacks in five out of ten comparisons (with one tie) for cities, but in only three comparisons (with one tie) for suburbs.

It is interesting that black women in the suburbs do not face the same position relative to white women in consumer-services employment that black men face relative to white men. Apparently there is not the same restriction of access. In part, this is no doubt due to the fact that black women are more frequently hired as domestics, a relatively important occupation in the affluent suburbs. It may be due, also, in part, to the very nature of the jobs they typically fill. As both women and blacks, they are the lowest-paid group in the total work force, performing menial services in hospitals, retail stores, motels, and restaurants. If there are constraints due to difficulty of competing for jobs in the dispersed suburban economy, there are very likely offsetting factors arising out of the large demand for very low wage-workers in a heavily consumer-service-oriented economy.

OCCUPATIONAL COMPOSITION OF EMPLOYMENT BY SEX AND RACE

In Chapter 4 it was observed that there were fairly consistent variations between occupational structure of jobs in cities and suburbs. Among males, the percentage of white-collar and service jobs is larger in cities; the percentage of blue-collar jobs (excluding transport operatives) in suburbs. Among females, the percentage of white-collar jobs is again larger in cities, but, in contrast to males, blue-collar employment tends, also, to be relatively larger in cities and service-worker employment relatively smaller.

When occupational composition of black employment is examined (Table 5.4), the findings are consistent. A larger share of blacks hold blue-collar jobs in suburbs than in cities, and a larger share hold white-collar and service jobs in cities than in suburbs. More important, there is a strong tendency for blacks to hold the "low-end" jobs within these categories. For the white-collar grouping, a much smaller share of black, than of total male employment, is found in the higher-paying classifications—professional-technical, managerial-administrative, and sales workers—although the share of employment is comparable with that for total males in clerical, the lowest-skilled and lowest-paying white-collar employment. Within the blue-collar groupings, a smaller share of black male employment than of total male employment is found in craftsmen, where earnings are highest; a larger share in operatives and laborers. Not surprisingly, the share of employment in the low-wage service occupations is far higher for black than for total males.

Among black females, white-collar employment is more important in cities than in suburbs; blue-collar employment is roughly of the same importance, and service employment (which includes domestic servants), of much greater importance in suburbs. Black women fare relatively better in white-collar jobs than black men. In cities, the average share is 47 percent within this category (compared to 70 percent for total females), and the average share is 26 percent for black males (compared to 49 percent for total males). In suburbs, their average is 34 percent (compared to 68 percent for total females), whereas black males have an average share of 18 percent (compared to 43 percent for total males).

Black female employment is largest in the lowest-paying classifications. Thirty-six percent of black females in cities are service workers, 50 percent in suburbs. Twenty-nine percent are in the lowest-paying classifications of white-collar workers, clerical, in the city; 18 percent in the suburbs. Virtually all black female blue-collar workers in the city and suburbs are operatives.

Table 5.4. Percentage Distribution of Total and Black Employment, by Occupation, by Sex, Ten Metropolitan Areas, 1970[a]

| | CITIES | | | SUBURBS | | | 1970 Median Earnings (Dollars) SMSA |
| | Distribution | | Ratio: | Distribution | | Ratio: | |
	Total	Black	Black/Total	Total	Black	Black/Total	
Male							
White-collar	48.7	25.9	0.53	43.1	18.4	0.43	
Professional-Tech.	16.5	6.9	0.42	16.4	7.4	0.45	11,192
Mgrl. & Admin.	12.4	3.9	0.31	11.7	2.6	0.22	12,199
Sales workers	8.3	2.8	0.34	7.5	1.8	0.24	9,087
Clerical	11.0	12.0	1.09	7.7	7.1	0.92	7,300
Blue-collar	41.3	54.5	1.32	45.2	62.2	1.38	
Craftsmen	19.0	14.3	0.75	21.7	16.3	0.75	8,522
Operatives (reg.)	10.2	15.9	1.56	12.3	20.5	1.67	6,903
Operatives (transp.)	6.5	11.2	1.72	4.7	9.1	1.94	7,138
Laborers	5.4	11.7	2.17	6.0	14.3	2.38	5,141
Service	8.9	18.5	2.08	8.0	14.8	1.85	5,143
Other	0.8	0.6	0.75	3.1	4.2	1.35	

Female

White-collar	69.8	46.6	0.67	67.6	33.5	0.50	
Professional-Tech.	15.2	13.1	0.86	18.2	10.5	0.58	6,094
Mgrl. & Admin.	3.7	1.8	0.49	3.6	1.4	0.39	5,894
Sales workers	6.3	3.3	0.52	9.3	2.6	0.28	2,463
Clerical	44.7	28.5	0.64	36.9	18.2	0.49	4,429
Blue-collar	13.0	16.1	1.24	11.9	16.3	1.37	
Craftsmen	1.7	1.4	0.82	1.6	1.2	0.75	4,605
Operatives (reg.)	10.4	13.2	1.27	8.9	13.3	1.49	3,678
Operatives (transp.)	0.3	0.3	1.00	0.6	0.3	0.50	2,910
Laborers	0.8	1.3	1.63	0.9	1.5	1.67	3,260
Service	16.4	36.0	2.20	20.0	49.5	2.48	2,498
Other	[b]	[b]	[b]	0.5	0.5	1.00	

[a] All data shown are modified averages, i.e., highest and lowest values among ten places omitted in computing. Employment data reported at place of work.
[b] Two or more places with no significant employment.

Source: *U.S. Census of Population, 1970*, PC(1) D37, Table 190.

123

STABILITY OF EMPLOYMENT, 1968[6]

The distinction between full-time and part-time employment is important for several reasons. The proportion of total employment accounted for by full-time work is a measure of both quality of employment and opportunity for part-time work. Where persons who seek full-time employment find only part-time work available, or are laid off intermittently, their earnings are reduced and they may be regarded as partially unemployed.[7] On the other hand, part-time employment is highly desirable for some. Those seeking less than a full workweek (e.g., students, working mothers, partially retired persons, candidates for moonlighting jobs) are often unable or unwilling to accept employment on any other basis. Thus, a measure of full-time employment (which we call stable employment) is a somewhat ambiguous measure in social-welfare terms.

Nevertheless, an analysis of the extent of stable employment will provide insights into the nature of individual city and suburban labor markets by providing some indication of the relative importance of such work in each type of place. Somewhat crude estimates of stable workers were computed by counting as non-stable those workers who earned less than $750 per quarter (roughly $1.50 per hour, forty hours per week for thirteen weeks) during any quarter of the year 1968.[8]

These measures, though subject to certain weaknesses, make it possible to distinguish with rough accuracy the percentage of the total work force which may be regarded as stable or established, and to make city-suburb and intermetropolitan comparisons of these percentages for various sex, race and industry categories.[9]

Such comparisons reveal that for whites, both male and female, the suburban economy is characterized by less stable employment than the city economy (Table 5.5). This is consistent with earlier findings that suburban economies tend to have a higher percentage of very young workers and, except in manufacturing, a lower wage structure.

City-suburb comparisons vary, however, depending on the industry group examined. For white males, stability of employment is higher in most suburban manufacturing sectors, but this is not the case for white females. In MBS and in MCS the evidence points to a tendency toward greater employment stability in cities than in suburbs both for white males and white females.

For blacks, sample size is less adequate and findings are more tentative. It appears that male employment is more stable in suburbs; female employment, more stable in cities.

Not surprisingly, when comparisons of stable-worker percentages are made among the ten metropolises, we find variations which appear to reflect, at least in part, differences in the nature of their economies.

The most striking variations are observed between the two most highly developed service centers, New York and Boston, and the two places which are clearly distinguishable as manufacturing centers, Cleveland and St. Louis. The former rank among the lowest in terms of percentage of stable workers. The latter rank at the top of the list. The observation holds for males and females, cities and suburbs.

Such a finding is consistent with the essential differences between well-developed service centers and manufacturing places. Manufacturing activities are more highly organized. Establishments are larger, and work flows are subject to the cost discipline of high overhead. Work flow must be relatively constant if costs are to be minimized. Moreover, workers are primary wage earners, working full-time, and protected by union contracts. Service centers, on the other hand, are characterized by many small establishments and feature a variety of supportive functions. Work schedules are variable, and the strategy of cost minimization is often to make as full use as possible of part-time help—workers who are likely to be secondary wage earners. Clearly, cities heavily committed to manufacturing will, by the nature of their industrial structure, have a lower percentage of part-time or part-year workers than those specialized in services, although they may, of course, be subject to greater fluctuations in employment during the course of a business cycle.

Closer analysis reveals, in addition, that ranks based on percentages of stable workers tend to be more or less uniformly low for manufacturing, business services, and consumer services in cities and suburbs for New York and Boston; high in these same major groupings in Cleveland and St. Louis. In short, the characteristics of low or high levels of employment stability observed above appear to cut across industrial lines. Apparently, terms and conditions of employment in the export sector influence the terms and conditions of employment which obtain throughout the labor market.

It is more difficult to interpret the findings for the remaining metropolises, however. With one exception (Baltimore), their percentages of stable workers lie in the intermediate range—well below Cleveland and St. Louis and well above New York and Boston—and there is no apparent correlation between their ranks based on stable-worker percentages and their ranks based on percentages of employment in manufacturing (see Table 3.3). Moreover, Baltimore presents a puzzle. As Table 5.5 shows, it finds a place alongside New York and Boston at the bottom of the list in almost all comparisons for males (city and suburbs), and ranks relatively poorly in virtually every comparison for females. Yet Baltimore does not display the characteristics of a well-developed service center, ranking fourth in manufacturing and eighth in MBS-TCU (see Table 3.3).

There is no explanation at hand. It may be that the low percentages of

Table 5.5. Percentage of Employment Which Is Stable: Total Industries and Selected Categories, Ten Metropolitan Areas, 1968[a]

	All Industries			Manufacturing			Mainly Business Service			Mainly Consumer Service		
	Average[b]	C>S	S>C	Average[b]	C>S	S>C	Average[b]	C>S	S>C	Average[b]	C>S	S>C
Cities												
Male	81.1	9		86.1	3		83.7	6		69.9	9	
White	83.0	9		87.5	3		84.7	6		71.7	10	
Nonwhite	74.2	2		80.2	4		78.6	3		63.7	2	
Female	69.5	9		75.1	6		74.7	7		64.2	9	
White	71.3	10		76.4	5		75.7	7		65.5	10	
Nonwhite	64.4	6		69.2	6		62.8	c		61.0	5	
Suburbs												
Male	78.4		1	86.9		7	83.0		4	64.6		1
White	78.9		1	87.9		7	84.1		4	63.8		0
Nonwhite	76.7		8	79.2		6	80.9		7	69.8		8
Female	65.1		1	70.7		4	70.9		3	60.9		1
White	66.2		0	74.2		5	71.6		3	61.2		0
Nonwhite	60.9		4	62.1		4	c		c	59.6		5

	All Industries		All Industries		Manufacturing		Mainly Business Service		Mainly Consumer Service	
	Male	Female	Male	Female	Male	Female	Male	Female	Male	Female
Cities										
Atlanta	82.2	70.3	6	7	7	6	6	6	2	7
Baltimore	76.6	59.4	9	10	8	8	7	10	10	10
Boston	75.1	61.9	10	9	9	9	9	'	9	9
Cleveland	86.5	76.0	1	1	1	1	3	4	1	1
Denver	82.5	73.5	4	3	2	5	4	3	4	
Houston	80.8	71.2	7	4	4	4	8	2	8	
New Orleans	82.3	70.6	5	5–6	3	2–3	1	1	6	5
New York	77.1	63.1	8	8	10	10	10	8	7	8
Philadelphia	82.8	70.6	3	5–6	6	7	5	7	5	6
St. Louis	84.9	74.9	2	2	5	2–3	2	5	3	3
Suburbs										
Atlanta	76.1	64.3	8	7	10	7	2	5	7	7
Baltimore	76.2	60.2	7	8	6	5	6	7	8	9
Boston	74.3	57.9	9	9	8–9	9	8	8	10	8
Cleveland	80.3	69.8	4	2	5	4	1	2	6	3
Denver	78.0	66.0	6	6	2	2	3	3	4	6
Houston	83.8	66.7	1	5	1	10	10	1	2	4
New Orleans	78.8	66.9	5	4	7	6	7	9	5	2
New York	73.0	55.9	10	10	8–9	8	9	10	9	10
Philadelphia	81.7	68.9	2	3	4	3	4	6	3	5
St. Louis	81.6	72.7	3	1	3	1	5	4	1	1

[a] Covered employment at place of work.
[b] Averages are modified, i.e., highest and lowest values among ten places omitted in computing.
[c] Deleted because of small sample size.
[d] Indicates rank of stable worker percentage among cities or suburbs.
Source: Tabulations from Social Security Administration, *Continuous Work History Files.*

127

stable workers are due, in part, to the bias of wage rates. Baltimore ranks ninth among cities in average earnings; and low wage levels, *ceteris paribus*, tend to reduce the number of persons who qualify as stable workers. But this hardly explains the equally low ranks in the suburbs. Baltimore suburbs show relatively high average earnings, ranking sixth among all places.

COMMUTER FLOWS AND SUBMETROPOLITAN LABOR MARKETS[10]

Commuting (that is, traveling regularly to work in a community other than the one of residence) may differ in significance among the employers and employees concerned. For workers, it widens the labor market and increases job opportunities, while at the same time it increases competition in the job market for those opportunities. Residential choice is increased similarly. For employers, a larger commuter shed means access to a larger labor supply, increased competition with other employers, and, for some, an erosion in preferential labor-market position.

But widespread commuting bears with it additional significance; it reflects a spatial organization of production and residential functions which results in long journeys to work. Such journeys involve costs for those who find employment, and they may operate as an obstacle to securing employment for others who do not. Location in the suburbs usually represents an improvement over former situations for those who have moved from the city—upgraded plants and more desirable housing. On the other hand, as was shown in Chapter 2, the spatial organization of the suburb has been strongly influenced by a number of factors, including the arrangement of highways, the development of new institutional arrangements, and the arbitrary actions of communities as regards zoning and other restrictions.

IMPORTANCE OF COMMUTER FLOWS

Chapter 4 revealed that suburb-to-city commuting is of considerable importance, measured either in terms of share-of-city employment, or as a percentage of workers residing in the suburbs. It was also observed that the number of suburb-to-city commuters increased in the period 1960-70. It is interesting that, measured relative to the size of the city's work force (i.e., total jobs in the city), suburb-to-city commuting increased in importance in every metropolis, but that measured in terms of the proportion of all suburban resident workers (i.e., persons living in the suburbs but working in suburbs or city), it decreased in every metropolis (see Table 4.5). This seeming paradox is readily explained by the fact that employment in cities has been growing slowly, or declining, while the employment in the suburbs has been growing rapidly, due largely to growth in the suburban local-sector.

Increases in commuter flows to the city that account for larger shares of city jobs may comprise a smaller percentage of the total employed persons living in the suburbs.

In analyzing commuter flows, it is important to determine also the extent to which workers residing in the suburbs commute considerable distances to jobs which are within the suburbs, or in places outside the metropolitan area. Data indicating commutation across county lines within the suburbs, or to points outside the SMSA, permit rough estimates of the extent of significantly distant commutation (Table 5.6).

The number of suburban residents who daily cross county lines to employment within the suburbs, or to points outside the SMSA, is substantial. In four metropolitan areas (Atlanta, Baltimore, Boston, and Philadelphia) it was more than 16 percent of all suburban resident workers (Table 5.6). In every area but one (Houston), it is more than ten percent. When these percentages are added to the percentages commuting to the city, we find that from 41 to 60 percent of employed suburban residents find work in the city, or outside of the county of their residence.

When 1960 and 1970 data are compared, we find that intra-suburban county-to-county commuting grew as a percentage of employed suburban residents in eight of the nine suburbs for which data were available, and suburb-to-outside SMSA commuting increased similarly in six places out of ten. The net result of this decline in importance of suburb-to-city commuting, and increase in importance of other surburban commuting (relative to the number of resident suburban workers), was that the percentage of "non-commuters" (defined as those who do not commute to the city or cross county lines in their journey to work) showed little change from the beginning to the end of the decade in most suburban areas.

The one glaring exception to this generalization is St. Louis, where there were relative declines in commuting of all types by workers residing in the suburbs. This finding is consistent with earlier observations regarding suburban and city employment change (see Chapter 3, Table 3.3). In suburban St. Louis, employment grew by 56 percent during the sixties, while the city's employment declined by almost five percent. At the same time, the suburban manufacturing sector declined in importance from 45 percent of total suburban employment to 35 percent, and the consumer-services sector increased from 28 to 40 percent. Such a growth in the suburban local sector is consistent with a reduced emphasis on commuting in the suburbs. Even so, the percentage of employed suburban St. Louis residents who commute was an impressive 42 percent in 1970 (Table 5.6).

Thus, our general finding is that even with rapid development of suburban local sectors, where wages tend to be lowest and journeys to

Table 5.6 Suburban Commuters as Percentage of Suburban Resident Workers,[a] The Metropolitan Areas, 1960, 1970

	Atlanta	Balti-more	Boston	Cleve-land	Denver	Houston	New Orleans	New York	Phila-delphia	St. Louis	Modified[b]
1970											
Commuters to city	42.8	34.6	26.3	43.5	42.3	46.9	42.3	28.0	23.4	30.2	
Commuters within suburb[c]	14.2	9.5	11.3	7.2	10.4	2.6	2.9	7.4	13.4	10.5	9.1
Commuters to outside	2.9	6.6	5.6	4.4	2.2	2.9	7.1	5.3	7.9	1.7	4.6
Total, other than to city	17.1	16.1	16.9	11.6	12.6	5.5	10.0	12.7	21.3	12.2	13.7
Total commuters	59.9	50.7	43.2	55.1	54.9	52.4	52.3	40.7	44.7	42.4	49.5
Non-commuters	40.1	49.3	56.8	44.9	45.1	47.6	47.7	59.3	55.3	57.6	50.5
1960											
Commuters to city	49.0	40.8	29.3	52.4	43.3	46.2	44.6	31.6	26.0	35.1	40.0
Commuters within suburb[c]	8.5	4.6	7.9	2.8	7.5	[d]	0.5	4.8	9.2	18.9	6.5
Commuters to outside	5.1	4.9	4.1	2.5	2.3	2.9	4.4	2.0	5.5	9.9	4.1
Total, other than to city	13.6	9.5	12.0	5.3	9.8	2.9	4.9	6.8	14.7	28.8	9.6
Total commuters	62.6	50.3	41.3	57.7	53.1	49.1	49.5	38.4	40.7	63.9	50.5
Non-commuters	37.4	49.7	58.7	42.3	46.9	50.9	50.5	61.6	59.3	36.1	49.5

[a] Employment at place of work. Suburban resident-workers include workers who work outside SMSA.
[b] Highest and lowest values among ten places omitted in computing modified average.
[c] Workers commuting across county lines within suburbs.
[d] Only one county in SMSA.

Source: *U.S. Census of Population, 1960*, PHC(1)-37, Table P-3, *U.S. Census of Population, 1970*, PHC(1)-45, Table P-2.

130

work shortest, an important share of suburban workers (on average close to half) continues to commute across county lines to their daily employment. This reveals much about suburban labor markets. Place of work and place of residence tend to be widely separated. Such a labor market favors those who have access to private transportation and works a hardship on those who do not.

Finally, Chapter 4 indicated that city-to-suburb flows are smaller than those from suburb to city, but that from 1960 to 1970, city-to-suburb flows increased more than those from suburb to city (Table 4.5). The increased importance of these flows indicates the outward movement of some activities, the establishment of suburban branches, and a growing attraction of suburban labor markets (i.e., upgrading of suburban jobs) to city dwellers. In all likelihood it reflects also the inability of many to find suburban homes near their work. Where housing opportunities are restricted, workers tend to resort to commuting.

FEMALE COMMUTATION

Female commutation is larger than seems to be generally recognized and is expanding. In 1970, female commuting accounted for about 31 percent of total suburb-to-city flows, on average, and 33 percent of city-to-suburb flows (Table 5.7). Moreover, women's shares of total flows both from suburb to city and city to suburb increased in every metropolitan area from 1960 to 1970. Measured as a percentage of total female jobs in the city, female commuter flows averaged 32 percent in 1970, whereas male commuter flows averaged 43 percent of male jobs in the city. For city-to-suburb commuting, comparable figures were 14 and 16 percent.

These flows, though somewhat smaller than for men, are greater than would be expected in the light of wage differentials between male and female commuters. On average, estimated wages of female commuters were only 48 percent of those of male commuters in the ten cities in 1970.[11] The usual explanation of the effect of wage levels on commuting distance is that jobs located farther from the worker's residence tend to involve higher search costs and higher commuter costs, both in terms of monetary outlay and time in transit. But other factors enter, particularly when the commuting practices of men and women are compared.

Such factors are complex. For one thing, there must be an acceptable alternative to the distantly located low-paying job. That workers will travel great distances, if necessary, is evidenced by the fact that, in some cities of the undeveloped world, workers walk many miles daily for the opportunity of earning a pittance. Further, the worker must be aware of alternative job opportunities and will be influenced by how attractive the job is in a non-monetary sense. It will be seen, in a later section, that a

Table 5.7. Measures of Relative Size of Male and Female Commuter Flows, Ten Metropolitan Areas, 1960 and 1970[a]

	Atlanta	Balti-more	Boston	Cleve-land	Denver	Houston	New Orleans	New York	Phila-delphia	St. Louis	Modified[b] Average
A. Female commuters as % of total commuters											
Suburb-to-city											
1960	31.7	28.5	31.1	26.9	26.2	27.7	25.9	14.6	23.7	26.3	27.0
1970	36.5	32.9	35.9	31.0	32.2	29.9	31.1	16.2	26.6	31.5	31.4
City-to-suburb											
1960	31.5	20.5	30.8	27.9	25.0	20.7	24.3	23.5	23.9	32.3	26.0
1970	37.9	35.2	34.4	32.1	34.7	29.8	29.8	30.1	30.0	38.2	33.0
B. Male in-commuters as % of total male empl. in:[a]											
City											
1960	39.0	29.5	52.1	40.5	31.5	13.6	16.5	12.6	26.7	44.5	30.2
1970	55.3	41.5	58.5	57.3	43.9	24.7	31.2	15.7	32.5	59.6	43.1
Suburb											
1960	13.4	22.3	9.3	14.6	19.2	23.5	18.7	13.2	9.4	7.3	15.0
1970	16.1	20.6	9.0	19.7	17.5	24.0	23.1	12.0	10.7	8.9	16.1
C. Female in-commuters as % of total female empl. in:[a]											
City											
1960	29.0	21.2	40.7	31.6	20.7	10.4	10.6	4.1	15.8	30.9	21.3
1970	45.0	30.6	44.6	45.0	33.6	18.0	21.4	5.0	19.5	44.0	32.1
Suburb											
1960	12.4	13.7	7.3	10.7	13.4	16.6	15.7	7.3	6.2	7.6	11.0
1970	16.0	20.5	6.9	15.6	15.4	21.7	19.7	7.4	8.2	9.3	14.0

[a] Employment at place of work.

[b] Highest and lowest values among ten places omitted in computing modified average.

Source: See Table 4.3.

large proportion of women commuting from suburb to city are employed in clerical jobs, the lowest-paying jobs of the white-collar category. These young women come to the city because jobs there are easy to find, and because the city offers a relatively attractive work environment (e.g., nearby places to shop at lunch and after hours, opportunities to meet other young people).

But there is still another point. The city is highly visible, and transportation arrangements are typically convenient. In contrast to the city dweller seeking employment in the widely scattered economy of the suburbs, the young woman seeking employment in the highly concentrated economy of the CBD faces a relatively easy task. Job openings are readily discovered in the major newspapers, or through centrally located employment agencies. Major transportation arteries converge upon the central city and provide well-defined modes of public transportation. Car pools are more easily arranged to the central city than to selected locations in the suburbs.

AGE CHARACTERISTICS OF COMMUTER FLOWS

Young workers comprised a larger share of total commuter flows of women than of comparable flows of men in 1960.[12]

	% Less than 25 years[a]
Male commuters, total	
suburb-to-city	8.8
city-to-suburb	13.2
Female commuters, total	
suburb-to-city	20.9
city-to-suburb	16.1

[a] Modified averages

This is not unexpected, since men tend to make a lifetime commitment to work, whereas women frequently drop out of the work force. Accordingly, young male workers comprise a smaller percentage of total male workers, and young male commuters comprise a smaller percentage of total male commuters. It may also be due, in part, to the fact that the number of young men less than twenty-five years of age is reduced because they tend to remain in school somewhat longer, but there is no direct evidence on this point.

RACIAL COMPOSITION OF COMMUTER FLOWS

Commuter flows of blacks from city to suburb are larger, both relatively and in absolute numbers, than commuter flows of blacks from suburb to city. In 1970, blacks accounted for 28 percent of all persons commuting from city to suburb, but only 4 percent of persons commuting from suburbs to city (Table 5.8). In terms of their importance in the suburban work force, commuters comprised 52 percent of all blacks holding suburban jobs in 1970. Moreover, these black city-to-suburb commuter flows increased sharply during the sixties, accounting for 72 percent of increases of black suburban employment.

The larger flow of black commuters from city to suburb than from suburb to city must be interpreted carefully, however. The share of employed blacks residing in the city, which is accounted for by black city-to-suburb commuters, is smaller than the share of employed blacks residing in the suburbs accounted for by black suburb-to-city commuters.[13] The larger flow from city to suburbs reflects the much larger number of blacks who live in the city.

OCCUPATIONAL COMPOSITION OF COMMUTER FLOWS

The occupational composition of commuter flows is strongly influenced by the occupational composition of employment in the cities or suburbs to which workers commute. Where specialization of employment is in blue-collar activities, there will be a relatively large share of blue-collar commuters; where specialization is in white-collar activities, a relatively large share of white-collar commuters.

And yet, as noted in Chapter 4, there are tendencies for commuter flows to be consistently heavier in some occupations, lighter in others, than would be expected on the basis of the extent of occupational specialization of city or suburban work forces alone. This is shown in Table 5.9, which presents, for males and for females, figures indicating for each occupational class the number of instances in which shares of commuters are greater or less than shares of employment in the respective work places.

Where the tallies indicate disproportionately high, or low, levels of commuting, the most reasonable line of explanation is that wage levels are the major intervening variable (although, as we have seen, there are other factors at work as well). Relatively high wages act to loosen up the financial constraints and, hence, result in increased commuting; relatively low wages act to discourage commuting. As discussed above, this is more likely to hold for the primary worker than for secondary workers in the household, who may allocate a larger share of earnings to the journey to work.

The SMSA occupational earnings data (Table 5.9) indicate that wages are highest for males in the professional-technical, managerial-administrative, and sales-worker occupations and that it is in these occupations that male workers commute from suburb to city in relatively large numbers. Such employees presumably earn sufficiently large salaries to

Table 5.8. Measures of Relative Size of Black Commuter Flows, Ten Metropolitan Areas, 1960 and 1970

	Atlanta	Balti-more	Boston	Cleve-land	Denver	Houston	New Orleans	New York	Phila-delphia	St. Louis	Modified[b] Average
A. Black commuters as % of total commuters											
Suburb-to-city											
1960	3.1	2.1	0.9	0.5	0.7	12.3	6.6	1.8	2.3	2.5	2.5
1970	4.1	3.0	1.2	4.8	0.4	6.0	5.9	2.7	3.3	5.6	3.8
City-to-suburb											
1960	19.2	32.4	10.4	19.7	4.2	19.2	28.6	9.9	25.5	27.7	20.0
1970	44.7	41.8	12.1	31.7	6.8	21.1	35.1	14.9	25.8	39.3	27.7
B. Black city-to-suburb commuters as % of black suburban employment[a]											
1960	22.7	46.3	50.4	71.9	45.8	46.0	26.4	18.8	24.3	29.9	36.5
1970	58.0	64.2	53.0	76.8	75.4	45.7	44.0	20.7	32.3	44.4	52.1
C. Percentage of black job increases in suburbs accounted for by increases in commuters[a]											
1960–1970	97.8	85.9	62.5	78.6	114.5	45.6	63.2	30.7	77.7	61.5	71.6

[a] Employment at place of work.

[b] Highest and lowest values among ten places omitted in computing modified average.

Source: See Table 4.3.

Table 5.9. Percentage Distribution of Emplo
by Occupation, by Sex, Ter

	Total Employment	Commuters to City (All Races)	CITY Number of Places Where % Commute Greater(+) less(−) than % Employed		Black Commuters to City
			+	−	
Male					
White-collar	48.7	56.5			33.8
Professional-Technical	16.5	20.1	9	1	12.1
Managerial-Administrative	12.4	16.1	9	0	5.8
Sales workers	8.3	9.7	9	1	3.4
Clerical	11.0	9.8	0	10	12.0
Blue-collar	41.3	37.8			51.0
Craftsmen	19.0	21.1	9	1	15.1
Operatives	10.2	8.3	0	9	13.5
Transport	6.5	5.1	1	9	10.5
Laborers	5.4	3.1	0	10	10.7
Service	8.9	5.0	0	10	13.4
Other	0.8	0.7	3	7	1.2
Female					
White-collar	69.8	81.0			57.9
Professional-Technical	15.2	16.4	6	4	18.6
Managerial-Adminsitrative	3.7	4.0	8	2	2.6
Sales workers	6.3	6.2	5	5	2.9
Clerical	44.7	53.7	10	0	33.7
Blue-collar	13.0	9.8			14.9
Craftsmen	1.7	1.8	8	0	1.4
Operatives	10.4	7.3	0	9	11.6
Transport	0.3	0.2	4	2	c
Laborers	0.8	0.6	1	9	1.2
Service	16.4	8.3	0	10	27.0
Other	c	c			c

[a] Percentages are modified averages and need not add exactly to 100. Employment measured at place of work.
[b] Modified averages of SMSA Median incomes for sex-occupational classifications indicated i.e., highest and lowest values among ten places omitted in computing.

136

| Total Employment | SUBURB | | | Black Commuters to Suburbs | SMSA Median Earnings (average)[b] |
| | Commuters to Suburb (All Races) | Number of Places Where % Commute Greater(+) Less(−) Than % Employed | | | |
		+	−		
43.1	38.9			18.9	
16.4	14.5	3	6	6.9	11,192
11.7	8.9	2	8	2.2	12,199
7.5	6.2	4	6	1.8	9,087
7.7	9.1	10	0	7.8	7,300
45.2	50.3			66.5	
21.7	21.5	5	5	18.2	8,522
12.3	15.3	9	1	23.9	6,903
4.7	6.0	9	0	9.4	7,138
6.0	7.6	7	2	13.5	5,141
8.0	8.4	6	4	14.0	5,143
3.1	1.3	1	9	0.9	
67.6	60.5			31.0	
18.2	18.8	5	5	10.8	6,094
3.6	2.7	0	9	0.9	5,894
9.3	6.6	0	10	2.4	2,463
36.9	32.4	1	9	17.3	4,429
11.9	14.5			18.4	
1.6	1.8	7	1	1.3	4,605
8.9	11.4	9	1	15.1	3,678
0.6	c	0	8	c	2,910
0.6	1.1	7	1	1.8	3,260
20.0	25.1	7	3	49.6	2,498
0.5	c			c	

[c] Two or more places with no significant employment.

Source: See Table 4.3.

137

permit them to live in the suburbs and commute over considerable distances. Among the blue-collar classifications, only the relatively well-paid-craftsman category is over-represented. The remainder of blue-collar workers, along with service workers, are relatively under-represented.

When we turn to the commuter flows of men to suburban employment we find, not unexpectedly, that commuting is disproportionately heavy in most of the blue-collar occupations and light in most of the white-collar occupations. As shown in Chapter 3, manufacturing wages in the suburbs tend to be relatively high, compared to those of the city. These differentials give rise to the well-known "reverse" commuting of many city industrial workers, who seek out these jobs, but do not wish to live, or are prevented from living, in the suburbs. In white-collar occupations, wages are unlikely to be as high as in the city. Moreover, these are occupations for which openings can readily be filled by suburban applicants. Under such considerations, it is hardly surprising that male white-collar employment in the suburbs tends to be relatively under-represented by commuters.

Surprisingly, however, there is one white-collar occupation, male clerical workers, in which the share of out-commuters to the suburbs is larger in all ten places than the share of male employment in the suburban work force. Lacking city and suburban wage data which show commuter earnings, we can only speculate regarding the explanation. Apparently, there are a sizeable number of clerical jobs in the suburbs which represent "good" jobs to the city resident in much the same way as do operatives' jobs in manufacturing plants (SMSA average earnings are slightly higher in clerical than in operative jobs). These are likely to be clerical positions in office parks and in back-office operations of major firms, where pay and fringe benefits are especially attractive and, possibly, where there is greater job security and opportunity for advancement. They may also include postal, or similar, jobs which are open to blacks.

Among female commuters to the city, 81 percent, on an average, hold white-collar jobs, a share which is significantly larger than the proportion, 70 percent, of total female city employment in this group of occupations. The important observation is that the over-representation of white-collar employees is accounted for principally by clerical workers (54 percent of female commuters to the city). These are the young women previously mentioned who exhibit a clear preference for work in offices largely within the CBD. The attractiveness of the CBD in terms of its amenities, its opportunities to meet people, to shop, and to find entertainment are thus key factors in its economic strength. The advantage which it offers in recruiting qualified clerical labor is an essential ingredient in its continuing role as a center for office activity. In contrast, among females commuting from city to suburbs, white-collar employment is under-represented and blue-collar and service employment over-represented.

Table 5.9 also presents average percentages of black commuters accounted for by the various occupations. For black commuters, the principal finding relating to city-to-suburb commuting is that two-thirds of male black commuters are blue-collar workers and one-half of female black commuters are service workers.

Regarding the flow of blacks from suburb to city, the major finding is that relatively few of these commuters travel to well-paying jobs. Among the black male suburb-to-city commuters, only 12 percent, on an average, are classified within the professional-technical category, and only 6 percent within the managerial-administrative. Among black female commuters, the proportion in the professional-technical category is somewhat larger (19 percent) than for black males, but it will be observed that, in this category, earnings for women are scarcely more than half of the earnings for men.

The commuter data do reveal, however, that there is a tendency for better-paid blacks to seek residence in the suburbs. The shares of black (male and female) suburb-to-city commuters in the professional-technical and management-administrative group are well above the share of black employment in the city, which are accounted for by these categories (see Tables 5.4 and 5.9).

SUMMARY AND CONCLUSIONS

This chapter examines a number of characteristics of city and suburban labor markets grouped under four headings: (1) Labor Force Participation and Unemployment; (2) Composition of the Work Force; (3) Stability of Employment; (4) Commuter Flows Within the Metropolitan Area.

Key findings are:

1. White male residents of the suburbs fare relatively better than those of the city. Rates of labor-force participation are higher, and rates of unemployment are lower. Moreover, younger workers account for a larger percentage of the white males employed in the suburbs than in cities, reflecting not only a younger labor force, but also greater availability of low-wage, entry-level-type jobs than in the city—especially in the large suburban consumer-service sector.

2. Black males fare slightly better in suburbs than in cities in terms of unemployment rates, but there is little difference in participation rates. Moreover, the percentage of black males employed in the suburbs which is accounted for by young men is typically lower than in the city, and the percentage of black males employed in consumer services is

smaller. Apparently, the more mature black males employed in the suburbs (a combination of black suburban residents and city-to-suburb commuters) find jobs which compare favorably to those in cities, but young black males find difficulty in securing suburban low-wage, entry-level-type service jobs.

3. Female jobs comprise a larger share of total employment in cities than in suburbs. This is due almost entirely to the fact that the industrial structure of cities is more heavily weighted with industries which typically hire a relatively large number of women. There is no evidence that cities tend to "over-employ" women (i.e., to employ a higher than national SMSA average percentage of women in given industries). On the other hand, some suburbs are found to employ a somewhat larger percentage of women in selected industries than is typical for all metropolitan economies within the United States.

4. Among white females, suburban-participation-rates are lower than in cities, but unemployment rates are roughly the same. At the same time, there are relatively larger numbers of white women in the suburbs than in cities who leave the work force for marriage and family responsibilities and return in middle life.

5. Among black women, there are fewer city-suburban differences. In both cities and suburbs, they enter the work force in relatively larger numbers than do white women and experience higher rates of unemployment. Moreover, young black women do not face the restricted access to suburban employment that is experienced by young black men. This is due, in a large measure, to the fact that jobs are available in the suburbs to black women, but not black men, in low-wage service activities.

6. In general, employment is more stable in city than in suburban economies. This is not true for manufacturing, where employment is typically more stable in suburban economies, but holds for all other industries and for males and females. Inter-metropolitan comparisons show marked differences among places in terms of percentages of stable workers, with employment being more stable in manufacturing centers than in major service centers.

7. By any measure, commuter flows are large and influence labor markets significantly. On the average, almost half of all suburban resident workers commuted in 1970 (i.e., suburb-to-city, city-to-outside, or across county lines within suburbs). Women comprise a substantial proportion (roughly, a third) of all commuters from suburb-to-city and city-to-suburb. A larger share of female commuters than of male commuters is less than twenty-five years of age, and a relatively larger share of city-to-suburb commuters is black than is true for suburb-to-city commuters. In terms of occupations, there is relatively more suburb-to-city commuting in white-collar than in blue-collar or service employ-

ment, and relatively more city-to-suburb commuting in blue-collar than in white-collar employment. In general, commuting is greatest in those occupations in which wage rates are relatively high, although this is not true for female clerical jobs in the city. These jobs account for more than half of all suburb-to-city commuting by women, but average pay is relatively modest.

REFERENCES

1. These remarks are drawn largely from the analysis in Chapter 3, which was based on Social Security data, and relate to employment measured at place of work.

2. This section, except for Part 4, makes use of Social Security data in which cities and suburbs are defined on a county basis. See Appendix A. All data refer to employment at place of work. The occupational analysis in Part 4 is based on *Census of Population* data examined on a place-of-work basis. See Appendix A.

3. Our procedure is to prepare for each city and suburb an "expected" estimate of total female employment by applying "standard" female-employment percentages (i.e., female-employment percentages computed separately for each 2-digit classification from Social Security data covering all SMSAs in the year 1970) to employment (both sexes) in the respective industrial classifications. Estimates of female employment in individual industries are then summed up and a single "expected" female employment percentage computed for each city and suburb. Computation of actual and expected female employment percentages for a hypothetical city or suburb is shown below:

Component (2-digit)	Total Employ-ment	Total Female Employ-ment	Actual Female Employ-ment %	Standard Female Employ-ment %	Expected Female Employ-ment
1	600	200	33.3%	20%	120
2	1200	240	20.0	30	360
3	300	100	33.3	40	120
Total, Industry Class A	2100	540			600

Actual Female Empl. % $= \dfrac{540}{2100} \times 100 = 25.7$

Expected Female Empl. % $= \dfrac{600}{2100} \times 100 = 28.6$

4. The procedure for computing expected female percentages for major industrial groupings is the same as that described above for computing such percentages for an entire suburb or city.

5. Since both actual and adjusted percentages are based on the same industrial composition of total (both sexes) employment, they may be compared directly.

6. This section makes use of Social Security data in which cities and suburbs are defined on a county basis. Employment is measured at place of work. See Appendix A. It should be noted that the analysis relates to a year of business-cycle-prosperity (1968). Had a recession year been examined, the result would have, no doubt, been somewhat different.

7. The group of workers employed on a less-than-full-time basis has been described by Dean Morse as the peripheral labor force. See Dean Morse, *The Peripheral Labor Force* (New York, N.Y.: Columbia·University Press, 1969).

8. Those persons who failed to show earnings in all quarters because they had previously in the year attained maximum salaries for which Social Security deductions are made were not so treated, but were regarded as full-year, full-time workers.

9. This measure is deficient in several ways. In the first place, it does not distinguish between a person who earned less than $750.00 in one quarter, because he worked part-time, from the person who failed to qualify as a stable worker simply because he entered the work force too late, or left too early in the year to earn the requisite $750.00 in each quarter. Secondly, it fails to record as unstable employment those cases in which individuals actually work part-time, but at rates of pay sufficient to cause income to be above $750.00 in each of four quarters. Third, it does not distinguish between those who are employed part-time through preference (e.g., housewives who wish merely to augment family income) and those who cannot find full-time work.

10. Analysis of commuter flows makes use of *Census of Population* data which shows both place of work and place of residence. See Appendix A.

11. These estimates were made using average SMSA earnings in each male and female classification, weighting these wages by the average percentage of commuters in each occupation, and computing average earnings separately for male and female commuters.

12. Data for 1960 are used here because the 1970 census journey-to-work statistics do not provide age-characteristics data separately for males and females.

13. In 1970, black city-to-suburbs commuters accounted for, on an average, 19.4 percent and 14.2 percent of black male and female workers, respectively, residing in the city; black suburb-to-city commuters accounted for 28.1 and 30.3 percent, respectively, of black male and female workers residing in suburbs.

[6

Labor-Market Flows

Traditionally, there has been a tendency to speak of job opportunities in terms of those net additions to employment which occur through growth. Yet, because there is a continuous stream of departures due to retirement, out-migration, death, and simple withdrawal from employment, job openings far exceed net change in employment in any period. This is not to deny the importance of growth, for expansion of the economy brings with it additional opportunities for employment, and, accordingly, is associated with increases in all the entry flows. Nevertheless, an analysis of net change alone, even of net changes in component industry groups, provides limited insights into how employment opportunities arise.

This chapter examines the magnitude and nature of worker movements into and out of city and suburban work forces (measured at place of work) during the period 1960-70.[1] The analysis focuses on the issue of how the labor market accommodates itself to change and, hopefully, sheds light on possible problems of adjustment in the years ahead.

In any period, economic expansion and upgrading of the labor force are facilitated by three different inflows of manpower: (1) *new entrants* (those who were not on the employment rolls in any city, suburb, or non-metropolitan area at the beginning of the period); (2) *in-transfers* (entrants from another part of the same metropolitan area, i.e., workers entering suburban employment from city jobs, or entering city employment from suburban jobs); and (3) *in-migration* (entrants into a particular city or suburban work force from places outside the same metropolitan area).

At the same time, outflows are occurring in three similar streams: (4)

departures (those departing from the work force entirely); (5) *out-transfers* (those transferring from city employment to suburban employment or from suburban employment to city employment); and (6) *out-migrants* (those migrating from employment in the city, or suburb, of a particular metropolitan area outside that area). Streams 2 and 5 are the same, but viewed from different vantage points. Finally *stayers* are those who continue to work in the same city or suburb.

A breakdown of these flows for New Orleans, covering the period 1965-1970, is presented below. All data are expressed as a percentage of total employment in the city, or suburbs, in the base year (e.g., new entrants into city employment during the period 1965-70 are presented as a percentage of all persons working in the city in 1965). Both the in-migrants and the out-migrants are divided into two categories, "inside BEA area" and "outside BEA area." The BEA area is a grouping of counties, including not only the SMSA but counties more or less contiguous to it, which have been classified by the Bureau of Economic Analysis, Department of Commerce, as being within its economic orbit, judged in terms of commuting and certain other economic factors. It is possible, therefore, to observe in a rough way whether or not in-migration and out-migration are largely related to the "exurbs" (rural fringes or hinterland), or to areas at greater distances.

	City[a]	Suburb[a]
Stayers	48.8	40.6
Inflows, total	60.1	112.3
New entrants	36.2	59.8
In-transfers	2.9	19.6
In-migrants	21.0	32.9
within BEA	2.8	7.3
outside BEA	16.1	22.2
military[b]	2.1	3.4
Outflows, total	51.2	59.4
Departures	29.2	28.3
Out-transfers	4.7	12.1
Out-migrants	17.4	19.0
within BEA	3.1	7.1
outside BEA	13.5	11.0
military[c]	.7	.9
Net Change	8.9	52.9

[a] Figures indicate numbers of employees expressed as a percentage of total employment in 1965.

[b] Persons entering work force from military service.

[c] Persons departing work force to become members of military.

In the New Orleans metropolitan area, outflows and inflows were large relative to net employment change, indicating a high level of turnover within the work force. During the five-year period, 51 percent of the initial workers in the city (59 percent in the suburbs) left the work force, transferred or migrated, and would have had to be replaced simply to maintain employment at its original level. Inflows amounted to 60 percent of the original employment in the city, 112 percent in the suburbs.

Among flows into the work forces of city and suburb, new entrants are the largest category (36 and 60 percent), with in-migrants the second largest (21 and 33 percent). Among the latter category, in-migrants from outside the BEA area comprise a large majority (16 and 22 percent). The magnitude of the flows reflects, to some extent, overall growth rates during the five-year period. For example, the flow of new entrants is relatively larger for suburbs than for city, reflecting the effect of higher suburban growth rates.

Among outflows, departures are the largest group (29 and 28 percent of beginning employment) with out-migrants (17 to 19 percent of beginning employment), the second largest. Among the latter, those migrating to areas outside the BEA are the major component.

MAGNITUDES AND COMPOSITION OF FLOWS

MAGNITUDES OF FLOWS

These streams have been measured in the ten metropolises. Table 6.1 presents modified average rates (averages for ten places, excluding lowest and highest values) for each type of flow and for stayers. Rates were computed separately for males and for females, for cities and suburbs, and for each five-year period.

Inflows appear to be most affected by variations in growth rates. All categories of inflows in both cities and suburbs show higher average rates for the second period when rates of growth are higher. Variations in the rates are greatest among suburban new entrants and in-migrants.

There are also marked differences between inflows of males and females in both city and suburb. Female new entrants come into the work force in relatively larger numbers than male new entrants (e.g., during the 1965-70 period, 55 percent compared to 28 percent in the cities, 81 percent compared to 39 percent in the suburbs).

To a degree, this was because women were becoming a larger part of both city and suburban work forces, with the the result that their rates of net employment change and of new entry were higher than for men. But the higher rates at which women were entering the work force reflect also the tendency for women to enter and leave the work force more

Table 6.1. Relative Size of Stayers, Inflows and Outflows, by Categories, By Sex, Ten Metropolitan Areas, 1960–65, 1965–70

	Males						Females					
	Cities			Suburbs			Cities			Suburbs		
	1960-65	1965-70		1960-65	1965-70		1960-65	1965-70		1960-65	1965-70	
	Flow[a]	Flow[a]	Share[b]	Flow[a]	Flow[a]	Share[b]	Flow[a]	Flow[a]	Share[b]	Flow[a]	Flow[a]	Share[b]
Stayers	56.7	54.9		52.4	51.5		50.3	49.3		45.2	44.2	
Inflows	46.4	54.1		61.2	82.9		56.9	70.0		86.2	115.3	
New entrants	23.5	27.9	51.6	29.2	38.9	46.9	44.9	55.0	78.6	65.4	81.1	70.3
In-transfers	4.3	4.6	8.5	14.8	16.6	20.0	2.4	3.0	4.3	11.1	13.0	11.3
In-migrants	18.1	21.4	39.6	17.2	27.9	33.7	8.8	11.6	16.6	9.7	13.9	12.1
Within BEA	1.5	1.8	3.3	3.1	4.1	4.9	0.8	1.3	1.9	1.6	2.6	2.3
Outside BEA	13.3	15.9	29.4	10.6	19.0	22.9	7.8	10.1	14.4	7.4	11.2	9.7
Military	3.3	3.8	7.0	3.6	4.9	5.9	0.0	0.1	0.1	0.1	0.1	0.1
Outflows	43.3	45.3		47.7	48.5		49.7	50.6		54.8	55.8	
Departures	20.2	21.3	47.0	18.7	20.5	42.3	36.2	35.3	69.8	37.3	36.6	65.6
Out-transfers	5.5	6.8	15.0	9.9	11.5	23.7	3.7	5.0	9.9	8.3	8.1	14.5
Out-migrants	16.6	16.4	36.2	18.0	16.1	33.2	9.7	10.4	20.6	9.4	10.5	18.8
Within BEA	2.1	2.0	4.4	3.1	2.9	6.0	0.9	1.1	2.2	1.6	1.8	3.2
Outside BEA	13.9	13.6	30.0	13.3	11.5	23.7	8.6	9.3	18.4	7.6	8.7	15.6
Military	1.1	1.1	2.4	1.2	1.4	2.9	0.0	0.0	0.0	0.0	0.0	0.0
Net Change:	3.3	8.8		12.0	34.9		7.1	17.8		30.1	52.7	

[a] Figures shown are modified averages of rates for stayers, flows or of net employment change (expressed as a percentage of male or female employment in initial year of period). Covered employment at place of work.

[b] Modified averages of shares of total inflows or total outflows. These average shares need not add to exactly 100 percent.

Source: Tabulations from Social Security Administration, *Continuous Work History Files.*

than once. This means that the turnover of female work force is higher than for men, since men tend to enter only once (in their late teens or early twenties) and to remain in the work force, more or less continuously, for the rest of their working lives.[2] Accordingly, the new entry data for women include both persons entering the work force for the first time and those entering for the second or third time, whereas the new entry data for men include largely persons entering for the first time.

Related to these patterns is the differential effect of migration on male and female workers. Male rates of in-migration are roughly twice the comparable rates for females (e.g., during the 1965-70 period they were 28 percent for males, 14 percent for females in the suburbs), reflecting the much greater tendency for males to migrate from one labor market to another. Whereas males change residence with a change in location of their jobs, females may give up employment when their husbands' employment requires migration. Rates of flow for in-transfers are, in general, much smaller than for migrants, and vary less between men and women. Nevertheless, they are greater for men (e.g., 17 percent for males in the suburbs, 1965-1970; 13 percent for females).

Outflows reflect the same general tendencies sketched above. The sharply higher proportion of departures for females (e.g., 37 percent compared to 20 percent for men in suburbs during the 1965-70 period) again reflects the tendency of women to enter the labor force more than once: to find employment, to subsequently leave the work force to assume child-rearing responsibilities, and to return at a later date. The lower rates of out-migration of females (e.g., 10 percent in suburbs during the 1965-70 period compared to 16 percent for men) reflects their lower tendency to migrate for employment reasons and a higher probability of their leaving employment entirely when the primary worker migrates to take a new job. On an average, women move somewhat less readily than men within the labor markets of the metropolitan area (i.e., from suburb to city, city to suburb) (e.g., out-transfer rates for women were 8 percent in suburbs in the 1965-70 period, compared to 12 percent for men).

SHARES OF FLOWS COMPARED: SUBURBS AND CITIES

Differences in composition of city and suburban flows may be highlighted by examining shares of total entrants and departures accounted for by each type of flow during the period 1965-70 (Table 6.1). The data indicate that for both males and females:

1. New entrants and in-migrants from outside BEA areas comprise a larger share of flows into city employment than of flows into suburban employment.

2. Transfers contribute more to total flows of workers into suburban employment than into city employment.

3. Departures from the work force and out-migrants to jobs located outside BEA areas are a more important share of total city outflows than of total suburban outflows.

The observation that city labor markets draw from distant points (i.e., from national labor markets) to a relatively greater extent than do suburban labor markets (and that migration to such points is also relatively larger) is not surprising. City employment is comprised, in a larger measure, of higher-level executives and professionals, and the market for the labor of these people is much broader than the market for lower-level employees.[3]

On the other hand, the observation that new entrants comprise a larger share of total flows into city employment than into suburban employment is unexpected in view of the earlier finding (Chapter 4), that job increases in cities during the sixties, especially in the female clerical occupational class, were accompanied by very sizeable increases in commuters.

Why do these large increases in commuters to cities not show up in the Social Security data as in-transfers? It is quite likely that many of these young commuters found their first regular employment after high school or college graduation in the offices of the central cities' business districts. Estimates of new entrants are prepared by comparing first-quarter employment at place of work at the beginning and terminal year of the five-year periods. Thus, young workers who had only summer employment in the beginning year, but full-year employment in the terminal year, are picked up as new entrants. A suburban worker employed only in the summer of 1965, or, for that matter, working only during summers from 1965-69, but employed full time in the city in 1970, would be classified as a new entrant into the city's work force.

The large share of suburban inflows, accounted for by in-transfers, reflects the importance of movement of workers from city to suburban employment. Many such changes have occurred in the past as workers followed manufacturing firms in movements from the city. Moreover, the establishment of branches of city retail stores, banks, insurance agencies, and the like also causes a significant movement of service-type personnel from city-to-suburb employment.

AGE COMPOSITION OF FLOWS

Not surprisingly, flows of workers into, and out of, the job market vary in terms of their age composition, for they represent quite different groups (Table 6.2). New entrants are, to a large extent, young people coming into the job market for the first time. In-migrants are persons transferring their employment from other places and are likely to have more work experience and earn higher wages. Men usually leave the work force for an extended period only at the end of their careers, while women may show two periods of relatively high rates of departure, one at time of family formation, another in later life.

In addition to supporting the generalizations sketched above, the 1965-70 data shown in Table 6.2 also lead to the following observations:

1. There are a relatively greater number of entry-level jobs for young males in suburbs than in cities. Among new entrants, the percentage of males under twenty-five years of age is much higher in suburban jobs than in city jobs (65 percent compared to 58 percent).

2. Female new entrants are, on an average, older than male new entrants. There is a relatively smaller percentage of females under twenty-five years of age than males (43 percent compared to 65 percent in suburbs and 49 versus 58 percent in cities). This, presumably, reflects the greater tendency for females to enter (or reenter) the work force in middle life. But the number of female new entrants over thirty-five years of age is larger in the suburbs than in cities (39 percent compared to 32 percent), suggesting that there are relatively more older women (presumably housewives) entering the job market in suburbs than in cities. This is, of course, consistent with all that has been said about the suburbs: the importance of the local sector and of part-time employment and the availability of housewives as a source of labor.

3. Among male in-migrants, those entering from beyond the borders of the BEA are older than those entering from within BEA areas. There are fewer under thirty-five years of age and more over thirty-five.

4. Males entering suburban employment from the city work force tend to be older than males entering city employment from the suburban work force. Presumably, this reflects movement of firms to the suburbs and promotions to branch offices. Highly skilled workers tend to remain with firms that have shifted to suburban locations, whereas low-skilled and clerical staff tend to remain in city jobs, but change employers. The tendency to remain with employers who change location is strong for men over forty-five, many of whom may be assumed to have acquired a number of years of seniority and pension rights.

EARNINGS BY CLASS OF FLOW (WHITE WORKERS)

Just as persons within the various classes of flows vary in terms of age characteristics, they vary in terms of typical earnings. In the present section, average earnings of white workers are analyzed for cities and suburbs by sex grouping for each class of flow and for stayers (Table 6.3). White and black workers are not combined because wage dif-

Table 6.2. Age Distribution of Major Flow Categories, by Sex, Ten Metropolian Areas, 1965–70[a]

	New Entrants		In-Transfers[b]		In-Migrants (Within BEA)		(Outside BEA)		Departures		Out-Migrants (Within BEA)		(Outside BEA)	
	C	S	C	S	C	S	C	S	C	S	C	S	C	S
Male														
Less than 25	57.7	64.9	10.3	6.8	7.8	9.2	6.0	5.0	4.5	6.2	7.0	c	5.1	7.1
25–34	18.3	13.9	35.0	33.4	36.9	38.7	34.3	33.7	16.6	17.8	32.3	39.6	34.0	35.6
35–44	9.3	7.9	22.4	23.8	21.3	20.2	27.1	29.6	14.8	15.9	27.2	24.1	27.7	27.2
45–64	12.4	10.8	28.4	32.9	29.5	30.7	30.7	31.1	35.8	34.5	30.2	28.3	31.0	27.6
65 and over	2.8	1.7	c	3.8	c	c	2.1	1.4	28.5	25.1	c	c	2.2	2.0
Female														
Less than 25	48.9	42.9	12.3	5.2	18.1	c	9.4	6.7	8.7	8.5	c	c	8.6	12.6
25–34	18.6	16.9	25.6	27.8	27.9	31.1	36.1	33.5	35.5	32.0	36.1	c	36.0	33.8
35–44	15.0	19.1	19.3	22.3	20.7	c	20.0	23.7	13.7	16.7	18.9	c	21.3	21.4
45–64	16.0	19.7	38.2	41.9	28.9	34.8	31.7	33.2	26.8	32.2	35.8	39.6	31.9	31.7
65 and over	1.1	c	c	c	c	c	2.6	c	15.6	10.4	c	c	2.3	c

[a] Covered employment at place of work. All data shown are modified averages, i.e., highest and lowest values among ten places omitted in computing modified average.

[b] Since in-transfers to city are out-transfers from suburbs and in-transfers to suburbs are out-transfers from city, these flows are shown only once, i.e., no out-transfers are shown.

[c] No data for two or more places.

Source: Tabulations from Social Security Administration, *Continuous Work History Files*.

ferentials between the two races are too great to justify combining them. Furthermore, earnings of black workers have not been analyzed separately because sample size is inadequate. Average earnings of white workers in given groupings are expressed as earnings indices, which are ratios of earnings to average earnings for all workers (all sex-race classes) in the SMSA.[4]

1. Clearly, male in-migrants (outside BEA) and out-migrants (outside BEA) represent above-average levels of skills and experience in both cities and suburbs. Indices for in-migrants, cities and suburbs, were 1.33 and 1.32 respectively; for out-migrants, 1.37 and 1.21. In contrast, earnings of female in-migrants (outside BEA) and out-migrants (outside BEA) were not especially high, even in comparison with earnings of females in other flow classes. Indices for in-migrants, cities and suburbs, were .63 and .62 respectively; for out-migrants, .62 and .54. On the other hand, in-migrants (inside BEA) and out-migrants (inside BEA) have somewhat lower earnings, at least for men.

2. In-transfers to suburbs have higher average wages than in-transfers to cities. For males, indices are 1.19 compared to 1.06 percent; for females, .62 compared to .51. This reflects, at least in part, the tendency observed earlier (Table 6.3) for workers transferring from city to suburban jobs to be somewhat older than those shifting employment from suburb to city.

3. Earnings of new entrants to the cities were significantly higher than earnings of new entrants to suburbs for males, an average index of .76 in cities versus .68 in suburbs; for females, .52 versus .45.

4. Departures are probably a relatively heterogeneous group. According to Table 6.3, they include a considerable number of relatively young workers, as well as workers over sixty-five and beyond the usual retirement age. It is likely that many of these workers are employed only part-time. Accordingly, departures do not represent a group of persons retiring at the height of their earnings experience. Indices for men are 1.06 and .97 in cities and suburbs in contrast to indices of 1.45 and 1.36 for stayers. Similarly, for women, indices for departures are .57 and .49 in cities and suburbs, whereas comparable indices for stayers are .74 and .65.

Thus, among white workers there are several groups moving into, or out of, the work force of the city, each with different wage characteristics. The largest group are new entrants whose wages are quite low, though well above those of the suburbs. As noted previously, these new entrants include young suburban commuters as well as local residents. The second are departures, a somewhat heterogeneous group with no more than average earnings, probably because of considerable part-time employment. The third group are relatively well-paid migrants moving from or into areas beyond the BEA borders. The fourth are transfers from the suburbs, very likely workers shifting employment to the CBD. For males, but not for females, their average pay is above that of new entrants. Finally, a fifth group are in-migrants from beyond the suburbs, but within the BEA area. These workers' average earnings are slightly below those of entrants from suburbs. Presumably, these workers bring with them fewer special skills and less training, since they typically found their previous employment in an outlying and less-developed area.

In the suburbs, earning levels of the various flow groups are, for the most part, somewhat different from those in the city. Earning levels for white new-entrants are below those in the city, as are those for departures. But those for in-migrants (outside BEA) are approximately equal. The fourth group, in-transfers, show higher wages for suburbs than for cities. It is important to observe that, included here, are city workers who locate better-paying manufacturing employment in the suburbs. Finally, in-migrants from outside suburbs, but within the BEA, are once again found to receive relatively low wages as compared to other flow groups.

Table 6.3. Indexes of Earnings for Major Flow Categories, White Workers, Ten Metropolitan Areas, 1965–1970[a]

	Male		Female	
	Cities	Suburbs	Cities	Suburbs
Inflows:				
New Entrants	0.76	0.68	0.52	0.45
In-transfers	1.06	1.19	0.52	0.62
In-migrants				
Within BEA	1.01	0.97	0.47	0.52
Outside BEA	1.33	1.32	0.63	0.62
Outflows:				
Departures	1.06	0.97	0.57	0.49
Out-transfers	1.19	1.06	0.62	0.51
Out-migrants				
Within BEA	1.15	1.04	0.65	0.50
Outside BEA	1.37	1.21	0.62	0.54
Stayers:	1.45	1.36	0.74	0.65

[a] Each index is computed by dividing average earnings for flow by average earnings in SMSA (all workers). All data shown are modified averages, i.e., highest and lowest values among ten places omitted in computing average. Covered employment at place of work.

Source: Tabulations from Social Security Administration, *Continuous Work History Files.*

RELATIONSHIPS OF FLOWS TO EMPLOYMENT CHANGE

What determines the magnitude of worker flows? The relationships between entrant and departure rates and employment changes are analyzed by use of regression analysis in which the various flows, expressed as rates, are related to rates of net employment change for males and for females, and for cities and suburbs. The analysis makes use of simple regressions in which the equations are of the form $x = a + by$, where:[5]

> x =rate of a given inflow or outlow. The rate for males, or females, is simply the number of workers moving into, or out of, the city or suburban work force as new entrants, transfers, migrants, or departures during the five-year period, expressed as a percentage of the number of workers (male or female) at the beginning of the period.
>
> y =rate of employment change. In order to avoid negative numbers, this rate has been computed by expressing end-of-period male, or female, employment as a percentage of number of workers (male or female) at the beginning of the five-year period. Thus, a 40 percent increase is expressed as 140 percent.
>
> a =coefficient indicating the value of x when the value of y is zero. It is important to keep in mind that in order to compute the rate of entry of departure under hypothetical no-growth conditions, we must compute x from the regression equation with the value of y equal to 100 (i.e., when end-of-period employment is 100 percent of beginning employment).
>
> b =regression coefficient indicating relationship between y and x. Since both x and y are expressed as a percentage of beginning employment, this coefficient indicates the incremental rate of change in x, associated with a 1 percent change in y.

The analysis sheds light on two questions:

1. How large would given types of flows into, and out of, the work force be under no-growth conditions?

2. Under conditions of net growth or decline in male or female employment, what rate of new entry, transfer, migration, or departure is associated with each 1 percent of net increase (or decrease) in employment?

NEW ENTRANTS AND EMPLOYMENT CHANGE

The analysis tells us much about the role of new entrant flows in the economies of cities and suburbs. The relationship between new entrants and net employment change is generally close (i.e., coefficients of correlation are high), although less so in the cases of male employment in the suburbs in the 1960-65 period than in other cases. Nevertheless, it is clear that a large number of job openings would develop for new entrants even if there were no growth. There would be a considerable number of new entrants simply to replace losses resulting from departures from the work force and from out-migration. Our estimates indicate that five-year new entrant flows under no-growth conditions expressed as a percentage of male or female employment at the beginning of the period would have been as follows:

	1960–65	1965–70
City		
Male	21.8%	24.6%
Female	39.1	41.3
Suburb		
Male	25.1	24.2
Female	38.1	36.9

Expressed on an annual basis, these estimates indicate that the number of new entrants required each year simply for replacement purposes would approximate 4 to 5 percent of male employment in the beginning-of-period year for men, and 7 to 8 percent of female employment in the beginning-of-period year for women. The higher rates of new entry for women under such conditions are consistent with the previous observation that female employment is characterized by higher turnover than is male employment.

When we turn to the association between net employment change and new entry flows, we find female new entrants respond more sensitively to net change in female employment than male new entrants respond to net change in male employment. The estimated change in new entrants (expressed as a percentage of base-year male or female employment) associated with a 1 percent net change in male or female employment are:

	1960–65	1965–70
City		
Male	.48%	.35%
Female	.86	.71
Suburb		
Male	.37	.42
Female	.86	.84

The larger flows of female new entrants for a given amount of female employment change may be explained by the fact already observed that, for women, new entrants have played a larger role, and in-migration a smaller role, in bringing about increased employment than is the case for men.

A final observation which concerns the dynamics of the relationship is perhaps the most important. The relationship appears to be stable over periods of differing growth rates. Under the high-growth conditions of the second period (1965-1970), the percentages (i.e., coefficients) do not decline from levels shown for the first period (1960-1965), at least in the burgeoning suburbs. This means that each percentage point of growth in employment is associated with a roughly unvarying relative increment in the flow of new entrants over a quite wide range of observations. The generalization holds for both males and females, although the coefficients are different.

Of course, increased employment must come from somewhere: from new entrants, in-migration, in-transfers, coupled, perhaps, with declines in departures. But there would seem to be no reason, *a priori*, to expect the sort of elasticity of supply from new entrants that is observed here. One might very well have hypothesized that higher rates of growth would encounter increasing constraints from the existing potential labor force so that marginal rates of new entry would decline sharply. The evidence that new entrants have provided, within the range of growth observed, a highly expansible source of new workers stands out as a major finding of this study. It is recognized, however, that the evidence is drawn from a sample of cities and suburbs in ten major metropolitan areas. Accordingly, it deserves further research, especially regarding the source of new entrants, i.e., are they commuters or workers who reside near the suburban or city work place?

IN-MIGRATION AND EMPLOYMENT CHANGE

The analysis also indicates a positive association between rates of in-migration and employment change, although the relationship is well established only during the period of fast growth, 1965-70. Apparently, there was a weak association between suburban growth and in-migration under the relatively slow growth conditions that characterized the 1960-65 period, at least for the ten places studied.

Rates of in-migrant flows under no-growth conditions were estimated to be considerably lower than for new entrant flows, and to be much lower for women than for men:

	In-migrants	
	1960–65	1965–70
To City		
Male	15.3%	15.1%
Female	6.8	4.3
To Suburb		
Male	17.9	9.7
Female	4.5	−2.0

These estimates are consistent with general observation: Where no growth is taking place we would not expect a very large number of in-migrants, even though we might expect a steady flow of young people replacing those who retire. Nevertheless, we would expect a larger in-migration of males than of females, because males have a greater tendency to move in order to secure the best possible employment.

The association between in-migrants and net change in employment is quite different from that observed for new entrants. For males, the estimated percentage change in flow associated with a 1 percent change in employment is higher than for new entrants; and for females, sharply lower:

	In-migrants	
	1960–65	1965–70
To City		
Male	.78%	.69%
Female	.36	.34
To Suburb		
Male	a	.54
Female	.18	.30

a Not statistically significant.

We must conclude that growth in male employment is facilitated to a larger extent by in-migration than by new entrants, i.e., that the in-migration flow is more closely associated with or sensitive to overall growth rates than is the new-entrant flow. Such is not the case, however, for female employment in which new entrant flows are considerably more sensitive to growth (see above) than are in-migration flows (e.g., during 1965-70, .84 versus .30 percent in suburbs and .71 versus .34 in cities).

IN-TRANSFERS AND EMPLOYMENT CHANGE

In-transfers are less closely associated with net changes in employment than are new-entry and in-migrant flows. Measures of correlation (coefficients of determination, R^2's) are smaller (see Appendix Table E).

Estimates of male in-transfers under no-growth conditions are larger than comparable estimates of female in-transfers, especially for suburbs. Perhaps more important, however, is simply the observation that these estimated flows under no-growth conditions are small, amounting to roughly a tenth of beginning employment over a five-year period, even for male city-to-suburb flows:

	1960–65	1965–70
To City		
Males	4.9%	6.8%
Females	3.6	4.3
To Suburbs		
Males	11.8	9.8
Females	4.1	2.7

Unfortunately, the association between in-transfers and net change in employment (i.e., regression coefficients) cannot be evaluated because the statistical relationships are poor for both cities and suburbs in the first period, and for males in the city in the second.

OUT-MIGRANTS, DEPARTURES, AND EMPLOYMENT CHANGE

As regards the relationship between out-migrants and employment change, only one general observation can be made: that such departures are positively related to employment change, but that the relationship is weak. Departures from work force were not found to be significantly related to employment change.

SIGNIFICANCE OF FLOWS FOR LABOR-MARKET ADJUSTMENT

While we cannot determine the extent to which institutional arrangements for education and training differ between city and suburb, our data do permit us to focus attention on the industrial occupational characteristics of jobs which are opening up and closing down, on the extent to which local-market workers must compete with workers drawn from elsewhere, and, of course, on the extent to which the overall demand for labor is growing.

NEW ENTRY POINTS

New workers do not gain access to employment with equal ease in every industry or in every occupation. There are a variety of barriers to entry, including level of skill and experience, union membership requirements, specifications regarding sex, knowledge of employment opportunities, and prejudice. Even in the most efficient and equitable labor markets, there are customary entry points. Some industries and occupations are much more accessible to the new entrant than others.

Table 6.4 presents average distributions of male and female new entrants among industries for cities and suburbs during the period 1965-

Table 6.4. Percentage Distribution of New Entrants Among Industrial
Classification, Actual and Normalized Shares,
Ten Metropolitan Areas, 1965–70[a]

	Males		Females	
	Shares[a]	Normalized Values[b]	Shares[a]	Normalized Values[b]
City				
Primary	1.1	132.3	0.6	164.4
Construction	7.3	89.3	0.9	81.9
Manufacturing	22.7	71.3	16.0	68.8
Low-wage	7.6	85.0	7.6	61.4
High-wage	14.7	65.6	7.8	78.0
TCU	7.4	65.9	6.1	92.1
MBS	24.3	108.6	27.8	117.0
Wholesale	10.3	90.1	6.3	97.5
FIRE	6.0	96.0	13.0	118.5
MCS	36.1	161.4	49.5	108.0
Retail	23.6	164.2	26.2	113.5
Suburb				
Primary	2.8	134.5	0.7	c
Construction	10.3	79.8	1.3	106.8
Manufacturing	28.9	69.2	18.6	64.0
Low-wage	6.4	68.1	6.2	51.3
High-wage	22.6	71.4	12.3	99.2
TCU	3.7	78.8	3.4	96.4
MBS	10.5	92.8	14.9	119.9
Wholesale	4.9	102.0	3.8	128.7
FIRE	2.0	c	6.6	99.6
MCS	41.9	168.6	60.3	111.5
Retail	32.4	172.2	35.6	116.0

[a] Data shown are modified averages of shares of new entrants. (Highest and lowest values excluded from averages.) Based on employment at place of work.

[b] Shares have been normalized in industrial class by dividing shares of new entrants by shares of employment at beginning of period. All data shown are modified averages for ten cities and suburbs.

[c] Two or more places with no new entrant data.

Source: Tabulations from Social Security Administration, *Continuous Work History Files.*

1970. It is immediately apparent that there are significant differences between sexes and between cities and suburbs. Males tend to have larger percentages of new entrants than females in construction, manufacturing, and TCU, regardless of whether we examine city or suburb. Females have higher percentages in mainly business services and mainly consumer services. On the other hand, suburbs tend to have higher percentages in construction, manufacturing, and mainly consumer services regardless of sex; cities in TCU and mainly business services.

The earlier analysis indicated differences between cities and suburbs in industrial composition of employment which will clearly influence patterns of entry into city and suburban work forces (e.g., suburban new entries in manufacturing and mainly consumer services are expected to be relatively large because employment in those categories is relatively large). Accordingly, it is useful to adjust the entry data to compensate for the effect of industry-employment composition. This has been done for the most recent period by normalizing the new-entrant-industry composition, dividing the percentage of new entrants in each industry (1965-70) by the percentage of employment in that industry in 1965. Modified averages of the normalized new-entry data, computed separately for males and females in each city and suburb, are shown in Table 6.4.

These normalized data indicate wide differences among industries. For males, the average normalized value for mainly consumer services is considerably more than twice as large as for manufacturing in both cities and suburbs; almost twice as large as for business services in the suburbs; and half again as large as for business services in the cities. For females, the average values range less widely among major groups. The important difference between females and males is that the normalized share for females in the business services is larger, but in the consumer services it is smaller. In relative terms, male new entrants appear to be favored in consumer services; while female new entrants are favored in business services.

The latter comparison must be interpreted with care, however. The normalized figures are ratios relating share of new entrants with share of employment at the beginning of the period. In the case of women the actual shares of new entrants accounted for by consumer services are larger than is the case for men in both cities and suburbs. The normalized value is smaller only because new entrants for women are not so large relative to the even larger shares of female employment in consumer services.

UPWARD MOBILITY AND THE OPENING-UP OF ENTRY-LEVEL JOBS

It is, of course, entirely appropriate that some industries receive a relatively larger share of new entrants than others, for such industries are characterized by a larger proportion of so-called entry-level jobs (i.e., low-skill, low-wage jobs). Thus we expect retailing and certain low-wage branches of manufacturing to receive a disproportionately large share of young persons entering the job market.

It is important, however, that there be upward mobility within the job market. Entry-level jobs become available through continuous movement of workers from lower to higher level jobs, as well as through continuous out-migration and retirement of workers from the labor force. Also, high levels of growth bring about high levels of new entrants. The corollary to this observation is that in the years that follow a period of rapid growth the large cohort of new entrants can find opportunity for upward mobility only if growth is sustained.

In this context we must note that 1957 marked the beginning of the decline in birthrates for the nation as a whole and that the number of young people under twenty-five years of age will not begin to recede until 1982, declining only gradually thereafter. Thus the need for accommodation of a rapidly emerging labor force can be confidently projected well into the 1980's.

How well this accommodation proceeds will be largely determined by the way in which effective demand for labor unfolds. A rising generation of young adults to a large extent creates the demand for its own labor in the nation as a whole (though not necessarily in given cities and suburbs), especially if latent demand for durables, new housing, and other capital infra-structure is translated into active demand.

Age structure of employment in selected industry classifications is analyzed in Table 6.5. As expected, the shares of workers under twenty-five are larger in 1970 than in 1960 because of demographic trends. Employment under twenty-five years of age increased for males from 13 to 18 percent in cities and from 17 to 23 percent in suburbs; and for females from 22 to 26 percent in cities and 22 to 27 percent in suburbs.

The percent of employment under twenty-five years of age in a specific industry is an indication of the extent to which the industry has accumulated young workers. These workers must, over time, be assimilated into higher level jobs within the industry or into other industries if subsequent new entrants are to be satisfactorily accommodated. Should upward mobility not be adequate to provide fully for much accommodation, adjustments of other sorts are required. Migration may partially relieve the pressure on a particular metropolis, but this will also tend to be accompanied by higher unemployment and lower labor-force participation. Perhaps the most obvious result, however, will be the increasing tendency for workers to find themselves in "dead-end" employment (i.e., men and women in boys' and girls' jobs).

The percentage of young workers increased in all classifications in

Table 6.5. Percentage of Workers in Selected Industrial
Classifications Who Are Less Than Twenty-five Years of Age,
Ten Metropolitan Areas, 1960, 1970[a]

	Males			Females		
	Shares		Change	Shares		Change
	1960	1970	in Shares 1960–70	1960	1970	in Shares 1960–70
City						
Industry						
Construction	10.1	13.3	3.2	b	b	b
Manufacturing	12.4	14.7	2.3	3.8	18.2	4.4
TCU	6.7	11.3	4.6	33.0	34.5	1.5
MBS	11.4	15.8	4.4	29.7	32.3	2.6
MCS	22.1	31.4	9.3	20.9	26.5	5.6
Retail	24.3	36.0	11.7	22.8	29.5	6.7
Total	13.4	17.9	4.5	21.9	26.3	4.4
Suburb						
Industry						
Construction	13.2	16.7	3.5	b	b	b
Manufacturing	12.3	16.9	4.6	18.5	20.2	1.7
TCU	b	17.1	b	32.3	b	b
MBS	15.3	16.5	1.2	27.1	27.1	0.0
MCS	29.3	41.8	12.5	21.9	29.9	8.0
Retail	32.0	44.7	12.7	24.3	33.6	9.3
Total	16.8	22.8	6.0	21.9	26.7	4.8

[a] Covered employment at place of work. All data for shares are modified averages. (Highest and lowest values excluded in averaging). Based on covered employment at place of work.
[b] Sample in some places too small to permit computation.

Source: Tabulations from *Social Security Administration, Continuous Work History Files.*

both cities and suburbs, but there is variation among industry classes. Consumer services showed the largest percentages of young male workers in both cities and suburbs.

In general, the shares of employment accounted for by women under twenty-five are quite high, significantly higher than for men. This, of course, reflects the tendency for women to leave the labor force following their early years of work. Moreover, percentages of workers less than twenty-five vary less among industrial categories for women than for men, suggesting that young women performing clerical tasks play an important role in all industries. It is in the consumer services, however, that percentage of employment is highest and has risen the most—from 21 to 27 percent in the cities and from 22 to 30 percent in the suburbs.

In interpreting these data for both males and females, it must be kept in mind that in the decade of the sixties the rising generation of workers entering employment was accommodated in suburbs to an important extent by absorption into a rapidly building consumer-services-sector, which depended for its growth in part on the one-time-only fillip of import substitution. The large number of young people in this sector at the end of the decade raises questions as to how and when the needed upgrading will occur in the years ahead. Such upgrading is required to offer young people in this industry, as well as in others, jobs of sufficient responsibility and challenge as they develop, and at the same time to make possible the assimilation of a continuing inflow of new workers. This level of adjustment will require substantial growth in some or all of the other sectors: manufacturing, construction, TCU, business services, and the public services.

It must be recalled that in cities, where employment grew more slowly (or declined), entry rates were generally lower than in suburbs, although female entry rates were much higher than those for males. The more rapid rise in demand for young women than for young men has been due to the rapid growth of the business-services sector, the increase in office activity generally, and the rise in importance of health and education services. In all these activities there is a relatively heavy demand for female labor, much of it white-collar clerical.

Thus a serious question is raised regarding the outlook for adequate functioning of city labor markets in the years ahead. If, in the recent past cities (at least those growing slowly or declining) have not been absorbing the emerging male labor force, on what grounds may we expect a more satisfactory performance in the years that lie immediately ahead? Moreover, if life styles and values change in such a way as to cause young women to demand the right to stay in the labor force during their entire adult life, can the labor market of specific cities and suburbs take up such a supply? Will not the problem become even more critical?

SUMMARY

The preceding analysis results in a number of findings, the most important of which are: (1) that flows into and out of the labor force are very large, and that the labor market will accommodate a substantial number of new entrants annually, even under no-growth conditions; (2) that new entrants' rates are quite elastic to increasing rates of growth. Incremental responses of new entrants to overall employment growth did not decline, even under very high-growth conditions in suburbs during the 1965-70 period; (3) that cities draw more heavily upon national and regional labor markets than do suburbs; (4) that new entrants have flowed much more heavily into some industrial classifications, especially consumer services, than others, resulting in disproportionately large numbers of young workers in these classifications.

Upward mobility may emerge as a future problem created by the rapid growth of the recent past. If the relatively large number of young men and women in certain classifications are not to become stymied in boys' and girls' jobs, there must be an appropriate pacing of future development. It is not at all clear that sufficient growth lies ahead to take up the emerging young labor force and to offer needed upward mobility for the young people already within the labor force.

REFERENCES

1. The entire analysis in this chapter is based on Social Security data in which cities and suburbs are defined on a county basis. See Appendix A.

2. This does not mean that males do not change employment or drop out for short periods but rather that, measured in terms of periods as long as the five-year spans examined here, the employment is generally continuous.

3. The data, of course, relate to place of work—not place of residence.

4. Beginning earnings are used in every case except for new entrants. Since this group has no beginning earnings, end-of-period earnings are used. To permit comparisons, all earnings are expressed as a percentage of beginning-of-period average SMSA earnings (all sex-age categories), with the exception of earnings of new entrants, which are expressed as a percentage of end-of-period average SMSA earnings.

5. Results of the regression analysis are presented in Appendix G, where correlation, regression coefficients, standard errors of coefficients, and estimates of entry rates under zero-growth conditions are shown. All estimates presented in this section are shown in this appendix table.

[7

The Unskilled Worker
in Cities and Suburbs

City and suburban economies vary in terms of the problems which face the unskilled worker, a category which includes many disadvantaged workers—the old, the young, and the ghetto dweller. The central thesis of this chapter is that problems facing the low-wage worker in the city and in the suburbs arise, in the main, from different causes. In the city the low-income worker faces difficulties in getting and holding employment because of structural changes in the city's economy. Upgrading, job erosion, and suburban shift have resulted in changes in the type of labor demanded, changes which have sometimes occurred under conditions of low growth or declines in overall employment. In the suburbs, which have been favored by rapid rates of growth, shifts in relative importance of types of labor have been less marked, and increased employment in all categories have more than taken up any slack created by declining sectors. Here the problem lies, rather, in the failure of the labor market to provide access for workers from low-income households, due to difficulties of job search and lack of communication.

The discussion which follows falls into four parts. The first examines the problems facing the unskilled inner-city resident, particularly the ghetto dweller, in finding employment in the city. The second examines problems facing unskilled workers from low-income households, residing in either city or suburbs, in obtaining and holding suburban jobs. The third examines the "mismatch controversy,"which concerns the availability of jobs for city minority workers, i.e., whether or not suitable jobs exist in the city.

Finally, the fourth assesses the minority experience—the extent to which blacks have been able to gain employment and improve incomes in cities and suburbs.

PROBLEMS OF THE UNSKILLED WORKER
IN THE CITY LABOR MARKET

As documented earlier (Chapter 4), most job increases in cities are in white-collar occupations; a majority of these job additions are filled by women. Most decreases are in occupations usually filled by men. Patterns of job change in the suburbs are different. White-collar employment is also the largest source of job increases, and there are relatively large gains by women; but blue-collar and service occupations play a more important role. Moreover, suburbs are growing rapidly so that there is typically at least some growth in every type of employment.

This contrast between employment changes in cities and suburbs serves to put into focus the problems faced by the unskilled worker, particularly the ghetto resident. In the city, changes extending back over more than a decade have not favored work establishment of ghetto workers or of any workers without the skills or social orientation for white-collar jobs. Moreover, they have worked a special hardship on the ghetto male, for he suffers the double disadvantage of being black and male. As a black, he is generally regarded by employers and educators as a candidate for only blue-collar or service-maintenance type employment; as a male, he is frequently ineligible for clerical employment.

This does not mean, of course, that there are no job opportunities, for, as we have learned, there are sizable flows within the labor market even where no growth occurs. Nor does it deny, as evidenced in a subsequent section, that blacks have made significant gains in a number of places. Yet the point stands: the ghetto worker is disadvantaged to the extent that the unskilled labor supply is expanding while suitable employment is declining.

Evidence supporting this point was presented earlier (see Table 5.4). In cities shares of black male jobs were disproportionately large in the declining or slow-growth blue-collar and service-worker occupations, disproportionately small in expanding white-collar classifications. The single exception was clerical jobs, which accounted for a slightly larger share of black male employment than of total male employment. Within this classification, males are found principally in the detailed classifications of mail carriers, postal clerks, shipping clerks, and stock clerks, jobs which have long been available to black men.

There is still another factor which operates to limit access of minorities to the job markets of cities: competition from commuters. In Chapter 5 it was noted that commuters provide a substantial percentage of the city's work force (an average 43.1 percent for males and 32.1 percent for females in 1970). Table 5.9 indicates that commuting is most important in white-collar employment, the category most favored by recent growth trends. Moreover, the percentage of city employment comprised by commuters has increased sharply in all occupations.

Increased commutation means that, within the city, ghetto residents face competition from suburbanites for entry-level employment. When the city applicant does not meet fully the desired qualifications for the job (e.g., being able to work easily with suburban-type professionals and technicians), the employer need not make adjustments to accommodate the job to the worker or to provide necessary training. An acceptable alternative is ready at hand in the commuter—by tapping the suburban labor market. Such competition is most important (i.e., commuter percentages are largest) in those occupations where employment trends are most favorable—the white-collar jobs. It is least important in the less desirable blue-collar and service-maintenance jobs. The conclusion that commuters compete with local residents for employment is inescapable.[1]

Part of this competitive edge of commuters, especially the young commuters, reflects the fact that priorities of the boards of education and manpower agencies in the suburbs are more likely to reflect contemporary manpower needs than are those of the more entrenched bureaucracies in the larger and older central cities. In fact, few cities have even surveyed employment opportunities for low-wage workers in expanding white-collar occupations—an essential first step in the establishment of meaningful priorities.[2]

PROBLEMS OF THE UNSKILLED WORKER IN THE SUBURBAN LABOR MARKET

THE MINORITY CITY WORKER IN THE SUBURBAN LABOR MARKET

While the unskilled city resident has experienced difficulty in gaining access to employment in the city, he also has not found ready employment in the rapidly expanding suburbs. Many suburban labor markets are new and they pose special problems for the job-seeker residing in the city. Under conditions of rapid growth when new work forces are being assembled, a wide variation in wage rates and poor access to job information are to be expected. With time these markets will mature, information flows will improve, and the labor market will function more efficiently. Nevertheless, employment patterns will tend to be perpetuated and will continue to pose problems to the outsider.

David Gayer, in a detailed study of two New York suburban industrial parks (Lake Success in Nassau County and Deer Park in Suffolk County), has provided a number of valuable insights into the nature of suburban labor markets.[3] His major thesis is: ". . . housing, transportation, and worker characteristics are not as great an impediment to the acquisition of low-skill jobs as are the defects of the market itself."[4]

The following are the more important findings of Gayer's study:

1. Poor workers have low mobility as regards the area of job search. Among workers earning above $10,000, less than a third had found employment within a half hour's commuting from their homes. For those earning less than $5,000, however, the share was well over four-fifths.

2. A major factor restricting job search among low- and middle-income workers, especially blue-collar workers, was the employers' practice of recruiting principally by word-of-mouth. Consequently, unless a firm was already well staffed with blacks or other minorities, there was virtually no opportunity for members of these minorities to learn of job openings.

3. Wide variations in wages for similar jobs existed among employers. These variations, coupled with variations in fringe benefits (of which the job-seeker is generally ignorant), make the search for work a haphazard and uncertain affair. The ghetto resident cannot determine with certainty whether or not worthwhile jobs are available in the suburbs, and, should he decide to search, whether or not he is being offered favorable employment.

4. To these difficulties must be added the heavy cost of job search in the spatially dispersed suburban economy. The city ghetto worker who seeks employment in the suburbs faces heavy transportation costs and subsequent time losses. In the suburbs, low density of employment, lack of public transportation, and wide dispersion of manufacturing complexes (often on newly created streets) make the job search at once an expensive, formidable, and uncertain undertaking. This contrasts sharply to the job market of cities such as New York, where workers are able to search in relatively concentrated areas such as the garment district of mid-Manhattan, the industrial core of downtown Brooklyn, or the market area of Hunts Point, the Bronx.

On the other hand, if the worker is successful in obtaining a job, the pay differential between suburban manufacturing and employment in the city may be substantially above commuting costs. There was evidence that, for a large number of city ghetto job-seekers, transportation costs alone were not necessarily a barrier to accepting suburban employment.[5]

The Gayer study is not the only research related to the problems facing the low-income city resident seeking work in the suburbs. John Kain, in a study of Chicago and Detroit, provided evidence that substantial numbers of blacks are unable to gain suburban employment because of residential segregation.[6] Schultz and Rees have shown a clear relationship between earnings and length of journey to work. This latter finding strongly implies that the low-wage city worker is unlikely to be employed at any considerable distance from his place of residence.[7]

THE UNSKILLED SUBURBAN WORKER IN THE SUBURBAN LABOR MARKET

The previous section has dealt principally with the difficulties facing the city ghetto worker in finding employment in the suburbs. These problems are not restricted to the unskilled worker of the city, however. They may be generalized to include the unskilled workers of all races who reside in the suburbs. If reliance on word-of-mouth recruitment tends to break down communications between employers and job-seekers, then dwellers of the suburbs, like those of the city ghetto, will experience difficulty in learning of employment options (though perhaps to a lesser extent). If there is uncertainty as to what terms of employment are being offered and where job vacancies are located, the suburban worker will encounter difficulties in finding the best employment available. Finally, if there are high costs and special problems related to the job search in suburban labor markets, these difficulties will apply to many unskilled residents of the suburbs as well as to those of the city.

There are two additional factors which make the suburban labor market generally dysfunctional in meeting the needs of the unskilled worker.[8]

First, unskilled workers often depend on second jobs to supplement household income. Such employment involves additional job searching and commuting, and the time for each must be found after regular working hours. If job search in the suburbs is difficult for primary employment, it is even more difficult for secondary employment. In an economy in which firms are loosely scattered over broad areas, the likelihood that a second job can be found in proximity to the first job is poor. Commutation to two jobs located in widely different areas becomes a difficult if not impossible assignment. Thus the spatial organization of the suburban economy tends to make it difficult for the worker to command more than one source of income.

Second, spatial diffusion poses problems for families that need a second or third earner to supplement their income. Since public transportation is poor or non-existent, a second car may often be necessary if an additional member of the family is to enter the labor market. Given the low wages and reduced hours which typify secondary employment, especially in the service sectors, the purchase of an additional automobile is not economical in low-income familes.

It was noted earlier (Chapter 4) that in the suburbs there are few low-income tracts but a large number of low-income jobs. The suggestion was offered that these workers were largely second or third workers in middle-income families.[9] Such workers in a sense stand in competition with unskilled primary earners. The wives and children of well-paid executives, professionals or tradesmen are likely to have access to private auto transporation and to labor-market information through relatives and friends. Moreover, they are in a better position to tolerate irregular hours and low pay, since the family as a unit enjoys a higher level of income. It is small wonder that relatively few of the poor, especially minority workers residing in the inner city, have been successfully absorbed into the suburban economy.

THE MISMATCH CONTROVERSY

In recent years an important controversy has raged regarding the cause of high levels of unemployment among blacks and other minorities who inhabit the ghettos of the city. On one hand, it has been argued that because employment growth (viewed mainly as increases in blue-collar jobs) has taken place largely in the suburbs, high unemployment of minority city residents is due largely to their lack of access to suburban labor markets. The result is said to be a surplus of jobs in the suburbs and an excess of workers in the city: a mismatch of demand and supply. Others observe, however, that the ratio of jobs to residents of working age is far higher in cities than in suburbs, and that this ratio is increasing. The problem is, therefore, not one of lack of potential employment, but one of racial barriers.[10]

Interesting research reflecting the latter point of view has been conducted by Charlotte Fremon.[11] In an analysis of eight metropolitan areas (six of which were among those which we have examined), Fremon found that the share of employment increases accounted for by high-skilled jobs was slightly, but not importantly, higher in cities than in suburbs. This finding is combined with two observations to draw a major conclusion regarding the problems facing minority workers in the city. First, job-to-labor-force ratios are higher in cities than in suburbs. Second, the proportion of additional jobs taken by women (from 1965 -1967) was approximately proportional to the number of women in the work force in the middle year of this period (1966). The major conclusion is:

> The urban employment problem, the fact that central-city and suburban residents experience very different unemployment rates and income levels, cannot, then, be explained by purely structural arguments. The jobs are there, and are growing, and are not skewed dramatically in favor of high-skilled or female applicants. The problem is clearly more subtle. For one thing, it is largely racial. Unemployment rates are much higher for central city than for suburban residents, but they are not higher for white central-city residents than for white suburban residents. In fact, in 1968, nonwhites living in the suburbs had higher unemployment rates than nonwhites living in central cities. That fact alone requires a good deal of explaining. In the same vein, all of the increases in jobs in central cities is being absorbed by suburban commuters, at a time when job opportunities are

expanding rapidly in the suburbs. This means that central city employers face some competition in recruiting suburban labor in all categories. The amount extra they are willing to pay, therefore, to induce suburban residents to commute to the central city, is a certain measure, then of the extent to which employers prefer a (white) suburban work force to a (black) central city work force.[12]

The fact that jobs in central cities are being absorbed by suburban commuters is unassailable, but the thrust of the findings presented in earlier chapters is at variance with Fremon's. Her analysis of change in skill requirements and sex characteristics is based on special estimating procedures and requires explanation.[13] All covered employment (i.e., nine EEOC occupations) was classified within three major categories: high-skilled, semiskilled, and low-skilled. (There was also a category, government, for which information on skill is not available.) The high-skilled category includes officials and managers, professionals and technical workers; the semiskilled category, sales workers, office and clerical workers, craftsmen and operatives; the low-skilled, laborers and service workers. On the basis of this classification scheme, employment change is examined in terms of skill level for both cities and suburbs. Unfortunately, no differentiation is made between jobs traditionally filled by males and those traditionally filled by females. Hence the tendency for growth in female jobs to offset declines in male employment is overlooked.

The data presented in this study differentiate white-collar, blue-collar, and service employees of each city rather than treat all jobs at a given skill-level as one group. This evidence indicates important obstacles to minority employment arising out of changes in occupational distributions. There is no reason to expect that individuals who move readily into unskilled or semiskilled blue-collar employment can qualify for white-collar employment of the same skill-level (an assumption which is implicit in Fremon's analysis). This is especially true for minority males seeking clerical jobs, where the female labeling of the job becomes, itself, a barrier to employment. Moreover, Fremon's estimates of the importance of female employment are shown to be incorrect by subsequently published census materials. These materials show women's shares of job *increases* to be far higher than women's *average* proportion of city employment. For the ten cities studied, the average share of job increases (1960-70) accounted for by females was 67 percent (Table 4.2), whereas the average share of employment (1960) was only 34.0 percent.[14]

The evidence presented in the preceding two sections does not, strictly speaking, support or contradict the mismatch hypothesis as it has usually been set forth. But it does show that the unskilled minority worker faces structural problems as well as discrimination in gaining admission to the jobs in both the city and the suburb. In the city such a worker, unlike his predecessors in the earlier generations of immigrants, does not find the entry-level employment for which he is best qualified—that of laborer, operative, or even service worker—to be in high demand.

It seems unlikely that the problem of adequate employment opportunities for minorities can be solved by concentrating all efforts on opening up the suburbs through low-income housing, on cheap mass-transit for reverse commuting, or on policies for creating jobs in the city. As the following section will show, minority workers are becoming established in both city and suburban labor markets, but the gap is far from being closed. What is needed is a concerted effort to assimilate workers whom informal labor markets do not serve, to press for greater equality in hiring practices, and to inaugurate programs within the public educational system which prepare minority young people for employment in those sectors which are growing.

Also needed, but within a longer time frame, is the upgrading of inner-city neighborhoods to stem the out-migration of upwardly mobile households and the local-sector jobs which are associated with them. Ultimately, cities may be able to attract a number of medium- and high-income workers back into the city, putting additional employment within reach of low-skilled city residents as the local sector is rebuilt.

THE MINORITY EXPERIENCE[15]

Despite serious obstacles, blacks have achieved employment gains in city and suburban labor markets, and have increasingly found opportunities in more responsible jobs. In eight out of ten cities, and in half the suburbs, the share of black employment increased during the decade of the sixties, though often the increases were small:

	Cities		Suburbs	
	Change in share 1960–1970	Share 1970 %	Change in Share 1960–1970	Share 1970 %
Atlanta	+1.7	21.1	−3.6	14.0
Baltimore	+4.8	25.9	− .9	14.0
Boston	+3.3	7.2	+ .3	2.0
Cleveland	+1.8	14.4	+2.1	4.0
Denver	+ .6	4.3	.0	2.0
Houston	−1.2[a]	15.6	−2.7	12.6
New Orleans	−1.9	26.0	+3.7	25.5
New York	+3.5	15.7	+2.0	9.8
Philadelphia	+4.6	20.6	− .4	9.4
St. Louis	+4.9	16.5	+1.0	10.1

[a] Represents actual decline in employment.

MINORITY EMPLOYMENT EXPERIENCE IN CITIES

The rates of employment change for black males were greater than for whites in six out of ten cities (Table 7.1). In four of these cities (Baltimore, New York, Philadelphia, and St. Louis), there were substantial increases even though white male employment was declining. In only three places was the black male employment-increase less than 20 percent.

The greatest gains by black males were in the manufacturing sector, where total employment showed small increases or even declines. Not only was this the most important source of new jobs for blacks, but it was the most important in a relative sense (i.e., black male gains relative to white male gains were largest). In the six cities in which white male employment declined in manufacturing, black male employment increased in five and remained constant in one.

	Change in Manufacturing Employment	
	White Males	Black Males
Baltimore	−3,100	+6,100
Boston	−3,200	+2,200
Cleveland	−3,600	+6,500
New York	−88,600	0
Philadelphia	−59,100	+1,300
St. Louis	−17,100	+7,300

In other sectors, black males did not fare as well. In the slow-growing consumer services, changes were small relative to whites, except in New York and Boston. In New York black males gained 13.6 thousand consumer-service jobs, compared to only 3.5 thousand for white males. In Boston black male employment increased by 1.5 thousand at the same time that there was a net loss of 2.6 thousand white male jobs.

In general, black males also fared poorly in construction, but somewhat better in the relatively small TCU sector. In the important business-services sector, the experience was mixed. In New York, Philadelphia, Baltimore, Boston, Atlanta, and St. Louis, gains were substantial, while in the remainder of the ten cities, experience was relatively poor:

	Change in MBS Employment 1960–1970	
	White Males	Black Males
Atlanta	219,000	45,000
Baltimore	28,000	20,000
Boston	91,000	21,000
Cleveland	246,000	28,000
Denver	105,000	−1,000
Houston	403,000	55,000
New Orleans	26,000	−7,000
New York	549,000	339,000
Philadelphia	66,000	56,000
St. Louis	3,000	12,000

Black females fared better than black males in cities. Rates of change in total employment were higher in every comparison (Table 7.1). Black women's gains compare favorably to those of white women. In every city, rates of growth were higher, with gains occurring in Baltimore, Philadelphia, and St. Louis under conditions of declining white female employment.

Gains in employment of black women (relative to whites) tended to be greatest in manufacturing and consumer services, and in most places were substantial in transportation, communications, utilities, and in business-services as well. Measured in numbers of jobs, the gains were typically largest in consumer services and second largest in business services.

To sum up, blacks in the city made considerable gains in employment, though not necessarily in growing sectors (nor, as we know from earlier analysis, in the best jobs). In general, black females fared better than black males. However, these gains were made from relatively small bases so that black employment was in no instance more than 26 percent of total employment in 1970 and in six of the ten cities was less than 17 percent.

MINORITY EMPLOYMENT IN SUBURBS[16]

In suburbs the growth of black employment relative to the growth of white employment has not been so favorable as in the cities (Table 7.1). In cities, employment growth-rates for black males were higher than for white males in seven out of the ten comparisons, and rates for black females higher than for white females in every comparison. In suburbs, male growth-rates were higher than for whites in only five comparisons; among females, higher in seven.

MINORITY-EARNINGS EXPERIENCE

Evidence regarding the minority experience may also be found in black-white comparisons for average earnings in 1970 (Table 7.2) and changes in average earnings, 1960-1970 (see Table 4.4).

The following observations can be made for cities:

1. Earnings of both black males and black females have shown more rapid rates of increase than have earnings of their white counterparts. Earnings have risen more rapidly for black females than for black males.

2. Earnings of black males are much lower relative to whites (ranging from ratios of .49 to .65) than are earnings of black females relative to whites (ranging from ratios of .68 to .96). It should be kept in mind, however, that earnings of white women were also low, typically no more than half the levels of white men.

The data indicate similar trends for the suburbs. Earnings of blacks

Table 7.1. Employment Changes by Sex and Race, Ten Metropolitan Areas, 1960–1970[a]

	Rates of Net Change (%)				Net Change in Jobs (000's)				Job Change, Blacks, as Percentage of Job Changes, Whites[b]							
	Cities		Suburbs		Cities		Suburbs		Cities						Suburbs
	White	Black	White	Black	White	Black	White	Black	Constr.	TCU	MFG	MBS	MCS	Total	Total
Male															
Atlanta	40.0	31.2	133.4	57.9	57.6	11.9	38.7	4.4	15.8	12.6	43.2	20.5	14.3	20.7	11.4
Baltimore	-2.3	14.4	33.7	18.7	-4.0	7.2	32.6	3.6	e	30.3	e	71.4	46.9f	e	11.0
Boston	3.6	83.5	22.7	69.5	8.8	7.1	81.7	4.1	12.3	e	e	23.1	e	80.7	5.0
Cleveland	11.9	23.6	49.3	366.7	43.2	12.6	10.2	1.1	1.4	e	e	11.4	12.3	29.2	10.8
Denver	28.2	20.0	83.1	90.9	33.7	1.0	34.5	1.0	g	e	9.9	g	7.9	3.0	2.9
Houston	65.1	39.8	67.3	37.0	141.4	18.8	11.3	1.0	10.4	19.5	28.8	13.6	1.7	13.3	8.8
New Orleans	25.9	-3.9	59.3	134.4	22.7	-1.5	15.9	8.6	c	e	16.7	g	g	g	54.1
New York	-1.4	31.4	35.0	60.6	-24.9	71.3	118.3	18.8	d	107.8	d	61.7	388.6	e	15.9
Philadelphia	-9.6	14.3	31.0	11.6	-39.8	10.7	96.5	4.4	38.0	44.6	e	84.8	g	e	4.6
St. Louis	-9.3	25.3	36.8	35.8	-20.8	7.3	53.1	5.7	31.9f	333.3	e	e	81.8f	e	10.7
Female															
Atlanta	39.2	114.4	183.6	276.9	30.6	17.5	23.5	3.6	c	20.0	216.7	31.5	85.6	57.2	15.3
Baltimore	-1.0	56.2	83.7	127.8	-1.0	13.6	27.8	4.6	c	525.0	e	40.6	518.2	e	16.5
Boston	12.8	122.8	31.8	17.1	19.7	9.7	69.2	0.7	33.3	32.3	e	16.8	88.7	49.2	1.0
Cleveland	21.4	57.3	68.9	133.3	34.4	13.0	8.6	0.4	11.1	e	1050.0	32.7	19.4	37.8	4.9
Denver	37.1	140.0	164.5	200.0	23.9	2.8	27.3	0.4	d	5.0	46.7	6.9	11.3	11.7	1.5
Houston	77.8	100.0	95.8	41.7	71.2	15.3	4.6	0.5	c	36.7	30.3	13.7	26.6	21.5	10.9
New Orleans	26.3	65.2	122.1	40.6	12.3	9.0	9.4	1.3	c	44.4	27.3	26.7	256.0	73.2	13.8
New York	8.6	45.3	59.3	142.5	86.3	71.5	106.0	18.1	38.5	117.8	68.7f	97.1	52.9	82.9	17.1
Philadelphia	-2.8	44.2	63.1	115.9	-6.6	21.6	84.8	12.4	e	e	e	66.0	81.5	e	14.6
St. Louis	-10.9	53.0	97.7	214.0	-13.2	8.8	56.4	9.2	25.0	e	e	e	e	e	16.3

a Covered employment at place of work.
b Changes in numbers of blacks employed as a percentage of changes in number of whites (1960–1970).
c Change in black employment is zero; change in white employment is positive.
d Change in black employment is zero; change in white employment is negative.
e Change in black employment is positive; change in white employment is negative.
f Change in black employment is negative; change in white employment is negative.
g Change in black employment is negative; change in white employment is positive.

Source: Tabulations from Social Security Administration, Continuous Work History Files.

174

Table 7.2. Comparisons of Average Earnings between Race and Sex, Ten Metropolitan Areas, 1970[a]

	Atlanta	Baltimore	Boston	Cleveland	Denver	Houston	New Orleans	New York	Philadelphia	St. Louis
City										
Males										
Ratio: Black/White	0.49	0.63	0.57	0.65	0.61	0.57	0.52	0.58	0.61	0.61
Females										
Ratio: Black/White	0.73	0.96	0.78	0.88	0.89	0.71	0.68	0.86	0.89	0.93
Ratio: Female/Male										
White	51.4	50.0	48.6	43.8	50.3	47.4	49.8	52.0	49.2	49.5
Black	76.5	76.4	66.4	59.8	73.8	58.5	64.4	76.9	72.0	75.2
Suburb										
Males										
Ratio: Black/White	0.63	0.69	0.67	0.82	0.77	0.58	0.61	0.64	0.67	0.65
Females										
Ratio: Black/White	0.74	0.93	0.97	0.81	1.06	0.92	0.70	0.91	0.86	1.02
Ratio: Female/Male										
White	52.7	54.7	45.9	48.8	46.2	41.3	41.1	50.6	48.4	44.5
Black	61.9	74.0	66.8	48.3	63.9	65.7	47.6	71.9	62.1	69.5
Ratio: Suburb/City										
Males										
White	91.0	98.4	89.9	81.8	88.1	82.6	94.0	91.5	93.3	86.4
Black	117.4	108.7	105.8	104.3	111.8	83.0	108.8	101.0	102.9	92.6
Females										
White	93.3	107.6	84.9	91.1	80.9	72.1	77.5	89.0	91.8	77.8
Black	95.0	105.3	106.5	84.2	96.8	93.2	80.5	94.4	88.7	85.6

[a] Covered employment at place of work.

Source: Tabulations from Social Security Administration, Continuous Work History Files.

(male and female) have tended to rise faster than those of whites; earnings of females faster than those of males. Once again, the ratio of black-to-white earnings is much higher for women than for men.

Relative to the earnings of white workers, black workers fare better in suburbs than in cities. For males, the ratio of black-to-white average income is higher in suburbs than in cities in nine out of ten metropolitan areas (the exception is Houston, where there is no significant difference), and for females in six out of ten suburbs. This reflects, presumably, the lower wage-scales of white workers in the suburbs, as well as the fact that employed blacks, in particular black males, tend to do better in suburbs than in cities in finding well-paying blue-collar jobs but experience difficulty in entering the consumer-services sector (see Chapter 5).

Finally, it must be kept in mind that, although most job increases take place in the suburbs, wage levels are generally higher in the city (except in manufacturing.) Moreover, blacks account for only a small share of job increases in the suburbs and, on average, over half of black workers in the suburbs (typically the better paid ones) are commuters (Table 5.8).

SUMMARY

The central thesis of this chapter is that city and suburban economies vary in terms of the kinds of problems which face the unskilled worker in a low-income household. In the city he faces problems which are due largely to difficulties in getting and holding employment in a market in which growth is slow and employment shifts favor white-collar workers. Further, except in the declining or slow-growing sectors, he faces serious competition from suburban commuters. In suburbs the problem lies in the failure of the labor markets to function properly in respect to information, complicated by scattered work sites, and, more than in the city, the advantageous position of second and third wage earners in middle- and upper-income households in competing for secondary employment.

In spite of these difficulties, blacks made significant inroads into the work force of both cities and suburbs during the sixties. In cities black male employment increases in covered employment have been greatest in manufacturing, a declining sector.[17] Black female employment gains were better than those for black males in cities in terms of numbers of jobs and were more widely dispersed among industrial sectors.

Employment experience was less favorable in suburbs for both black males and black females. Measured in terms of rate of increase in earnings, the black experience has been favorable, but such increases were made from low base levels, and 1970 average earnings remained low.

Although we have not inquired in depth into the difficulties minority and other low-income workers face, we would attribute under-employment of city residents to the fragmentation of the metropolis and the drawing off of employment opportunities arising out of: (1) the upgrading of the city's export sector; (2) the increased utilization of females; (3) the erosion of blue-collar jobs in the city; (4) the suburban shift of local-sector service jobs; and (5) the imperfections of the suburban labor market.

A more complete understanding of how the labor market functions will undoubtedly result in a re-evaluation of solutions now being proposed or implemented. Low-cost transit and scattered-site low-income housing in the suburbs do not appear to offer more than partial solutions to the problem which must ultimately be dealt with in the context of regional developmental processes and over a considerable span of time. If the city is revitalized, some low-wage jobs will follow middle- and high-income residents back into the city. The prospects for such an eventuality are explored in the concluding chapter.

REFERENCES

1. It is, of course, quite possible that the availability of talented executives and professionals residing in the suburbs and elsewhere encourages growth and development of the city's economy and thereby opens up jobs for all. In this sense, commuters contribute as well as compete.

2. For an example of such services see: *Clerical Jobs in the Financial Industry in New York City* (New York: City Planning Commission, July, 1972); and *Employment Opportunities in Central Minneapolis* (Minneapolis: Minneapolis Planning and Development, March 1970).

3. David Gayer. *The Suburban Labor Market—Jobs for the Low Skilled*. Unpublished Ph.D. dissertation, New York University, 1970.

4. *Ibid.*, p. 5.

5. Other research has indicated that for low-wage workers commuting costs are a sizable obstacle. A survey conducted by the California State Business and Transportation Agency found commuting costs of suburban jobs accounted for as much as a third of daily earnings for jobs paying $2 or less per hour. Cited by Bennett Harrison, *Urban Economic Development: Suburbanization, Minority Opportunity, and the Condition of the Central City* (Washington, D.C.: The Urban Institute, 1974). p. 87.

6. John F. Kain, "Housing Segregation, Negro Employment, and Metropolitan Decentralization," *Quarterly Journal of Economics*, May, 1968.

7. George Schultz and Albert Rees, *op. cit.*

8. Gayer, *op. cit.*, pp. 133-137.

9. Evidence of the importance of second and third wage earners in suburban white families is presented by Harrison for 1965, showing that, although importance of male family head to family incomes increases from city to suburb, it amounted to only 53 percent in suburban sample areas, on an average (in contrast to 46 percent in central-city. poverty areas and 50 percent in other city areas). Thus, almost half of average suburban white-family incomes was accounted for by secondary employees. The study showed, in addition, that contributions of male family heads were somewhat smaller in non-white suburban families in both relative and actual terms. Bennett Harrison, *Education, Train-*

ing, and the Urban Ghetto (Baltimore: Johns Hopkins University Press, 1972), p. 108.

10. For an excellent review of the literature relating to this controversy, see Bennett Harrison, *Urban Economic Development . . . , op. cit.,* Chapter 3.

11. Charlotte Fremon, *The Occupational Patterns in Urban Employment Change, 1965-1967* (Washington, D.C.: The Urban Institute, August 1970).

12. Fremon, *op. cit.,* p. 29. Note that Fremon's findings regarding unemployment rates in cities and suburbs in 1968 differ from ours for 1970 (Table 5.1). The differences, presumably, reflect the differences in date of observation and the group of cities observed.

13. In preparing estimates of employment (at place of work), Fremon makes principal use of *County Business Patterns* data, augmented by data from other sources, estimating occupational composition from information provided by OEEC materials. Job-to-labor-force ratios were computed for five cities (New York, Philadelphia, St. Louis, Washington, and Baltimore) for 1959 and 1967. In investigating change-in-skill level and sex distribution of city work forces, she examines data for eight cities (the five named above, plus San Francisco, Denver, and New Orleans) for the years 1965 and 1967. Our data source for job-to-labor force and occupational analysis, however, was the 1960 and 1970 *Census of Population* (the latter census was not available for the Fremon study) for ten cities and suburbs, some of which are the same. Accordingly, there are possibilities for differences in findings, due to differences in time, data sources, and, to a small extent, places observed.

14. This average percentage of female employment was computed from *Census of Population* data and differs from the average (36.7 percent) computed from *Social Security* data for covered workers.

15. The data examined in this section are based on covered employment at place of work (Source: *Social Security* data). City and suburb definitions are based on county data. See note 2, Introduction, and Appendix A.

16. Analysis of suburban minority employment-experience is limited to examination of sex-race aggregates since sample size is inadequate for reliable measurement of employment change in terms of sex-race categories at the industry level.

17. The tendency for minority groups to make both relative and absolute employment gains in industries experiencing slow growth or moderate decline has been demonstrated by Hiestand in a study of the American economy covering the period 1890 to 1960. Dale L. Hiestand, *Economic Growth and Employment Opportunities for Minorities,* (New York, N.Y.: Columbia University Press, 1964), pp. 75-77.

[8

Metropolis
at the Crossroads

Proposals for development of the city and its suburbs should be considered in the context of the total metropolitan economy. Most proposals which are advanced are deficient because the recommended solutions are limited to political or administrative issues, limited in terms of the time frame in which they are operative, or limited in terms of their regional impact. Their true significance can be assessed only when linkage among the various parts of the metropolitan system have been made explicit and when implications for economic development have been examined.

Four general findings provide such a perspective.

First, central cities are in the midst of a transition toward greater specialization as service economies, a transition which has been associated with a continued commitment to the CBD as a work place. The importance of these changes and the promise they hold for future vitality vary from place to place, but the evidence examined indicates that such transition is significant everywhere.

Secondly, there has been a "sorting out" of functions within the metropolis in which the suburbs have picked up manufacturing, some back-office and wholesaling-distributing activities, and local-sector activities associated with their residential role.

Third, unlike cities, suburbs are widely viewed as a desirable place to live. For a majority, they offer a life style more attractive than that offered by the city. They have also been more able to adapt to a complex variety of economic functions through new institutions. Regardless of what new problems may lie ahead, the viability of suburban economies seems established. What is at issue is the extent to which developments in the years to come will continue to favor the suburbs or will tend to bring about a revitalization of central cities as a place of residence.

Finally, the suburbs are related to the city in a vital symbiosis. Far from being independent, suburbs draw lifeblood from the cities. Not only does a large share of suburban income originate in the city's economy, but suburban firms and residents depend upon the city for a variety of services, both business and consumer, and upon the city's great markets. At the same time, the city draws upon the suburbs for much of its professional, technical, and executive talent.

The corollary to this conclusion is that weakness in either suburb or city will ultimately weaken the entire metropolis. Modern cities and suburbs carry out their economic roles within a dynamic and competitive national system of metropolitan economies. With many of the older production-oriented export functions becoming increasingly footloose, and with new firms, new industries, and new technologies continuously coming on stage, metropolitan economies must remain attractive and competitive if they are to retain or improve their positions. The penalties for failing to do so are the loss of income and employment to other metropolitan areas here and abroad.

In such an environment, cities and their suburbs must increasingly find common cause, striving to complement each other rather than seeking solutions in terms of narrow and short-range interests. Deterioration in the quality of the city's business services and medical, educational, and civic facilities tends to be reflected in the profit and income levels of both suburban and city firms and residents. At the same time, a failure of suburban institutions and housing markets, or the loss of the suburb's attractiveness as a place to live, reduces the ability of firms and institutions anywhere within the metropolis to recruit the most intelligent and talented graduates, professionals, technicians, and executives.

The physical, social, and cultural dimensions of the quality of life become more critical as the city is upgraded. With development, the comparative advantage of a metropolis, which underlies its export sector, is based increasingly upon a critical core of institutions, the effectiveness of which depends, in turn, upon the expertise that can be recruited and developed. The attractiveness of a city and its suburbs, therefore, affects the caliber of expertise available to the city, and, consequently, the effectiveness of its key institutions. Thus, the quality of life affects the competitive position of the city and its place within the metropolitan hierarchy.

CURRENT PROBLEMS OF CITIES AND SUBURBS

That most large cities are in trouble today has been widely observed. Their problem arises because of a loss of manufacturing employment, of medium-and upper-income residents, and of associated local-sector employment opportunities for workers in low-income households within the city. The loss of tax revenues has followed upon these reversals. Moreover, cities have been unable to cope successfully with the increasing incidence of poverty in their impacted ghettos, at least within an acceptable time frame, and now face major problems of dealing with inflation and budget deficits, of maintaining public services, and of providing employment for a disproportionately large cohort of young men and women entering the labor market.

What has been less evident is that suburbs also face a variety of problems. With improved access to the city and to metropolitan markets through improvement of the highway system and with rapid development, suburban real estate prices and housing costs have soared. At the same time, fiscal imbalances arising from mismatches in the distribution of taxable properties and the demand for public services among many small suburban communities have created heavy strains upon a large number of suburban taxpayers. Many suburban communities now face problems similar to those of the inner city: congestion, pollution, deteriorating public services, rising crime rates, and fiscal squeeze.

In addition, increased costs of energy, automobiles, and road maintenance, all of which must be calculated as a cost of low-density land use, act to erode suburban advantages in terms of the real wages of its residents. (Automobile costs of $2,000 per year represent $1 per hour worked).

FORCES OF CHANGE

Combined with the problems enumerated above are a number of other critical factors which, together, are moving the modern American metropolis toward a position from which new patterns of development are likely to emerge. These factors, which are to be distinguished from general forces such as structural changes in the national economy leading to increased service employment everywhere, may be grouped under seven general headings: (1) changes in demographic patterns; (2) growth of high-income households; (3) changes in life styles; (4) changes in crime rates; (5) filtering and the conservation of housing; (6) improved understanding of the costs of sprawl; (7) recognition of new approaches to designing urban settlements.

CHANGES IN DEMOGRAPHIC PATTERNS

Perhaps the most important factor is changes in the demographic composition of cities and suburbs. The changes which will unfold in the years immediately ahead stem from abnormally high birthrates during the period extending roughly from the beginning of the fifties until the late sixties, followed by a sharp drop in birthrates, which is still continuing. During this latter period, the rate dropped from an expected 3,700 births per 1,000 women at completion of childbearing age (as of 1960) to 1,950 (as of 1973).[1] These dramatic demographic developments influence the outlook for labor supply, the expected rates of family formation, the role of women in the labor force, and the types of housing that will be demanded.

Table 8.1 presents estimated changes in all age categories from 1972 to 1980 and 1972 to 1990 for the United States as a whole. The most striking disclosure is the rapidity with which the age group 25-34 years builds up: by 35 percent from 1972 to 1980, by 53 percent from 1972 to 1990. The next older group, 35-44, increases by 11 percent by 1980, but shows the largest increase of all, 62 percent, by 1990. Two additional observations are also important. The first is that there are sharp increases in the 65 years and older bracket—15 and 32 percent—and significant decreases in the 5-17 age group.

What these estimates of change reveal is that, in the years immediately ahead: (1) there will be sharp increases in the number of young people who will be forming households and will require full-time employment; (2) there will be a sharp increase in older people of retirement age; and (3) there will be a substantial decline in public-school enrollment.

These predictions require special interpretation for suburban areas. Since the suburbs were settled in the fifties and sixties largely by couples who raised larger-than-average families, these outlying areas have dis-

Table 8.1. Population Changes by Age Groups:
United States, 1972 to 1990
(Percent Change)[a]

Age Groups	1972–80	1972–90
All Ages	6.2	14.5
Under 5 years	− 2.4	3.0
5–17 years	−11.7	−13.4
18–24 years	13.0	− 3.8
25–34 years	35.1	52.8
35–44 years	11.4	62.0
45–54 years	− 5.0	4.3
55–64 years	10.4	6.6
65 and over	14.8	32.6

[a] Assumes 1.8 average births per woman in childbearing-ages 15 to 44.

Source: Adapted from *State of the Cities* National League of Cities, 1974. Table 13, page 22. Data are from *U.S. Bureau of Census*.

proportionately large cohorts of the baby-boom generation and of their parents. Accordingly, it is to be expected that percentage increases in young adults who must either find employment or migrate, and of persons of late middle age who are moving into the retirement age, will be larger in suburbs than in cities. If the tendency toward lower birth-rates is widespread and if, in addition, young city-resident couples who choose to have children do not move to the suburbs in considerable numbers, the greatest percentage decline in school-age children will also occur in the suburbs (where they were previously the most numerous).

It is interesting to contemplate the shifts in demand for physical facilities and the kind of adjustments needed. Lower birthrates plus later and fewer marriages suggest increased demand for apartments. Moreover, as the baby-boom generation of the suburbs leaves home, many parents will tend to reduce housing consumption (although a number may simply find themselves locked into oversized houses with low interest, or paid-up mortgages). Both of these trends point toward an increased demand for smaller residences located in higher-density areas, with less orientation towards the needs of children (i.e., high-rise apartments, condominiums, or planned unit-developments), and to a greater orientation towards the needs of the elderly, single persons, and childless couples.

Although scattered experiences of labor shortages have been noted, the previous analysis (Chapter 6) does not indicate that adequacy of the labor supply has been a serious problem. The marginal rates of new entry and of entry from outside do not appear to have declined during the sixties, even at very high rates of employment increase. And yet, very important difficulties may lie ahead. We have seen that the local sector comprises a major share of the total demand for labor in the suburbs, and that, thus far, it has drawn from a pool of young workers and housewives. As the average age of the oversized baby-boom cohort increases, these young men and women will become a less appropriate labor supply for the local sector.

GROWTH OF HIGH-INCOME HOUSEHOLDS[2]

During the postwar period, suburbanization became, for many, a major goal in its own right. For households that shared in the post-depression, postwar baby boom, this goal took the form of a home fully furnished and applianced, with two cars for mobility, and a variety of services at hand (schools, stores, and local government). It was in the realization of this goal that employment opportunities and financial assests were created, providing, in turn, for even further development of the suburbs. The prosperity of the fifties continued into the sixties, and per capita real disposable income increased 39 percent. Moreover, with a slackening of the birthrate and increased participation of women in the labor market, rapid growth in the number of high-income households ensued.

It is changes in the distribution of income measured on a household basis which now provides a major source of suburban growth, and which contributes further to the disparity between living standards in the city and the suburbs. This explosion of upper-income households appears to be due in large part to the contribution of the second and third wage earners who take over low-paying jobs that, if located in the city, would employ members of low-income households. Between 1960 and 1970, households earning over $15,000 (1972 constant dollars) more than tripled from 5.5 million (12 percent of all families) to 16.5 million (30 percent of all families). The total income of these households increased from 30 billion in 1960 to 80 billion in 1970, and is expected to double to 160 billion by 1980.

The acceleration in the growth of per capita real disposable income from an increase of 15 percent during the fifties to one of 39 percent during the sixties is accounted for by the slowdown in the population growth, which reduced the dependent population; the change in age mix, which moved the largest share of the population into work-age categories; and an increase in the proportion of women employed. As a result of the post-war baby boom, the share of population of working age dropped during the fifties from 61 to 55 percent, stood at that same level again at the end of the sixties, and will rise during the seventies to reach 60 percent by 1980. The growth of the labor force (only 13 percent in the fifties) has accelerated to 19 percent in the sixties and seventies, thus pushing up income on a per capita basis.

Increased participation of women in the labor force is especially important in bringing about the rapid growth of high-income households, which have traditionally settled in the suburbs. For the nation as a whole, the number of working women doubled from nine to twenty million between 1950 and 1970, increasing the percentage of women working from 25 to 42 percent. A recent analysis by the Conference Board reports that three out of five working women are married and two out of five are married to men earning over $10,000. Especially significant is the finding that, in half of the housholds earning over $15,000, the woman of the house is employed. Moreover, in half of these cases, it is the supplementary paycheck of the woman that places the family in that earning class. This helps explain the explosion of high-income households.

These data suggest that many women are working by election, not by necessity, and are thus in a very favored position in terms of competing for jobs with members of low-income households who must support an entire household from their earnings. Some second wage earners may actually be subsidized by their households as they become established in the work force, for in the early stages of the work experience the household may not come out ahead financially after all work-related expenses, additional household expenses, and taxes are considered.[3]

This trend towards multiple earners in high-income households raises serious problems for those residents of low-income areas in the city who seek work but are unable to subsidize work establishment. Unless there is an overall increase in employment, competition for existing jobs will increase as women continue to enter the labor market. If jobs continue to be shifted to second and third wage earners, the rise of high-income suburban households will continue, while unemployment rates rise in low-income city neighborhoods. This shift of opportunity will steadily undermine the employment and income base of low-income areas in the city, contributing to the decline of economic viability and to an increase in unemployment, welfare, crime, and other social disorders. In the city of Cleveland, for example, analysis of employment and population flows indicates that each year the number of persons entering the labor force exceeds the number of job openings by a minimum of 5,000.[4]

Over time, the distorted income distribution of suburban residents promises to bring about a distorted distribution of available labor in terms of quality, with shortages of low-skilled workers and an excessive supply of well-educated candidates for better-paying employment. The problem of an excessive supply of well-educated workers will become more serious as young suburbanites born in the fifties and sixties enter the period of family formation and face the need for the kind of employment which is appropriate to their training and necessary for the maintenance of an accustomed standard of living.

On the demand side, the composition of local-sector employment will change in response to demographic changes in the community. For example, the demand for health-care services and public transportation increases with the aging of a population.

Given the major shifts in the age- and income-distribution that lie ahead, consideration should be given to the changing needs of specific groups. The end of a rapid growth-period can be traumatic if not planned for, as the recent experience of many institutions of higher education testifies. Suburbs may, however, anticipate these changes; some may opt to address the needs of the elderly; others, the needs of families; and still others, the requirements of a more heterogeneous population. Each community should develop along those lines best suited to its resources and the values of its citizens. Once objectives are defined, they can be attained by adjusting the mix of the services offered, meeting the needs of those it wishes most to retain or to attract.

CHANGES IN LIFE STYLES

Along with later age of marriage and lower birthrate, one observes changes in life styles and values, especially among younger Americans. Increasingly, young women are insisting on equal opportunities for full-time employment and freedom from being restricted to roles as home-makers, while many young men resist patterns of work which involve long daily commutation to the city.

To a considerable extent, this demand can be satisfied by new types of housing within the suburbs—more clustered living and the develop-ment of better recreational and cultural suburban activities. The sub-urban communities are capable of considerable adjustment. Already one may witness scattered renovations of single-family houses to make possible multiple-family living or to provide apartments for aging par-ents. Such activity rarely finds its way into the housing statistics but is, nevertheless, an interesting possible augury of the future. Further, there is a significant amount of interest within the suburbs in organizing senior-citizen programs, as well as in the construction of retirement homes and other facilities for the aging. Clearly, the suburbs offer certain advantages over the more-congested cities in terms of physical environment for the elderly (lawns, trees, gardens, etc.) and, typically, in terms of the cost of rendering care.

At the same time, new opportunities will arise for increasing the popularity of the city as a place to live. The suburbs have long tended to specialize in providing for the needs of the family with children—better schools, ample space. But the city offers for many a greater proximity to work and a greater urbanity (more cultural institutions, more entertain-ment and excitement). Where marriages are late and families are small, the city becomes a more attractive place to live.

CHANGES IN CRIME RATES

All of the above assumes, of course, that negative aspects, such as lack of housing and high incidence of crime, do not countervail. Three observations regarding the incidence of crime are especially relevant: (1) that crime is more prevalent in large cities; (2) that crime is growing most rapidly in suburbs and in smaller cities; (3) that young males are much more prone to commit criminal acts than any other group.

Crime statistics are difficult to interpret because of the variety of types of crime, variations in accuracy of reporting, and varying inci-dence of crime among different racial and income groups. Neverthe-less, the above observations seem valid, as witnessed by the following:[5] (1) the rate of violent crimes (measured in number of crimes per 100,000 population) in 1973 was 1003.4 for cities over 250,000 population, but only 220.7 for cities of 10,000 to 25,000 population; (2) the increase in the rate of violent crime from 1970 to 1973 was 2 percent for cities over 250,000, but 40 percent for suburban areas. A similar comparison for burglary shows the increase in rates to be less than 1 percent and 21 percent, respectively; (3) in 1965, rates of arrest per 100,000 for males under twenty-five years of age were 7.7 for criminal homicide, 64.2 percent for robbery, 592.5 percent for larceny, but for males twenty-five years and older, comparable rates were 4.4 percent, 9.9 percent, and 63.8 percent respectively.

One must be cautious in drawing conclusions based solely on demographic trends, but the implications are interesting. They indicate that, although cities have much higher rates of crime than suburbs, the relative position of cities is improving. Furthermore, they imply that, with a sharply changing age structure, the problem of crime in both city and suburb should improve. Such a development should be more favorable for the city than for the suburbs, since crime has been generally regarded as a serious deterrent to living in the city.

FILTERING AND THE CONSERVATION OF HOUSING

The principal instrument for bringing about a more heterogeneous income mix of households in the suburbs (as in the city) has been generally thought to be the filtering of housing—a process by which the affluent seek new housing (in the past, located on the outlying fringe), leaving previous residences for the next lower-income groups, who, in turn, leave theirs for still lower-income groups. The redistribution process is one which should also lead to a more normal distribution of income in the central city as the oldest housing is recycled. Filtering should redistribute the residences of the poor outward, leaving open land in the city for rebuilding, and offering new opportunities for resettlement of middle- and upper-middle-income groups.

There is considerable evidence, however, that the filtering process has failed to work to the best interest of the city. As a result of a variety of federally induced incentives to the construction of single-family housing in the suburbs (e.g., through tax deductions for mortgage financing and property taxes, availability of government insured mortgages), middle- and upper-income families have been motivated to build in the suburbs, leaving behind their previous stock of housing. This has set off a filtering process which has encouraged abandonment and obsolescence of housing stock within the city, while, at the same time, making for job erosion as the city's local sector is undermined by suburban shift of jobs.

The processes at work are complicated and not easily reversed, but two factors should tend to bring about at least a partial shift away from filtering and toward new patterns of building and adaptation to the housing stock. The first is a shift in the attitudes of suburban governments relative to the desirability of building new residences. In the years when suburbs were growing most rapidly, they were still relatively open. Growth was not a threat to the ordinary citizen and was looked upon as a boon to the owner of underveloped land, to the developer, and to merchants and public officials. But the weight of power has shifted from those who favored expansion to those who favor conservation. Today, many suburban residents have come to experience congestion, higher living costs, and a threat to the semi-rural or small-town life style which they value so highly. Few stand to gain and many to lose from further growth. The weight of opinion has been thrown toward no-growth policies, conservation, and cultural enrichment.

Coupled with this new emphasis on no-growth is the rise in cost of housing. According to recent estimates, the cost of housing rose by 14.3 percent during the six months ending in September, 1974, and 38 percent over the previous five years.[6]

Such factors suggest a trend toward new types of adjustment in the housing market. It is unlikely that action will occur on a single front, for there will surely be construction of multi-family dwellings in cities and suburbs alike, and there will be filtering of the aging housing of each. But it seems probable that the constraints upon suburban growth, along with demands stemming from new life styles and continued high building costs, will strengthen the attractions of the city as a place to live. Moreover, it seems likely that, in city and suburb alike, there will be greater attention paid to the possibilities of modernizing and adjusting the existing stock of housing to provide for the needs of young adult and older residents.

Economic and political realities suggest that redevelopment of the central city must be so arranged as to both create new residential options for middle- and high-income adults and to recognize the needs of low-income groups unable to exit the city. The policies and programs of the Urban Development Corporation (UDC) in New York and the Metropolitan Council of the Twin Cities area indicate an understanding of such priorities, although the recent need for refinancing the UDC has demonstrated the difficulties of implementation. Community-development policies to increase heterogeneity of income groups, if properly enacted, should go far to alleviate the city's problems, because the return of above-average-income residents to the city is of critical importance in terms of adding to the tax base, bringing back jobs in the local sector for low-skilled workers, and creating a more viable social fabric. Moreover, there is some indication that the current trends favor an increasing role of the middle-class resident.

In Boston, 19,000 young adults in the 20-34 age group returned to the city during the period 1970- 1973.[7] It seems likely that such trends are at least incipient in many other places and would be responsive to public policy.

As regards the suburbs, Wilbur Thompson has pointed out that, with appropriate planning and public investment, it would be possible to offer the suburban dweller the choice of two general patterns of settlement: one in which residences are clustered around high-quality, heavily subsidized public transportation, and a second in which the individual opts for more dispersed housing, providing his own transportation at relatively high cost.[8] Such a policy seems reasonable on both economic grounds and in terms of adjustment to emerging needs, especially the needs of older people and other transit-dependent populations.

IMPROVED UNDERSTANDING OF THE COSTS OF SPRAWL

It is important to recognize that the costs of suburbanization have never been made fully explicit. Single-family housing has been subsidized by federal housing programs and by tax concessions to home owners; the heavy costs of peak-load highway facilities designed to facilitate commuting have been shifted to an important extent to non-commuting motorists through taxes; and a large portion of the cost of new public facilities associated with new homes (water and sewer facilities, schools, etc.) has been financed by federal grants, deferred through extension of municipal debt or spread over all residences.

As communities have faced rising taxes due to higher prices and wages and to rising debt-service charges, they have increasingly been moved to identify the sources of tax increases and particularly to examine the costs of servicing new residences. For example, a study in Denver has estimated that each new residence costs taxpayers $21,000 for community services—almost as much as the new resident will pay the developer for the construction cost of his home.[9] Another recent study done in Minneapolis-St. Paul estimated that $1 billion in infrastructure costs could be saved from a total development cost of $3.7 billion dollars by building new housing units on undeveloped land in the city where infrastructure is already in place, rather than building new housing units in the suburbs where infrastructure would have to be developed.[10] Infrastructure costs were found to range from an estimated low of $2,200 per unit for six units per acre in the central city to a high of $10,900 for two to four units per acre in rural fringe areas.

The increased awareness of the costs of suburban development has resulted in a re-evaluation of suburban-growth policies. As noted above, pro-growth policies have increasingly been replaced by no-growth policies. According to a survey by the Department of Housing and Urban Development, some 226 cities have imposed moratoria on building permits, water or sewer connections, rezoning, subdividing, or other essentials of growth.[11] Some communities are trying to limit growth by the use of population ceilings or by rationing growth to a certain number of dwelling units per year. Although the legality of such action is currently being fought out in the courts, there can be no doubt of the resolve of suburban communities to constrain growth and to impose full costs on new developments. The old escape route from the city to the suburbs is being shut off. We can no longer assume that urban growth will be absorbed simply by movement to the suburbs, or by further annexation of suburbs by cities.[12]

And yet it is unwise to conclude that suburban development is everywhere more costly or that suburban growth is at an end. Some cities such as Houston and Phoenix grow through annexation. Moreover, growth in the suburbs does not necessarily require expensive new infrastructure, since past settlement has been spatially loose and there is much room for "filling in." In many instances, modest growth may proceed at little extra cost in terms of additional fixed facilities or services and at considerable gain in terms of additions to the tax base. In contrast, for some cities infrastructure (e.g., sewers, utilities) are obsolete and may require rehabilitation before additional residences can be serviced.

In the future, we may expect greater recognition of the importance of making available alternative patterns of development within the metropolis. The problem of accommodating population growth must somehow be approached from a metropolitan, rather than from a municipal, perspective. As this takes place, the urban problem will undoubtedly be redefined and approached in terms of new solutions which open up opportunities for substantial economies.

A new emphasis upon more rational urban settlement would, of course, lead to savings in terms of commuting, land, and energy costs. This has been partially documented by the results of the first comprehensive analysis of economic and environmental factors in urban sprawl recently released by the Department of Housing and Urban Development, the Council on Environmental Quality, and the Environmental Protection Agency. This analysis shows that a planned high-density suburban community, as compared with a typical low-density, sprawling community, entails 44 percent less in capital costs, 43 percent less in land costs and energy consumption, 35 percent less in water consumption, and 50 percent less in auto emissions.[13]

In the past, flight from the problems of the city, while offering temporary relief for some, has probably increased the long-run cost to society of the dysfunctional ghettos. Segregated schools or housing systems, restrictive zoning, red-lining (delineation of areas where financial institutions will not make mortgage loans), and suburban-growth controls cannot contain blight, abandonment, or crime in the central city.

If meaningful employment opportunities are not available, the social cost will spill over into the suburbs in terms of illicit activities, social stress, rising incidence of crime, public-health problems, and decline in personal safety and the quality of life. Without adequate employment opportunities, even generous public financial support will serve only to maintain, and to extend, the city's role as a reservation for the disadvantaged.[14]

RECOGNITION OF NEW APPROACHES TO DESIGNING URBAN SETTLEMENTS

As the costs of containment rise, and as the awareness of the ineffectiveness of such policies increases, more and more attention will be given to preventive methods. It is at this point that lessons can be learned from successful suburbs and from planned communities here and abroad regarding necessary conditions for a viable residential community.

For example, experience has shown that instead of allocating manpower and resources to control traffic and protect pedestrians or vehicles from harm, the problems can be approached by separating auto and pedestrian traffic and by designing street systems that do not require intersections or allow on-street parking. The two types of traffic may also be separated by a system of skyways, as has been demonstra- in Minneapolis-St. Paul, Cincinnati, and Atlanta.

Another characteristic of successful neighborhoods is that the presence of non-residents or through traffic is minimized, thus creating a more defensible and self-policing environment, as found in many suburban developments. But as Oscar Newman has demonstrated in his study, *Defensible Space*, the same design principle can be applied to effect a major decline in crime rates in public-housing projects with a very small investment.[15]

The potential cost savings and improvements in the quality of life that may be realized by the implementation of design principles deserve careful consideration.[16] The fact that vehicle accidents and pedestrian accidents can be eliminated by design, and that the need for police in residential neighborhoods can be reduced, should be particularly meaningful to our cities where a large share of the budget is spent on safety forces.

Even though the new towns which have incorporated these features were built in different countries for different populations, the evidence is persuasive.[17] The fact that a city of 70,000 persons (Tapiola, Finland) functions without requiring the service of a full-time policeman should indicate that we have much to learn from such experiments. In other planned environments, children walk to school and residents walk to local areas of shopping, business, and worship without crossing a street. Resources are freed to be allocated to other uses, with the result that a large proportion of taxes may be directed toward maintenance and construction of community facilities such as playgrounds and pools. As a result, residents have more confidence in public choices, take more pride in their neighborhoods and in their city, and become aware of the benefits that stem from sharing facilities.

It is interesting to note that such innovations in urban design are not necessarily socialistic experiments. The city, Tapiola, was built immediately after World War II entirely by private interests and against the wishes of the Finnish government.

Moreover, the "new town" movement is not limited to newly established towns or cities. New urban cores are also being established within major cities. In Paris such a project is La Défence, a new town-in-town which is integrated with the old city, as well as with five new satellite communities (a number of which are programmed to house from 250,000 to 500,000 persons). In the United States, the most interesting project would seem to be Houston Center, where thirty-three contiguous blocks in the center of the city are being developed as a complex by Texas Eastern, a large gas transmission utility. Major development plans are also growing out of San Francisco's new Bay Area Rapid Transit System.

ECONOMIC PRIORITIES FOR URBAN POLICY

Taken as whole, the analysis thus far provides three important guidelines for urban policy. First, top priority must be given to determining the nature of the export base and framing policy to assure its continued vitality. Second, the high level of interdependence between city and suburb makes it essential to plan and act on a metropolitan-wide basis to the greatest extent possible, and, even where such broad action is not possible, to base city or suburban policy on a thorough analysis of the entire metropolitan economy. Third, the public sector must be acutely sensitive to those new economic and social trends which promise significant discontinuities, since extrapolation of past trends is unreliable and can be extremely costly.

UNDERSTANDING AND ENCOURAGING THE EXPORT BASE

The first step in evaluating the metropolitan economy is to identify the institutions that form the economic base of the community, be they private industrial corporations, government facilities, research and development facilities, business services, universities, hospitals, or resort activities. If the critical role played by these institutions is recognized, then public programs that address the needs of the dependent population (e.g., education, manpower training, housing and community development, and transportation) may be formulated in a way that supports rather than undermines the economy. Recent legislation has moved in this direction, encouraging formulation of urban economic development policy. Community development block-grants and integrated grant applications provide mechanisms for such an approach.[18]

The problem of aligning public programs to economic trends in the private sector is particularly acute in cities where there has been a transition in the city's economic base, and where a large percentage of workers in expanding sectors commute in from the suburbs while a large percentage of voters are dependent on public assistance. The political organizations of the city find it necessary to be responsive to pressures from bureaucracies (e.g., police and sanitation departments, school boards) and from public-service employees' unions that deliver services to local constituents. They must also act within budget constraints, influenced heavily by state governments controlled by suburban and rural assemblymen in whose interest it is to prevent a further rise in taxes. The result is that city leadership often faces effective veto power from several directions which can, in addition to preventing further development of the economic base, create a hostile environment and cause strategically important institutions to move out. The result is a dismantling of the strategic elements of the community's economy and a widespread job erosion.

There is a need for increased recognition that the development of the city is critical to its suburban and rural hinterland. For this to happen, city strategy must be conceived within a framework focusing on the continued vitality of its leading sectors and the expansion of employment opportunities, rather than simply on the maintenance of its disadvantaged residents.

The emphasis that this study places on understanding the economic base and the growth dynamic in a community is born out of the observation that, in many large metropolitan areas, both the general public and the majority of public officials are unfamiliar with the economic base of their community. Few understand the relationship between the community and the metropolis, or between the metropolis and the rest of the world. Even fewer are familiar with the history of the region and its growth or are familiar with the region's present economic strengths.[19]

Such information about the region as is available is generated primarily by the media and by politicians and thus stresses more the weakness of the city (e.g., plant closings, layoffs, rising welfare rolls, and crime rates) than its strengths. Officials become defensive and the public reacts by focusing on the management of these problems, not by seeking to determine their underlying causes or by carefully considering alternative development strategies. To balance the bad news, the local chambers of commerce tend toward the opposite extreme by promoting the city with public-relations slogans.

Economic-development programs in urban areas are greatly influenced by the public's image of the region, and they tend to be more influenced by politics than by economics. The political approach is that something must be done to try to slow down the loss of jobs through various job retention, plant expansion, and new-plant-attraction schemes. Typical actions such as allocation of public funds to land banks, massive construction projects (e.g., stadiums or government office buildings), training programs, subsidies for plant construction, tax abatements, and special financing mechanisms are, however, unable to alter market forces sufficiently to change more than temporarily the powerful local, national, and international economic forces that dictate the location of production activity. While time may be bought in the short run, the discipline of economic forces eventually wins out as local resources become exhausted.

The first step in the formulation of economic development policy is to gain an understanding of the region: what kind of an economy it is, what businesses or institutions bring in income and how they are evolving, what attributes of the environment are most critical, and what the area's potential is for future development. Within this framework of regional development, the evaluation of the feasibility of alternative development strategies and public investment programs becomes manageable. Then, and only then, can the question as to what kind of city is desirable be considered and can a meaningful planning process be implemented. A major educational and informational program, based on carefully documented analysis, is required in order to overcome the distorted images of the city which have been created primarily by the bad news and booster syndrome.

Once a community or city is aware of its evolutionary nature and its unique growth dynamics or regional role, it can formulate a meaningful development policy, coordinate its public programs with local economic trends, and align short-run programs to long-term development objectives.

Obviously, a long-term regional development strategy is likely to call for a major change in past practices. In the past, the tendency has been to implement programs that will assure reelection of public officials. Many areas do draw up what are called comprehensive regional plans (especially under recent procedures of Section 701, Housing Act of 1970), but such plans tend only to emphasize recent trends and to stress the need for physical facilities, streets and sewers, as viewed by professional planners (typically physical/land-use-oriented planners). Such plans are usually implemented through zoning codes and building permits that pay little attention to the evolution of institutions that comprise the economic base, to human resources, or to any economic development strategy. For example, projected traffic volumes have been used to justify highway programs because no alternative economic development rationale was obvious.

Finally, it is of utmost importance that both planners and the public understand the logic of economic policy, and that the policy be meaningful to industrial leaders. The public needs more information regarding the acceptable alternatives if it is to make reasoned decisions at the polls. Recent revenue-sharing and mass-transit bills have greatly increased the need for such understanding, since responsibility for allocating federal funds has been passed down to local governments. If programs made possible by these expenditures are consistent with the region's potentialities for development, other resources will be more effectively marshalled and developed.

POLICY-MAKING WITHIN A METROPOLITAN FRAMEWORK

The importance of examining city economic policy within a framework which includes the entire metropolitan area is illustrated by the critical issue of determining emphasis to be placed on development of the CBD.

The rationale for continued high-density CBD development and the need for face-to-face activities has never been carefully examined. It seems reasonable that improved communications and changes in corporation organizational arrangements are acting to reduce dependence on continuous face-to-face consultations in some places, while increasing the need for offices to locate in close proximity in others. Where the former is the case and offices no longer have to be heavily concentrated in the CBD, then the high cost of land, congestion, commuting, and pollution, associated with high-density building, can be reduced and a broader spectrum of residential and cultural functions may once again be able to compete for space in a city freed by the suburbanization of commercial functions.

Office functions such as banks and ticket agents bid space away from retail stores, restaurants, and theaters in many large cities. Perhaps the best-known example is Fifth Avenue, once the most fashionable shopping street in the country and a major tourist attraction, which has become to an important extent a street of showplaces for airlines, branch banks, and government tourist and trade promotion centers. Department stores and restaurants have given way to those functions which can afford to pay higher rents. In so doing, they have completely changed the nature of the pedestrian traffic on the street. The street, once alive until late at night and through the weekends, is now active only during the primary office hours.

A further example of how policy requires analysis of the particular needs of the metropolis is found in the recent shift in interest away from road and toward fixed-rail transit systems. Such an emphasis requires reexamination in many cases. Typically, fixed-rail as opposed to road systems implies a major long-term commitment to the CBD. While a rationale for such a commitment may be appropriate for a service metropolis, it would be excessive for metropolitan regions not having employment concentrated in the CBD. A major investment in a fixed-rail regional transit system, such as BART in San Francisco, MARTA in Atlanta, and Metro in Washington, D.C., acts to increase suburban accessibility to the central city, pushing up land rents and hence changing land uses towards commercial and away from residentiary functions. This outcome may or may not be desirable. Such a transit system is costly in terms of investment, and it may exclude the possibility of developing a cosmopolitan environment or an acceptable density level (in terms of local residents). In terms of the future of the CBD, there is often a trade-off between density and ambience. Transportation policy must be formulated in the context of the region's development and coordinated with community-development and human-resources programs.

For these and other reasons, it is important that there be careful evaluation of the role of the city within the metropolis. The city is the focal point or base of operations for highly specialized and interdependent activities and for the complex life-support systems required for the maintenance and development of expertise. Many metropolitan areas have developed considerable capability for rendering services, some in the narrow range of education, insurance or medical services; others over a broad range of corporate and financial management, research and development, and producer and government services. For them, the central city tends to dominate the region, and the suburbs assume a secondary position as a place of work. There are other metropolitan areas, however, which have not cultivated such expertise and which must be regarded as being in a different stage or, perhaps, even a different process of development and as requiring different developmental policies. In such areas the CBD is likely to play a less prominent role.

It is important that a full range of metropolitan economies exist within the American system. Some will provide highly developed infrastructures and be constantly upgraded; others will provide more stable, lower-cost environments best suited for more routinized activities. Should all areas seek to upgrade their infrastructure equally, costs of doing business will rise, and many routinized jobs will be forced off shore to less-developed areas.

SIGNIFICANCE OF NEW ECONOMIC AND SOCIAL TRENDS

As we have seen above, changes in demographic patterns and life styles do not appear to favor a continuation of past rapid rates of suburban growth, particularly under conditions of rising costs of operating automobiles, deterioration of the suburban ambience, and an increased recognition of the costs of providing public services to newcomers and of a variety of social costs associated with suburbanization. It is unlikely, however, that well-developed past trends of filtering of the housing stock and now classic processes of suburbanization will soon be terminated. Instead, a complex of forces appears to offer a prospect for a renewed interest in the city as a place to live and work and a demand for new strategies in carrying forward further development of both the city and its suburbs.

All of this simply means that cities and suburbs alike face a twofold challenge: (1) economies must be viable within a larger national and increasingly global economy in which metropolises function in continuous competition with one another here and abroad; (2) urban populations, including a disproportionately large generation of young adults, must be provided with suitable employment, housing, and educational, cultural, and recreational facilities.

RESEARCH NEEDS

Hopefully, the analysis of the preceding chapters has shed light on a number of issues in urban economics: the essential differences between city and suburban economies, the nature of employment and the problems facing employees in each, the size and nature of flows into and out of these work forces, the types of urban growth process, and the nature of upgrading. But the analysis has also raised a number of questions which are left unanswered.

Many of these questions go to the very heart of any understanding of the American economy as a whole: What are the locational trends which face manufacturing and advanced service firms in the years ahead? Will plants continue to disperse, leaving the suburbs for lower-cost rural areas or off-shore locations? What lies ahead for the services sector (e.g., the legal, accounting, consulting, health, engineering, and educational services)? May recent trends towards increased shares of employment in the local sector, in the public sector, and in business services be extrapolated with any degree of confidence, or will a new era of cost-cutting and increased productivity work a special hardship on employment in certain segments of the services industries? Will employment opportunities become increasingly concentrated in high-income suburban households with more than one wage earner? What effect do increased unemployment and welfare levels have on the development of human resources in low-income neighborhoods isolated in the declining city? To what extent do cities differ in terms of the opportunities which are available to attract new business activity and to carry out successful transition? Finally, is there a need for a national urban-growth policy, or should each metropolis seek to find its own way?

Much can be accomplished by metropolitan leadership that is responsive to economic as well as political constituencies, that is willing to inform its voters and to present to them well-considered proposals. The ancient injunction, "know thyself," is as applicable for the metropolis as for the individual and presents to the social scientist as great a challenge as ever before.

REFERENCES

1. "The Burgeoning Benefits of a Lower Birthrate," *Business Week*, December 15, 1973, p.41.

2. This section is based on data reported in a paper prepared by Fabian Linden, titled "U.S. Consumer Spending Patterns" (The Conference Board [New York, N.Y., February 13, 1975]).

3. Subsidization of work establishment takes many forms: college paid by parents, subsidies by government, wives supporting graduate students, families supporting members in volunteer work which leads to a paid position, and the like.

4. Richard V. Knight, "The Job Market for Welfare Recipients," *Welfare to Work Study* (Federation for Community Planning [Cleveland, O., March 1975]).

5. National League of Cities, *State of the Cities, A Changing World of Problems for Urban Policy* (Washington, D.C., 1974), pp. 25, 35-37.

6. *Ibid.*, p. 43.

7. Boston Redevelopment Authority.

8. Wilbur Thompson, "A Preface to Suburban Economies," in *The Urbanization of the Suburbs*, L. M. Masotti and J. F. Madden (eds.) (Beverly Hills, Calif.: Sage Publications, 1973), p. 427.

9. Gladwin Hill, "Nation's Cities Fighting to Stem Growth," *New York Times*, July 28, 1974, p. 30.

10. Minneapolis-St. Paul Metropolitan Council Release, October 31, 1973.

11. Gladwin Hill, *op. cit.* p. 30.

12. When high-income residents move outside the city limits and the income differential between city and suburb widens, the welfare burden on the city rises, making annexation unattractive to the suburbs.

13. A study prepared by Real Estate Research Corporation, "The Costs of Sprawl: Environmental and Economic Costs of Alternative Residential Development Patterns at the Urban Fringe." Washington D.C.: Government Printing Office, 1974, as reported in *State of the Cities,. op. cit.*, p.53.

14. Norton E. Long, "The City as Reservation," *Public Interest*, Fall 1971, pp. 22-38.

15. Oscar Newman, *Defensible Space: Crime Prevention Through Urban Design* (New York, N.Y.: Collier Books, 1973).

16. It is interesting that many of these concepts were developed in the greenbelt towns built in the United States during the depression. Clarence S. Stern, *Toward New Towns for America* (New York, N.Y.: Reinhold Book Co., 1957).

17. See John B. Lansing, Robert W. Marans, Robert B. Zelney, *Planned Residential Environments* (Ann Arbor, Mich.: Institute for Social Research, 1970). In recent times, some of these features have been applied to the design of Reston, Columbia, Cedar-Riverside, and other new American communities.

18. Such grants are available under the New Communities Act (HUD) and Title IX of the Public Works and Economic Development Act of 1974.

19. These observations find support in a recent survey sponsored by the Kettering Foundation of the priorities of elected local officials and public-interest groups, which found that almost none of their time was spent on economic-policy consideration.

Appendices

Appendix A

SCOPE OF THE STUDY AND
NATURE OF DATA SOURCES

SCOPE OF THE STUDY

Except for a brief presentation of employment data extending back to 1939, the materials studied cover only the recent decade 1960-1970. Accordingly, the study is largely an analysis of current differences and similarities between city and suburbs and of recent transition in each.

Choice of metropolitan areas (SMSAs) was influenced by two criteria: (1) the need to select metropolitan areas in which central-city boundaries approximate the boundaries of the counties in which central city is located. This criterion was important if we were to make use of data drawn from the 1-in-100 Social Security continuous work-history file, since these data are available for no political unit smaller than a county. It was not a consideration in using census data, however, since these are available for each central city, as well as for each SMSA; (2) the need to study as representative a sample as possible.

There are only six SMSAs in the United States in which the central city has been designated as a county or is comprised of counties: Baltimore, Denver, New Orleans, New York, Philadelphia, and St. Louis. All of these were studied. In addition, the county of Suffolk, Ma. was considered to comprise a satisfactory approximation of the central city of Boston and was included.[1]

In the remaining three metropolitan areas studied (Atlanta, Cleveland, and Houston), the central-city counties overbound the central city (a small portion of Atlanta is also located in another county, DeKalb). Nevertheless, the economies of the central cities dominate these counties. These SMSAs were selected because they were considered to be especially interesting places in that two represented rapidly growing service centers of the South and Southwest and the other was an important manufacturing metropolis of the Great Lakes region.

Although there were annexations which altered city boundaries in only one city, Houston, during the period 1950-60, there were changes in definitions of some SMSAs through additions of outlying counties. The resulting problems of comparability of data were dealt with when using the Social Security materials by using the same (1970) definition throughout. It was not possible to do this when analyzing the *Census of Populations* data, but it is unlikely that significant distortions resulted, since the counties added to SMSAs between 1960 and 1970 were relatively unimportant to these metropolitan economies in 1960.

[1]The San Francisco SMSA was also a candidate but was excluded because it was felt that the location of the city of Oakland within San Francisco County introduced certain problems of comparability with other metropolises.

SOURCES OF DATA

The two major sources of data were the *Social Security Continuous Work History Files* and the 1960 and 1970 *Censuses of Population*. In addition, occasional use was made of *Census of Manufactures* and *Census of Business* materials. It is important to emphasize that the study involves principally an analysis of employment data, and that these data are examined entirely on a *place-of-work* basis, except in the analysis of commuter flows where both place of work and place of residence are considered.

The Social Security data are drawn from the files of workers covered under the provisions of the Social Security Act. Persons classified as employed in government, railways, agriculture, education and domestic services were excluded from the analysis either because they were not covered by Social Security or because coverage was incomplete.

Information on covered workers is provided by employers on a quarterly basis, and includes information on industrial classification of principal employer (there is no information on occupation), quarterly wages, age (date of birth), sex, and race. Accordingly, Social Security employment data indicate all persons employed at any time during a given quarter, rather than at one point in time. Our procedure was to make use of employment data for the first quarter of the year in question.[2] This minimizes the coverage problem which results when a person's cumulative income for the calendar year reaches the specified annual maximum ($5,000 during the latter years of the decade), resulting in income not being reported in subsequent quarters.

The unique attribute of the Social Security materials is that they permit the investigator to track the worker's employment through time. It was by taking advantage of this attribute that we were able to examine flows of entrants and departures into and out of city and suburban work forces in Chapter 6.[3]

On the other hand, there are certain limitations imposed upon the researcher who makes use of these materials. In addition to the limitations arising out of the fact that the data are available only on a county basis, and that employment in government and certain other types of employment are not covered, the data are based on a 1-in-100 sample. This means that cells may, in some instances, become quite small when data are cross-classified by more than one variable (e.g., black females in certain suburbs who are under twenty-five and employed in wholesaling). We have recognized this problem and have tried to deal with it in such a way as to avoid distortion of findings. Where cells are too small to provide usable results, this fact is noted, and the measures are withheld. Where sample size raises doubt as to reliability, but the measures are considered usable, the reader is warned that the results of the analysis must be regarded as tentative.

The *Census of Population* employment data are quite different in terms of

[2]This was not true of the special analysis of stable workers in 1968 (Chapter 5). Here information for all four quarters was examined.

[3]The term "work force" is used throughout to indicate persons employed in a given place. Thus, the work force of the city of Philadelphia is comprised of those persons who work there, regardless of where they reside.

both method of enumeration and coverage. Persons are enumerated at place of residence during a brief period every ten years, and worker status is determined simply by asking the individual whether or not he is employed and the industry and occupation of his employment. Individuals are also asked where they work, and census data on employed persons are published for SMSAs, indicating both place of residence and place of work. Information relating to both place of work and place of residence within an SMSA is further classified as being within the central city or outside the central city.[4] It is these data, classified in terms of work, that we have studied. It should be noted that information regarding employment status is obtained from a sample of all those enumerated. This sample is considerably larger (15 percent) than for the Social Security materials, and its adequacy does not comprise a serious problem in the analysis.

Advantages of the *Census of Population* materials are, therefore, that employment information is available for central city, not central city-county (when the two are different), that the data are published in such a form as to permit analysis of commuter patterns, and that occupational classifications are available. On the other hand, industrial classifications are less usable than in the case of Social Security materials (at least in the published forms), since classifications are less detailed, being often published in combinations which obscure the analysis (e.g., retailing and wholesaling are combined). For this reason, *Census of Population* data were not analyzed on an industry basis.

It is difficult to assess the quality of the *Census of Population* data. The Bureau of Census has indicated that there was roughly a 2.5 percent population undercount in the 1970 census for the nation as a whole.[5] We were advised by the Statistical Methods Division that there is a tendency for blacks to be less completely enumerated than whites; males to be less completely enumerated than females; and regions to vary as regards completeness of enumeration. There is no "formal evidence," however, that central cities are more poorly enumerated than the rest of SMSAs, and, further, there is no evidence that employment information reflects either more or less complete enumeration than does the published information relating to population. We were advised also that comparison with re-interview results indicated a high degree of consistency in reporting of occupational status when census questionnaires dealt with employment.

[4]The *Journey to Work* volume of the *Census of Population* also provides information on workers employed in the central city but residing outside the SMSA.
[5]PHCE #4 *Estimates of Coverage of Population, Sex, Race, Age: Demographic Analysis.*

Appendix B

ILLUSTRATIONS OF DEVELOPMENT PROCESSES
WITHIN A METROPOLITAN ECONOMY

In presenting these illustrations, it is important that they not be looked upon as forecasting devices and that they not be interpreted as implying that only the export sector plays an initiating role in the developmental process. To the contrary, we would argue that it is frequently the attractiveness of the local sector that induces export-oriented firms to locate within the metropolis.[1] Moreover, innovative local-sector firms are likely to expand their markets and become exporters.

In the models, the relationship between the export sector and the metropolitan economy is indicated in terms of employment and income multipliers.[2] The hypothetical metropolis examined below expands from 100,000 workers to 320,000 workers as it passes through different phases or periods of development. Since population would generally be about three times the work force, we may think in terms of the emergence of a metropolis of one million population.

The quantitative and qualitative aspects are modeled, first for growth originating in the export sector, second for growth originating in the local sector, and, finally, for growth from upgrading of the export and local sectors even in the face of declining employment in the export sector. In each case, the source of growth is indicated by boxing in the component changed.

It should be noted that the model is highly simplified in that only income streams for wages and salaries are treated. (Payments for rent, interest, and profit are ignored, and investment expenditures, non-local taxes, and transfers are omitted entirely.) Employment requirements are determined by dividing observed income streams by assumed average wages. In addition, it is assumed that the local sector adjusts fully to changes in the export sector within the period

[1]See Hans Blumenthal, "The Export Base of The Metropolis," R.W. Pfouts, ed., *The Techniques of Urban Economic Analysis* (West Trenton, N.J.: Chandler Davis Publishers, 1960), pp. 229-77.

[2]The values of the multipliers shown are, of course, hypothetical. They are not larger, however, than the *average* values of multipliers which were determined empirically for 368 American metropolitan economies 1940-1960 in Richard V. Knight, *Employment Expansion and Metropolitan Trade* (New York, N.Y.: Praeger Publishers, Inc., 1973).

The above study did not attempt to measure marginal-multiplier values, but it did determine that average values increased significantly in most places from 1940 to 1950, and again from 1950 to 1960, due to the increased importance of the local sector. These increases were due in a large measure to the growth of local medical and health services which occurred everywhere under conditions of rising per capita income and changed demographic patterns.

in which the changes occur. The time interval is conceptualized as a five- to ten-year period.

Two relationships are of special interest in the models. The first is that the income multiplier is based on the proportion of income spent by the populace within the local sector (in theoretical terms, on the propensity to consume locally produced goods and services).[3] The larger the proportion of income spent locally, the larger the income multiplier. Any broadening in the local sector through import substitution will increase the income multiplier, *ceteris paribus*. The second is that the size of the employment multiplier is determined jointly by the size of the income multiplier and by the relationship between wages in the export and local sectors. Acting alone, an increase in the income multiplier occurring through, say, import substitution in the local sector, will increase the employment multiplier, but an increase in wages in the export sector, without proportionate increase in local-sector wages, will also increase the employment multiplier relationship (see 1B).

PERIOD 1

At the beginning of period 1, employment is assumed to be as follows:

	Beginning of Period 1		
	Employment	Average Annual Wage $	Income $ (millions)
1. Export Sector	20,000	(10,000)	200
2. Local Sector	80,000	(5,000)	400
3. Total Metropolis	100,000	(6,000)	600
4. Export Multiplier (Row 3 ÷ row 1)	5[a]		3[b]

[a] Employment multiplier
[b] Income multiplier

Observations: The metropolitan work force is 100,000: one-fifth is employed in the export sector, with average annual earnings of $10,000; the other four-fifths are in the local sector, with average annual earnings of $5,000. The export-base-employment multiplier is 5, and the income multiplier is 3 (one-third of metropolitan income originates in the export sector).

Note: The multipliers will remain stable as long as no structural, or qualitative, changes occur in either sector.

During period 1, under assumption A, export employment increases 100 percent with no change in wages in either export or local (i.e., industry expansion). Under assumption B, with export employment having increased 100 percent, the export sector is then upgraded (wages increase 50 percent). Local-sector wages remain the same.

[3]The income multiplier is simply the numerical relationship between income generated in the export sector and total income received in the entire economy (export and local sector combined).

	End of Period 1					
	I-A Export Employment Increases 100%			I-B I-A plus Upgrading of Export Sector by 50% Wage Increase		
	Employment	Average Annual Wage $	Income $ (millions)	Employment	Average Annual Wage $	Income $ (millions)
Export Sector	40,000	10,000	400.0	40,000	**15,000**	600.0
Local Sector	160,000	5,000	800.0	240,000	5,000	1200.0
Total Metropolis	200,000	6,000	1200.0	280,000	6,429	1800.0
Export Multiplier	5		3	7		3

Observations: I-A. With an income multiplier of 3, an increase of $200 million income generated in the export sector results in an increase of $400 million in the local sector for an increase of $600 million in the economy. Since all wages remain the same, there is also a doubling of total employment.

Note: The employment multiplier is also unchanged, since there has not been a change in wages.

I-B. The upgrading of the export sector will increase the income originating in the export sector by 50 percent above I-A. Assuming that the multiplier relationship does not change, there will be an additional 50 percent increase in income and jobs in the local sector (local-sector wages are unchanged) as the local sector responds to increased income generated in the export sector.

Note: The income multiplier does not change, but the employment multiplier increases from 5 to 7 because there are more local-sector jobs in proportion to export-sector jobs.

PERIOD 2

During period 2, under assumption A, the local sector is broadened through import substitution (local-sector employment rises by 50 percent). Under assumption B, the broadening of the import sector is accompanied by productivity gains so that local-sector employment does not increase, but local-sector wages rise.

	End of Period 2					
	II-A Broadening of Local Sector By 50% Employment Increase			II-B Upgrading of Local Sector By 50% Wage Increase. No Local Sector Employment Change		
	Employment	Average Annual Wage $	Income $ (millions)	Employment	Average Annual Wage $	Income $ (millions)
Export Sector	40,000	15,000	600.0	40,000	15,000	600.0
Local Sector	360,000	5,000	1800.0	240,000	7,500	1800.0
Total Metropolis	400,000	6,000	2400.0	280,000	8,571	2400.0
Export-Base Multiplier	10		4	7		4

Observations: II-A. The increasing volume of business in the local sector induced from expanded export activity in I-A and I-B will lead to opportunities for broadening the local sector through import substitution. With import substitution, income that was previously spent to purchase imported consumer goods and services and which therefore left the metropolitan economy will be re-circulated through the purchase of the same goods and services produced locally. In theoretical terms, the propensity to spend locally has increased, and, accordingly, the income multiplier increases from 3 to 4.

Note: Since local-sector average wages have not changed, the increased spending in the local sector brings a rise in employment in the local sector, and an increase in the income multiplier from 3 to 4, and the employment multiplier from 5 to 10.

II-B. When broadening of the local sector is accompanied by increased productivity, the 50 percent increase in average wages in the local sector results in the same local sector increase in income as in II-A but with no change in employment. This is likely to occur as the upward pressure on wages intensifies pressure to increase output per worker. The employment multiplier remains at the same level as in I-B above. Income has increased with no net increase in employment.

Note: The employment multiplier remains at 7 as in I-B.

PERIOD 3

During period 3, under assumption A, export-sector employment declines to 30,000, with no decline in wages in either the export or local sector (i.e., no changes in either income or employment multipliers). Under assumption B, there is no decline in income generated within the export sector from the level at end of period 2, but, because of increased productivity in the export sector,. there is a decline in export employment (again to 30,000). Under assumption C, the conditions of III-B are repeated in the export sector, but there is a broadening in the local sector through import substitution. Local-sector wages remain the same as in III-B. Under assumption D, conditions of III-C are repeated, but there is an increased productivity of the local sector (average wages rise by 10 percent and employment is reduced accordingly).

End of Period 3

	III-A Export activity declines from II-B: job erosion			III-B Export activity remains same as II-B, but sector is upgraded: increased productivity		
	Employ- ment	Average Annual Wage	Income $ (Millions)	Employ- ment	Average Annual Wage $	Income $ (Millions)
Export Sector	30,000	15,000	450.0	30,000	20,000	600.0
Local Sector	180,000	7,500	1350.0	240,000	7,500	1800.0
Total Metropolis	210,000	8,571	1800.0	270,000	3,889	2400.0
Export Multiplier	7		4	9		4
Unemployment (Decline from end of II-B)	70,000			10,000		

	III-C			III-D		
	III-B, plus broadening of local sector			III-C, plus upgrading in local-sector activity: local-sector broadening plus increased productivity (10% wage increase)		
	Employment	Average Annual Wage $	Income $ (Millions)	Employment	Average Annual Wage $	Income $ (Millions)
Export Sector	,30,000	20,000	600.0	30,000	20,000	600.0
Local Sector	320,000	7,500	2400.0	290,000	8,250	2400.0
Total Metropolis	350,000	8,571	300.0	320,000	9,375	3000.0
Export Multiplier	11.7		5	10.7		5

Observations: III-A. Export activity has declined but there is no change in wages in either sector. Since export income and employment decline together, and there is no change in multiplier relationships from II-B, local-sector income and employment decline proportionately.

III-B. Export employment has declined, but this has been accompanied by upgrading in the export sector. There has been no decline in export-sector income and, accordingly, none in local-sector income and employment. The important observation here is that without upgrading the permanent loss of 10,000 jobs in the export sector would have eventually resulted in the loss of 60,000 jobs in the local sector and might have in time brought about the narrowing and downgrading of the local sector (the reversal of the mechanism outlined for period 2). This case illustrates the importance of considering qualitative changes in an area in transition.

III-C. Here we observe that import substitution has broadened the local sector sufficiently that total employment is 35,000 at the end of the period, well above the 280,000 at the end of Period 2 under II-B conditions. Here is illustrated the possibility that local-sector expansion may increase total employment, even when there are export-sector employment losses. It is important to note that where jobs in the export sector have been upgraded (III-B), there has in all likelihood been a shift of residence to the suburbs. Consequently, any import substitution in the local sector will occur in the suburbs also.

III-D. Here the processes are carried one step further. Export wages and employment are as before; income generated by the local sector is at the same level as III-C. But there has been an upgrading of the local sector, with the result that local-sector employment is lower than in III-B. Here again, higher real wages would suggest an upgrading of residents and continued suburban shift. *Note:* The employment multiplier is lower than in III-B (but higher than in II-B). Total employment has increased from 280,000 at the end of II-B to 320,000 at the end of III-D. Average annual wages increased from $8,571 to $9,375.

These cases illustrate fundamental processes of growth and transition underlying metropolitan development, and they thus provide a basis for considering intra-metropolitan development in the chapters that follow. For example, III-B demonstrates how the adverse effects of declining employment in the export sector (the closing of manufacturing plants in the inner city III-A) can be offset by continuing processes of upgrading in the export sector. Examples III-C and III-D illustrate broadening and upgrading of the local sector. Taken together, III A-D represent the combined effects of many growth processes typically at play in maturing metropolises such as Cleveland, St. Louis, Baltimore, and Philadelphia. These processes, accompanied by suburbanization (not shown explicitly), reflect the fundamental metropolitan growth-dynamics with which much of this book is concerned.

Appendix C

HOW CITY AND SUBURBAN EMPLOYMENT EXPORT-MULTIPLIERS DIFFER FROM THAT OF THE METROPOLITAN ECONOMY

The following highly simplified example demonstrates, in terms of employment, why city and suburban multipliers are smaller than the multiplier for the entire metropolitan economy:

Workers Employed in:	City		Suburb		Metro-politan Economy
I. Metropolitan Export Activities	Export Sector	Local Sector	Export Sector	Local Sector	
a. Live in city, work in city	50				50
b. Live in city, work in suburb	50[a]				50
c. Live in suburb, work in city			50[b]		50
d. Live in suburb, work in suburb			50		50
					——
Metropolitan Total, Export					200
II. Metropolitan Local Activities					
e. Live in city, work in city		200			200
f. Live in city, work in suburb	100[a]				100
g. Live in suburb, work in city			200[b]		200
h. Live in suburb, work in suburb				200	
	——	——	——	——	
City and Suburb Totals	200	200	300	200	
					——
Metropolitan Total, Local					700

City multiplier	(local + export ÷ export)	400 ÷ 200 = 2
Suburb multiplier	(local + export ÷ export)	500 ÷ 300 = 1⅔
Metropolitan multiplier	(local + import ÷ import)	900 ÷ 200 = 4½

[a] City residents commuting to suburban jobs are regarded as "hidden exports" of the city, since their earnings are received by the city.

[b] Suburban residents commuting to city jobs are regarded as "hidden exports" of the suburbs, since their earnings are received by the suburbs.

In the above, *a-d* represent employment in activities which result in exports of goods and services from the metropolitan economy. Lines *a* and *c* indicate employment in activities carried out in the city; *b* and *d* indicate employment in activities carried out in the suburbs. But *a* and *b* are a part of the export sector of the city, since these workers' earnings introduce income which is respent largely within the city. Similarly, *c* and *d* are a part of the suburbs.

The metropolitan economy local sector is also located partly in the city, partly in the suburbs. Employment in the city ((*e* and *g*) provides residentiary services principally for city residents, but also a variety of cultural, medical, educational, and governmental services for the entire metropolis. Employment in the suburbs (*f* and *h*) provides residentiary services principally for suburban residents, but also certain recreational and retail services to residents of the city. Line *f* is shown, however, as part of the city's export sector, since these workers commute to the suburbs and their earnings introduce income which is partially respent in the city. Analogously, line *g* is part of the suburban export sector.

It follows that, in computing city (suburban) export multipliers, we include those who live and work in the city (suburbs) and are engaged in metropolitan export-activities; plus those who commute to the suburbs (city), i.e., "hidden" export labor, regardless of whether such workers are employed in metropolitan export or local activities.

Thus, in computing the export multiplier for the suburbs, we include as exports:

(1) labor employed in the metropolitan export sector living and working in the suburbs (*d*), 50, (probably largely employed in manufacturing.

(2) labor employed in the metropolitan export sector, living in the suburbs and working in the city (*c*), 50, ("hidden" exports, probably largely employed in headquarters and advanced services.

(3) labor employed in the metropolitan local sector, living in the suburbs and working in the city (*g*), 200, ("hidden" exports, probably largely administrators, lawyers, police, teachers, doctors and salesmen).

Suburban local-sector employment consists of those living in the suburbs and engaged in local-sector activities (*h*), 200.

The suburban employment multiplier-relationship is thus computed as the ratio of total suburban employment (export plus local) to suburban export employment (computed as indicated above).

Appendix Table D. Additional Measures of Major Commuter Flows,
Ten Metropolitan Areas, 1960–1970[a]

	Atlanta	Balti-more	Boston	Cleve-land	Denver	Houston	New Orleans	New York	Phila-delphia	St. Louis	Modified[b] Average
Net suburb to city commuters as % of suburban resident workers[c]											
1960	41.3	26.2	22.4	45.2	31.5	31.4	32.6	23.1	19.2	30.4	29.9
1970	32.0	16.3	19.9	30.9	30.5	31.4	26.1	19.9	15.4	23.2	24.8
Net suburb to city commuters as % of total city employment[c]											
1960	28.0	16.8	34.5	30.8	19.8	8.3	10.2	6.6	16.8	33.6	20.5
1970	34.8	17.3	36.6	35.8	28.4	14.5	16.2	7.6	18.1	39.9	25.2
In-commuters to SMSA as percentage of out-commuters from SMSA[d]											
1960	271.9	96.9	285.2	391.4	94.1	132.3	166.2	258.8	67.9	341.4	205.9
1970	451.7	83.8	322.6	243.1	140.7	197.1	198.9	331.4	66.3	256.4	221.8

[a] Employment reported at place of work.

[b] Highest and lowest values among ten places omitted in computing modified average.

[c] Net suburb-to-city commuters computed by deducting city-to-suburb commuters from suburb-to-city commuters.

[d] In-commuters are those commuting daily to employment within SMSA (city or suburb) from outside SMSA boundaries. Out-commuter are those commuting daily to employment outside SMSA from inside SMSA boundaries.

Source: *Census of Population, Journey to Work, PC (2), 1960, 1970.*

Appendix E

ESTIMATING EXPORT SECTOR AND TOTAL RESIDENT EARNINGS OF THE SUBURBS

Estimates of earnings of suburb to city commuters ("the hidden export sector") were prepared by multiplying the number of male and female suburb-to-city commuters in each occupational classification by the median SMSA earnings (male or female, whichever is applicable) in that classification. It is very likely that the method of estimation used consistently underestimates the earnings levels of commuters, since these workers tend to be higher-paid professionals, executives, and technicians. Indeed, it is the fact that they are well-paid that makes it possible for them to live in the suburbs and to commute to the city.

Estimates of earnings for the remainder of suburban export activities are crude, but probably do not result in an underestimation. The procedure is to assume that earnings of all craftsmen and operatives who work and live in suburban areas represent total suburban earnings from manufacturing, and that manufacturing is the only other export of the suburban economy. Earnings of craftsmen and operatives are estimated by the techniques described above. Such a procedure overestimates earnings originating in manufacturing to the extent that it includes craftsmen and operatives in the important construction sector (not an export activity), but underestimates in that it excludes other occupations (mainly white-collar) within suburban manufacturing. It also underestimates to the extent that it ignores export activities other than manufacturing.

Estimates of total suburban incomes are prepared for each occupational classification by multiplying the total number of males and females living in the suburbs, and working in either suburbs or city, by the appropriate median SMSA earnings figure.

In preparing the 1960 estimates, 1960 employment data were used, but 1970 median SMSA earnings were applied in order to control for changes in wage levels.

In order to observe the extent of possible errors which could occur as a result of underestimation of suburban export sector employment within the suburbs (Table 3.8, Column D), we increased this estimate for 1970 by 25 percent in all places and recomputed commuter-related income as a percentage of suburban income (Column I). It will be observed in Table 4.5 that the estimated percentages are not changed sufficiently to alter the essential finding that hidden export sector is the principal contributor to suburban income when both direct and indirect effects are considered.

213

Appendix Table F. Selected Information relating to Central Cities, and Suburban Cities, Towns and Other Areas, 1970[a]

	County	Population ('000's)	Median Income ('000's)	% of Tracts Low Income	% of Tracts High Income	% Negro	% Commute by Auto	% Housing Constructed Pre-1940
Atlanta		1,389	10.7	23.9	19.4	22.3	84.6	18.1
Central city	3	47	7.9	49.6	11.9	64.3	73.3	39.7
	4	450	8.5			50.0	71.0	29.4
Suburbs		892	11.8	4.0	25.2	6.2	–	10.6
Cities-towns								
Marietta	2	27	9.6	14.3	28.6	14.0	91.2	17.6
East Point	4	39	10.7	14.3	28.6	8.4	87.2	16.0
Remaining parts of counties	2	169	11.4	0	5.0	2.6	94.2	8.6
	3	368	12.7	1.9	30.8	7.3	91.0	8.2
	4	118	12.2	0	45.4	7.7	90.3	16.1
Other counties	1	98	11.0	0	0	4.5	94.3	5.1
	5	73	9.6	14.3	0	5.1	–	–
Counties: Clayton (1), Cobb (2), Dekalb (3), Fulton (4), Gwinnet (5).								
Baltimore		2071.0	10.6	13.8	19.6	23.7	76.1	39.5
Central city	6	905.8	8.8	36.5	6.0	46.4	61.9	60.0
Suburbs		1165.2	11.8	1.6	26.8	6.0	86.4	21.6
Cities-towns								
Annapolis	1	30.1	10.3	16.7	0	29.5	76.9	38.2
Glen Burnie	1	38.6	11.1	0	0	2.8	90.1	8.4
Catonsville	2	54.8	12.6	0	33.3	6.4	84.8	24.8
Dundalk	2	85.4	10.7	4.2	0	5.8	83.9	18.1
Essex	2	38.2	9.9	10.0	0	1.0	86.3	16.9
Parkville	2	33.9	11.9	0	20.0	0.7	87.7	19.4
Pikesville	2	25.4	16.9	0	77.8	1.5	92.1	8.4
Randallstown	2	33.7	13.7	0	50.0	3.4	91.7	6.1

Towson	2	77.8	13.5	0	56.0	1.0	83.5	14.5
Woodlawn-Woodmoor	2	28.8	13.4	0	55.5	8.0	91.0	11.6
Remaining parts of counties	1	229.0	11.7	1.7	17.0	10.1	87.2	19.2
	2	243.0	11.9	0	28.9	2.4	87.5	24.0
Other counties	3	69.0	10.2	4.8	0	4.0	83.0	47.5
	4	115.4	10.8	3.1	12.5	8.2	84.7	25.7
	5	61.9	13.5	0	50.0	8.1	88.6	19.4

Counties: Anne Arundel (1), Baltimore (2), Carroll (3), Hartford (4), Howard (5), Baltimore City (6).

Boston		2,754.0	11.4	17.8	15.0	4.6	67.0	63.8
Central city	5	641.1	9.1	49.7	2.7	16.3	43.6	77.2
Suburbs		2,112.9	12.1	5.3	19.8	1.1	74.0	59.1
Cities-towns								
Beverly	1	38.4	11.3	0	0	0.4	81.3	62.5
Lynn	1	90.3	9.7	40.9	0	2.6	72.3	79.8
Peabody	1	48.1	11.6	0	0	0.4	88.3	37.5
Salem	1	40.6	9.9	14.3	0	0.5	76.2	78.0
Cambridge	2	100.4	9.8	23.3	6.6	6.8	41.9	81.2
Everett	2	42.5	10.1	0	0	1.3	61.9	83.8
Malden	2	56.1	10.2	0	0	1.3	65.4	76.7
Medford	2	64.4	11.1	0	0	2.5	65.3	80.9
Melrose	2	33.2	12.4	0	25.0	0.2	72.7	68.6
Newton	2	91.1	15.4	0	55.6	1.2	74.5	67.5
Somerville	2	88.8	9.6	6.7	0	0.8	55.3	89.9
Waltham	2	61.6	11.5	0	0	0.7	77.1	55.4
Woburn	2	37.4	11.7	0	0	0.6	84.4	43.5
Quincy	3	88.0	11.1	8.3	0	0.1	75.3	71.1
Chelsea	5	30.6	9.0	20.0	0	1.7	48.8	86.7
Revere	5	43.2	10.3	0	0	0.1	62.6	64.1
Remaining parts of counties	1	125.7	13.0	0	33.3	0.2	84.0	50.8
	2	476.6	13.5	0	34.2	0.6	80.3	44.8
	3	422.1	13.5	0	34.2	0.6	77.0	47.1
	5	20.3	11.7	0	0	0.2	60.7	79.4
Other counties	4	113.4	12.3	0	7.1	0.7	86.8	40.8

Counties: Essex (1), Middlesex (2), Norfolk (3), Plymouth (4), Suffolk (5).

Appendix Table F. continued

	County	Population (000's)	Median Income (000's)	% of Tracts Low Income	% of Tracts High Income	% Negro	% Commute by Auto	% Housing Constructed Pre-1940
Cleveland		2064.2	11.4	18.7	11.9	16.1	78.3	45.9
Central city		750.9	9.1	2.3	0.5	38.3	68.2	73.4
Suburbs		1313.3	12.6	0.8	20.4	3.4	83.7	28.4
Cities-towns								
Brook Park	1	30.8	12.5	0	0	0.3	89.5	2.6
Cleveland Hts.	1	60.8	13.4	5.9	41.1	2.5	76.5	72.8
East Cleveland	1	39.6	9.8	0	0	58.6	66.9	71.2
Euclid	1	71.6	11.8	0	0	0.4	85.8	17.3
Garfield Hts.	1	41.4	11.6	0	0	4.3	80.0	31.0
Lakewood	1	70.2	11.6	5.6	5.6	–	68.2	73.6
Maple Heights	1	34.1	11.8	0	0	2.0	83.2	16.7
North Olmsted	1	34.9	13.9	0	50.0	0.1	85.2	9.0
Parma	1	100.2	12.4	0	0	–	82.4	13.0
Parma Heights	1	27.2	12.9	0	0	–	85.3	4.6
Shaker Heights	1	36.3	19.9	0	100.0	14.5	72.7	45.7
South Euclid	1	29.6	13.3	0	0	0.1	81.1	16.0
Mentor	3	36.9	12.8	0	0	0.1	94.1	13.5
Remaining parts of counties	1	393.9	14.0	0	44.7	1.9	85.4	16.2
	3	160.3	11.8	0	5.9	1.6	90.6	25.4
Other counties	2	63.0	12.4	0	26.6	1.4	87.4	32.6
	4	82.7	11.2	0	0	0.8	88.5	38.1
Counties: Cuyahoga (1), Geauga (2), Lake (3), Medina (4).								
Denver		1227.5	10.8	13.8	22.4	4.1	85.2	26.3
Central city	4	514.7	9.7	28.8	19.5	9.1	80.1	40.9
Suburbs		712.8	11.5	7.1	23.7	0.4	89.0	13.1
Cities-towns								
Arvada	1	1.6	11.5	0	0	0.2	100.0	–

City / Area	County							
Aurora	5	45.2	12.0	0	22.2	0.1	93.6	4.9
North Glenn	1	27.2	9.5	0	0	1.9	83.2	6.8
Englewood	2	47.8	11.1	7.7	38.5	0.8	84.8	2.1
Littleton	1	27.9	11.7	0	25.0	0.5	92.6	–
Boulder	2	33.7	10.0	20.0	0	0.2	88.9	29.1
Lakewood	2	26.5	12.7	14.3	28.6	0.2	91.8	10.0
Wheat Ridge	3	66.9	11.4	25.0	31.3	0.9	78.1	21.8
	5	92.8	12.4	0	35.0	0.1	93.2	6.4
	5	29.8	11.7	0	33.3	0.1	89.2	12.1
Remaining parts of counties	1	129.1	10.2	6.5	0	0.5	91.4	10.1
	2	54.2	14.8	17.2	51.7	0.4	92.0	8.0
	3	65.0	11.0	6.7	13.3	0.1	90.3	24.3
	5	65.2	11.7	0	21.2	0.3	88.4	22.1

Counties: Adams (1), Arapahoe (2), Boulder (3), Denver (4), Jefferson (5).

City / Area	County							
Houston		1,985.0	10.2	17.2	16.5	19.3	86.9	15.3
Central City		1,232.7	9.9	26.6	17.1	25.7	84.7	17.3
Suburbs		752.3	10.5	11.5	16.2	8.7	90.9	11.6
Cities-towns								
Baytown	3	44.0	10.9	7.7	7.7	4.9	93.0	21.5
Pasadena	3	89.3	11.1	0	9.1	0.1	93.7	4.4
Remaining parts of counties	2	52.3	8.2	14.3	0	17.0	85.9	23.3
	3	375.9	11.3	1.8	21.4	8.5	91.9	9.0
	5	49.5	8.7	50.0	0	11.8	86.0	13.1
Other counties	1	108.3	10.4	19.3	0	9.4	89.8	12.5
	4	33.0	7.4	58.3	0	20.8	84.0	21.4

Counties: Brazoria (1), Fort Bend (2), Harris (3), Liberty (4), Montgomery (5).

City / Area	County							
New Orleans	2	1,045.8	8.7	25.5	21.0	31.0	69.7	34.2
Central city		593.5	7.4	36.9	16.9	45.0	58.7	49.4
Suburbs		452.3	10.0	8.5	27.4	12.5	84.1	11.0
Cities-towns								
Kenner	1	29.9	9.4	25.0	12.5	20.1	84.3	6.1
Marrero	1	29.0	8.9	0	12.5	31.5	83.3	12.7
Metairie	1	135.8	11.4	3.1	59.4	4.1	86.8	6.2

Appendix Table F. continued

	County	Population (000's)	Median Income (000's)	% of Tracts Low Income	% of Tracts High Income	% Negro	% Commute by Auto	% Housing Constructed Pre-1940
Remaining parts of parishes	1	142.9	9.5	11.8	14.7	14.8	81.1	12.8
Other parishes	3	51.2	9.6	0	12.5	5.1	85.7	7.7
	4	63.6	8.7	7.7	15.4	18.7	85.1	20.2
Parishes: Jefferson (1), Orleans (2), St. Bernard (3), St. Tammany (4)								
New York		11,571.9	10.8	19.7	20.1	16.3	40.5	53.8
Central city		7,894.8	9.8	25.7	10.7	21.1	25.9	62.1
Bronx		1,471.7	8.3	35.7	4.8	24.3	24.8	63.8
Kings		2,602.0	8.9	35.1	4.9	25.2	25.2	69.3
New York		1,539.2	9.0	45.6	25.9	24.7	10.2	66.5
Queens		1,986.5	11.6	4.8	13.7	13.0	36.4	49.2
Richmond		295.4	11.9	3.2	15.9	5.3	52.4	47.1
Suburbs		3,677.1	13.6	1.4	48.3	5.9	73.3	31.3
Cities-towns								
Baldwin	1	34.5	14.6	0	80.0	1.6	70.5	45.7
East Meadow	1	46.3	14.3	0	85.7	1.3	79.4	6.7
Elmont	1	29.4	12.6	0	20.0	3.2	70.4	22.6
Franklin Sq.	1	32.2	13.5	0	40.0	0.1	70.5	22.6
Freeport	1	40.4	12.8	0	14.3	18.5	68.9	39.8
Garden City	1	25.4	21.2	0	100.0	1.3	59.3	44.6
Glen Cove	1	25.8	12.9	0	25.0	6.7	76.9	39.5
Hempstead	1	39.4	11.5	0	14.3	35.8	70.5	35.1
Hicksville	1	48.1	13.9	0	71.4	0.1	79.5	12.0
Levittown	1	65.4	13.1	0	30.0	0.1	82.5	0.1
Long Beach	1	33.1	12.0	0	20.0	6.7	60.8	40.7
Massapequa	1	26.8	14.7	0	60.0	0.1	71.9	9.9
Merrick	1	25.9	17.5	0	80.0	0.4	66.7	25.7
Oceanside	1	35.4	14.6	0	66.7	0.3	67.4	26.8
Plainview	1	33.2	16.2	0	100.0	0.2	79.7	1.2
Rockville Center	1	27.4	16.8	0	60.0	3.9	60.0	52.9
Valley Stream	1	40.4	13.5	0	50.0	0.1	65.5	38.3

New City	2	27.3	16.3	0	100.0	1.1	89.6	13.0
Brentwood	3	27.9	11.9	0	0	2.2	83.9	6.2
Central Islip	3	36.4	11.6	0	10.0	5.2	85.7	11.0
Deer Park	3	32.2	12.8	0	0	5.9	80.7	5.3
Huntington St.	3	28.8	12.6	0	40.0	7.0	81.3	22.9
Lindenhurst	3	28.4	11.6	0	0	0.4	79.6	23.1
North Babylon	3	39.6	12.4	0	25.0	0.5	85.0	6.7
Mount Vernon	4	72.8	11.0	19.0	19.1	35.6	54.9	71.4
New Rochelle	4	75.4	13.2	0	33.3	14.4	62.0	56.0
Port Chester	4	25.8	10.7	0	20.0	13.6	71.7	69.3
White Plains	4	50.1	13.6	8.3	41.6	14.5	58.6	53.3
Yonkers	4	204.3	12.2	4.1	32.7	6.4	58.9	51.3
Remaining parts of counties	1	819.0	15.3	0.7	73.1	4.4	71.0	27.3
	2	202.6	13.5	0	45.1	6.3	82.7	29.7
	3	931.7	12.1	0.6	32.2	5.0	83.4	19.9
	4	465.7	15.9	1.0	67.0	5.3	67.3	45.7

Counties: Nassau (1), Rockland (2), Suffolk (3), Westchester (4)

Philadelphia	8	4,817.9	10.8	12.0	18.9	17.5	67.4	51.4
Central city		1,948.6	9.4	28.0	9.6	33.6	50.4	69.5
Suburbs		2,869.3	11.8	4.6	23.0	6.6	78.7	37.3
Cities-towns								
Fort Dix	1	26.3	7.3	100.0	0	16.0	15.5	5.9
Camden	2	102.6	8.0	60.0	0	39.1	61.8	70.1
Chester	6	56.3	8.5	47.1	0	45.2	70.8	66.8
Norristown	7	38.2	9.8	14.3	0	16.9	75.9	66.9
Pottstown	7	25.4	10.0	12.5	0	8.8	80.6	62.1
Remaining parts of counties	1	296.8	11.4	6.1	15.8	8.1	84.7	29.2
	2	353.7	11.7	0	20.7	3.4	79.4	35.0
	6	543.7	12.2	0.8	33.6	3.3	–	39.3
	7	560.3	13.2	0	37.5	2.5	81.1	34.3
Other counties	3	172.7	10.6	4.0	0	8.4	83.9	38.9
	4	415.1	11.7	0	13.4	2.0	86.5	24.9
	5	278.3	11.6	4.1	21.4	7.6	81.2	41.3

Counties: Burlington (1), Camden (2), Gloucester (3), Bucks (4) Chester (5), Delaware (6), Montgomery (7), Philadelphia (8)

Appendix Table F. continued

	County	Population (000's)	Median Income (000's)	% of Tracts[b] Low Income	% of Tracts[b] High Income	% Negro	% Commute by Auto	Housing Constructed Pre-1940
St. Louis		2,363.0	10.5	16.2	15.8	16.0	83.5	41.6
Central city		622.2	8.2	45.5	1.6	40.9	73.8	73.8
Suburbs		1,740.8	11.2	6.7	20.5	7.2	88.5	27.5
Cities-towns								
Alton	1	39.7	9.6	0	0	16.2	87.2	58.6
Granite City	1	40.4	10.3	12.5	12.5	–	85.8	42.2
Belleville	2	41.7	10.5	0	9.1	0.6	84.7	50.0
East St. Louis	2	70.0	6.6	69.3	7.7	69.1	74.5	55.1
St. Charles	5	31.8	10.9	0	0	1.6	88.3	29.7
Ferguson	6	28.9	11.8	0	14.3	0.9	90.8	15.6
Florissant	6	65.9	12.5	0	30.0	0.3	93.5	2.3
Kirkwood	6	31.9	13.9	0	71.4	6.4	89.6	29.0
Lemay	6	40.1	11.3	0	0	0.1	91.5	23.6
University City	6	46.3	11.8	0	33.3	20.0	83.8	44.7
Webster Groves	6	27.0	13.6	0	50.0	4.8	85.4	49.4
Remaining parts of counties	1	170.8	10.4	5.3	5.3	3.9	87.7	35.3
	2	173.5	10.2	15.9	6.8	8.6	87.0	27.5
	5	61.1	10.8	0	0	1.1	88.3	13.5
	6	711.3	12.4	2.4	36.2	4.6	90.3	19.1
Other counties	3	55.1	8.8	9.1	0	1.1	83.8	43.0
	4	105.3	9.7	0	0	0.8	91.0	22.5

Counties: Madison (1), St. Clair (2), Franklin (3), Jefferson (4), St. Charles (5), St. Louis (6).

Source: Department of Commerce, Bureau of the Census, *1970 Census of Population*, Census Tract Reports, PHC(1) Series.

a Low income is tract median income less than 75% SMSA median income, high income is tract median income 125% or more SMSA median income.

Appendix Table G. Regressions: Summary[a]

	1960–1965 City				1960–1965 Suburb				1965–1970 City				1965–1970 Suburb			
	R^2	a	b	a+100(b)[c]	R^2	a	b	a+100(b)[c]	R^2	a	b	a+100(b)[c]	R^2	a	b	a+100(b)[c]
New entrants (Y), Employment end of period (X)[b]																
Male	.78	−26.2 (.94)	.48 (.103)	21.8	.42	−11.9 (1.95)	.37 (.174)	25.1	.76	−10.4 (.94)	.35 (.080)	24.6	.92	−17.8 (1.52)	.42 (.049)	24.2
Female	.96	−46.9 (.64)	.86 (.077)	39.1	.83	−47.9 (2.29)	.86 (.159)[d]	38.1	.95	−29.7 (.81)	.71 (.066)	41.3	.91	−47.1 (2.07)	.84 (.108)	36.9
In-migrants (Y), Employment end of period (X)[b]																
Male	.96	−62.7 (.62)	.78 (.067)	15.3	.001	18.9 (1.77)	−.01 (.157)[d]	17.9	.79	−53.9 (1.63)	.69 (.144)	15.1	.94	−44.3 (.018)	.54 (.058)	9.7
Female	.58	−29.2 (1.08)	.36 (.125)	6.8	.40	−13.5 (1.27)	.18 (.089)	4.5	.85	−29.7 (.72)	.34 (.058)	4.3	.84	−32.0 (1.02)	.30 (.054)	−2.0
In-transfers (Y), Employment end of period (X)[b]																
Male	.025	9.9 (1.21)	−.05 (.026)[d]	4.9	.35	−6.2 (1.14)	.18 (.101)[d]	11.8	.25	21.8 (1.16)	−.15 (.076)[d]	6.8	.72	−6.2 (1.30)	.16 (.042)	9.8
Female	.05	8.6 (.76)	−.05 (.027)[d]	3.6	.53	−17.9 (1.21)	.22 (.084)	4.1	.85	−29.7 (.72)	.34 (.058)	4.3	.57	−16.3 (1.28)	.19 (.067)	2.7
Out-migrants (Y), Employment end of period (X)[b]																
Male	.75	−24.2 (.85)	.40 (.084)	15.8	.10	40.6 (2.55)	−.19 (.095)[d]	21.6	.19	−1.5 (1.49)[d]	.16 (.137)[d]	14.5	.29	8.3 (1.15)	0.6 (.037)[d]	14.3
Female	.71	−22.7 (.67)	.30 (.078)	7.3	.66	−12.7 (.73)	.17 (.051)	4.3	.29	−1.6 (.53)	.10 (.049)	8.4	.35	−1.9 (.86)	.08 (.045)[d]	6.1

[a] Covered employment at place of work. Numbers in parenthesis are standard errors for coefficients:

[b] Both X and Y variables expressed as percentage of employment in base year.

[c] Measures rate of flow at zero employment growth, i.e. when employment at end of period equals 100% of base year employment.

[d] Indicates that coefficients are not significant at .95 confidence level.

Source: *U.S. Census of Population, Journey to Work PC(2) 1960, 1970.*

Acknowledgments

It is not possible to acknowledge here the full extent of our debt to others. At almost every stage the work benefitted from the criticism and encouragement of one or more members of the staff of the Conservation of Human Resources Project—most importantly Eli Ginzberg, but also Ivar Berg, Charles Brecher, Robert Cohen, Anna Dutka, Marcia Freedman, and Dale Hiestand. David Hirshberg gave invaluable help as consultant in the programming of the Social Security materials. Suri Mehta and Tom Wong were enthusiastic, tireless, and skillful research assistants; and Victoria Brent was helpful in a variety of tasks related to typing and assembling the manuscript.

Index

DATE DUE

GAYLORD			PRINTED IN U.S.A.